Beihefte zur Zeitschrift für die alttestamentliche Wissenschaft

Edited by
John Barton, Reinhard G. Kratz, Nathan MacDonald,
Sara Milstein, and Markus Witte

Volume 562

Ezekiel's Sign-Acts

Methods and Interpretation

Edited by
Tyler D. Mayfield and Penelope Barter

DE GRUYTER

ISBN 978-3-11-151973-9
e-ISBN (PDF) 978-3-11-152101-5
e-ISBN (EPUB) 978-3-11-152123-7
ISSN 0934-2575

Library of Congress Control Number: 2024937901

Bibliographic information published by the Deutsche Nationalbibliothek
The Deutsche Nationalbibliothek lists this publication in the Deutsche Nationalbibliografie;
detailed bibliographic data are available on the internet at http://dnb.dnb.de.

© 2025 Walter de Gruyter GmbH, Berlin/Boston
Typesetting: Meta Systems Publishing & Printservices GmbH, Wustermark
Printing and binding: CPI books GmbH, Leck

www.degruyter.com

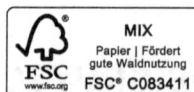

MIX
Papier | Fördert
gute Waldnutzung
FSC
www.fsc.org   FSC® C083411

Contents

Tyler D. Mayfield and Penelope Barter
Introduction

The Ezekiel passages describing the instructions for, and dramatization of, divine messages (Ezekiel 3–5; 12; 24; 37) are among the most bizarre and overlooked in the Hebrew Bible. The prophet is commanded to embody his message of judgment to Jerusalem, and these actions complement and clarify the oracles they surround. The literary presentation of these sign-acts often emphasizes the divine command and an interpretation of the action as if the actual performance of the action is either a given or unimportant. In addition, the acts frequently involve peculiar, and even impossible, actions. Yet, these sign-acts are frequently ignored within Ezekiel studies, which tend to focus on the book's strange visions and controversial oracles. This volume addresses this lacuna by inviting international senior and junior scholars to focus on the texts concerning Ezekiel's sign-acts through diverse methodological approaches. It aims to redirect scholarly attention to these often-unnoticed texts, which stand so central to understanding the nature of ancient prophecy as well as the overall book of Ezekiel.

The volume opens with an essay related to sign acts in general as it asks a central interpretive question in the field. Steven S. Tuell's "Show or Tell? Literary Sign-Acts in Ezekiel" explores the interpretive issues surrounding the observation that some of the prophet's sign-acts could not have been performed. He notes in fact that only two of the sign-acts in the book of Ezekiel claim to be performed by the prophet. Thus, Tuell suggests ways we can think of these acts as more literary and rhetorical. For example, the use of these sign-acts as a literary device highlights the literary nature of Ezekiel as a book, as a deliberately shaped piece of literature and not merely a haphazard collection.

The next two studies in the volume address the timely topic of trauma as it relates to prophetic sign-acts. C. L. Crouch focuses on sign-acts in both Jeremiah and Ezekiel – the biblical books most associated with these actions – while Brad E. Kelle reads a specific sign-act in Ezekiel 3 from the perspective of trauma hermeneutics.

"Jeremiah and Ezekiel's Sign-Acts through the Lens of Trauma" by Crouch argues that the prevalence of sign acts in the books of Jeremiah and Ezekiel when compared to other biblical books is linked to the traumatic aftermath of Judah's downfall in the sixth century BCE. The use of explicitly bodily forms of communication is explained by the "language difficulties characteristic of trauma survivors." What cannot be put into words is expressed therefore through the body.

Kelle explores the developing concept of moral injury as it relates to an individual sign-act in his "Ezekiel 3:24–27 and Prophetic Moral Injury: Trauma and

https://doi.org/10.1515/9783111521015-203

the Interdisciplinary Study of Ezekiel's Sign-Acts." Kelle notes that the theoretical framework of moral injury helps to foreground the textual elements of isolation, loss of social trust, and the prophet's inability to speak within the historical reality of destruction, war, and exile. These elements point to a sense of the prophet's "moral disjuncture, distress, and despair." This essay along with the following three studies address sign-acts in Ezekiel 3–5.

"Ezekiel's Confinement: From the Sublime to the Conspicuous" by Rosanne Liebermann examines Ezekiel 3:22–27, a passage in which the prophet is commanded to shut himself in his house, to bind himself with cords, and to not speak. Liebermann argues that the prophet's isolation secludes him from the impurity of his foreign environs and mirrors the Deity's isolation in the temple's deepest part. Ezekiel becomes a "high priest for the migration" with God's presence understood as with the Judeans outside of Judah.

Karin Schöpflin's essay "Predicting Jerusalem's Siege and Fall through Sign-Acts – Actual Performance or Literary Fiction in Ezekiel 4:1–5:4?" investigates the series of sign acts in Ezek 4 and 5. Schöpflin argues that they were intended to predict the siege and fall of Jerusalem and the consequences thereof with the later form of the text also looking toward conditions in exile. Alongside a historical-critical analysis, she discusses the likelihood of these sign-acts having actually been performed, using Jeremiah 13 and 19 as background.

Kelvin G. Friebel, whose 1999 monograph *Jeremiah's and Ezekiel's Sign-Acts: Rhetorical Nonverbal Communication* remains a key study of this volume's topic, explores the significance and function of the iron wall created by placing an iron griddle between the prophet and the city in his essay "The Enigma of Ezekiel's Iron Wall (Ezek 4:3)." Is the wall representational or figurative? Does the wall signify protection or attack or separation? Is iron mentioned to represent strength and impenetrability? Does Ezekiel represent God, the Babylonians, or himself? Friebel ultimately argues that the wall is a "figurative protective wall shielding the prophet from the reactant opposition of the people that is evoked by his contrary prophetic messages of judgment."

One of the central issues addressed thus far in the volume by Tuell, Schöpflin, and Friebel concerns the extent to which these biblical texts concerning sign-acts should be understood as purely textual phenomena. In "Ezekiel's Dark Tunnel to Exile", Stephen L. Cook explores the richly symbolic sign-act in Ezekiel 12, arguing that the text is not historical recollection, but an invitation into an intertextual world. Cook shifts scholarly attention from the redactional reconstructions of Ezekiel 12 to a discussion of the inner-biblical allusions and underworld imagery found in this sign act. Cook explores the intertextual connections between Ezekiel 12 and another priestly text, Genesis 15:7–21, including their anticipation of exile and use of symbols of darkness and death.

Next, the volume moves from the symbolism of exile in Ezekiel 12 to the symbolism of Ezekiel's loss of his wife as three contributions turn our attention to Ezekiel 24, each exploring the death of the prophet's wife as a symbol of the loss of Jerusalem from a different perspective.

"Where is Ezekiel's Wife? An Examination of Ezek 24:15–27 through the Lens of Performance Art" by John T. Strong examines the features that prophetic sign-acts share with performance art. Strong's contribution addresses not only issues of documentation and curation of time-based performance, but also the nature of the response to these performances. Just as Ana Mendieta's performance art elicited shock and revulsion, so Ezekiel's sign-act succeeds in its communication through the audience's emotional experience. By drawing useful comparisons between the performance art of Ana Mendieta and the sign-act in Ezek 24:15–27, Strong sheds new light on the theological significance of the forcible removal of Jerusalem – YHWH's consort and home to the temple – for both the prophet and his immediate audience.

Stefano Salemi's contribution, "Ezekiel's Wife's Death: Femicide, 'Divine Election,' Metaphor, or Mimic?", explores the loss of Ezekiel's wife as it points to the destruction of the beloved city of Jerusalem and the temple. The death of Ezekiel's wife is emphasized alongside his love for her, which lends itself well to visualizing the loss of Jerusalem, so loved by the people. The unusual behaviour of the prophet at his wife's death plays a role in the comparative framework of YHWH's relationship with his people and the people with the city and the temple. How can the death of a woman constitute a pivotal element in the experience of the exilic community within the theology of the book of Ezekiel? Is it an act of 'divine election'? A metaphorical element of a traumatic narrative? An essential characteristic of a bizarre sign-act of Ezekiel as YHWH's מוֹפֵת?

"Misogyny or Sign Act? Ezekiel's Embodiment of YHWH in Ezekiel 24" by Marvin Sweeney explores Ezekiel's Zadokite priestly identity as the reason the prophet was unable to mourn his wife's death. As an alternative, Ezekiel represented God in a sign-act meant to symbolically demonstrates God's refusal to mourn Jerusalem. The prophet is not an uncaring misogynist then but observes the proper priestly actions in the face of his wife's tragedy.

The volume turns next away from the prophet's symbolic refusal to mourn the city of Jerusalem to the promise of restoration found in the latter part of Ezekiel.

Penny Barter's contribution "Unity and (Compositional) Disunity" examines the role of the formulas in Ezekiel 37:15–28. While their role in determining the literary structure of the final form of the text is widely acknowledged, the relatively dense use of formulas in the sign-act and its interpretation(s) can also offer insight into the transformation of the text in its successive compositional layers.

The volume concludes by stepping back to explore how these sign-acts relate to each other and the role they play in the book. William Tooman in his essay, "'Is he not a Riddle Monger?' הלא ממשל משלים הוא – Ezekiel's Sign-acts as a Coordinated Sequence" begins with an examination of Ezekiel 12:1–20, focusing on its relationship to the book's other sign-acts. He argues that Ezekiel 12:1–20 is linked to chapters 2–5(6) and 24, and that it has been crafted to sit strategically between them. Then, he considers the whole sequence of sign-acts in Ezekiel and argues that they are a coordinated sequence, as signaled by the verbal, topical, temporal, and argumentative links between them. The result of this coordination is that the sign-acts present a progressive line of argumentation that speaks about the fate of five historical populations.

Abbreviations of Periodicals, Reference Works, and Series

AB	Anchor Bible / Anchor Yale Bible Commentary
AOTC	Abingdon Old Testament Commentaries
ATANT	Abhandlung zur Theologie des Alten und Neuen Testaments
ATD	Das Alte Testament Deutsch
BETL	Bibliotheca Ephemeridum Theologicarum Lovaniensium
BibInt	*Biblical Intepretation*
BJPsych	The British Journal of Psychiatry
BK	Biblische Kommentar Altes Testament
BLS	Bible and Literature Series
BWANT	Beiträge zur Wissenschaft vom Alten und Neuen Testament
BZ	*Biblische Zeitschrift*
BZAW	Beihefte zur Zeitschrift für die alttestamentliche Wissenschaft
CBQ	*Catholic Biblical Quarterly*
CBR	*Currents in Biblical Research*
ConBOT	Coniectanea Biblica Old Testament Series
DBAT	*Dielheimer Blätter zum Alten Testament*
ErFor	Erträge der Forschung
ETL	*Ephemerides Theologicae Lovanienses*
EvT	*Evangelische Theologie*
FAT	Forschungen zum Alten Testament
FOTL	The Forms of the Old Testament Literature
FRLANT	Forschungen zur Religion und Literatur des Alten und Neuen Testaments
HeBAI	*Hebrew Bible and Ancient Israel*
HSM	Harvard Semitic Monographs
HSS	Harvard Semitic Series
HUCA	Hebrew Union College Annual
ICC	International Critical Commentary
JANES	*Journal of the Ancient Near Eastern Society*
JBL	*Journal of Biblical Literature*
JNWSL	*Journal of Northwest Semitic Languages*
JSOT	*Journal for the Study of the Old Testament*
JSOTSup	Journal for the Study of the Old Testament Supplement Series
KeH	Kurzgefasstes exegetisches Handbuch zum Alten Testament
LHBOTS	The Library of Hebrew Bible/Old Testament Studies
NEB	Die Neue Echter Bibel
NICOT	New International Commentary on the Old Testament
NSKAT	Neuer Stuttgarter Kommentar Altes Testament
NTOA	Novum Testamentum Et Orbis Antiquus
OBO	Orbis Biblicus et Orientalis
OBT	Overtures to Biblical Theology
OTE	*Old Testament Essays*
OTL	Old Testament Library
RevExp	*Review & Expositor*

https://doi.org/10.1515/9783111521015-204

SBB	Stuttgarter biblische Beiträge
SBL-BS	Society of Biblical Literature – Resources for Biblical Study
SBLDS	Society of Biblical Literature Dissertation Series
SBLSS	Society of Biblical Literature Supplement Series
SBLSymS	Society of Biblical Literature Symposium Series
SOTSMS	Society for Old Testament Study Monograph Series
UBC	Understanding the Bible Commentary
VT	*Vetus Testamentum*
VTSup	Supplements to Vetus Testamentum
WBC	Word Biblical Commentary
WO	*Die Welt des Orients*
ZAW	*Zeitschrift für die Alttestamentliche Wissenschaft*

Steven S. Tuell
Show or Tell? Literary Sign-Acts in Ezekiel

Sign-acts were part of the standard repertoire of Israel's prophets, from Moses' metamorphosing staff (Exod 4:1–5) to Hosea's troubled marriage (Hos 1:1–9) to Isaiah's nudity (Isa 20:1–6) to Jeremiah's ox yoke (Jer 27:1–22). We can describe sign-acts broadly as non-verbal actions that Yhwh commands the prophet to perform, rather than words that the prophet is commanded to utter.[1] Yet beyond that description, it is difficult to generalize. Some sign-acts are supernatural portents, like the signs Yhwh gave Moses to perform before his enslaved people and before Pharaoh (Exod 4:1–8). Others are symbolic actions by which the prophet embodies what the Divine is doing or is about to do.[2] So Hosea's marriage to the unfaithful Gomer became a lived metaphor for the estrangement between Yhwh and Israel (Hos 1:2), while Jeremiah wearing an ox yoke effectively conveyed Yhwh's judgment upon Judah, and the necessity of submitting to Babylon (Jer 27:1–22). There does not appear to be standard Hebrew terminology to describe these enigmatic actions. The sign-act itself may be called a מופת (Exod 4:21; 7:9; 11:10; Ezek 12:6, 11; 24:24, 27;[3] Ps 105:27) or an אות (Exod 4:8–9, 17, 28, 30; Isa 8:18;[4] Ezek 4:3), or both (Deut 34:11; Isa 20:3),[5] or neither (e.g., Hos 1:1–9; Jer 20:1–22; Ezek 12:17–20). Nor

---

1 Kelvin G. Friebel (*Jeremiah's and Ezekiel's Sign-Acts: Rhetorical Nonverbal Communication*, JSOTSup 283 [Sheffield: Sheffield Academic, 1999], 14) defines sign-acts as "all the non-verbal behaviors (i.e., bodily movements, gestures and paralanguage) whose primary purpose was communicative and interactive" – a definition that seems overly broad. This study, by contrast, will distinguish between non-verbal sign-acts and actions performed by the prophet in conjunction with a verbal proclamation: e.g., Yhwh's command, at the start of a judgment oracle, that Ezekiel set his face (פנים with שׁים) against (אל) the mountains of Israel (6:2); false female prophets (13:17); the south (20:46; a slightly different form, with no preposition); Jerusalem (21:1); Ammon (25:2); Sidon (28:21); Pharaoh (29:2; again, a slightly different form, with על rather than אל); Mount Seir (35:2); and the symbolic final enemy Gog (38:2). In these and other like instances, the words of the prophet convey the meaning of the action. In sign-acts properly so-called, while an interpretation may follow, the actions stand alone.
2 Jeanette Mathews, *Prophets as Performers: Biblical Performance Criticism and Israel's Prophets* (Eugene, OR: Cascade, 2020), 66: "Prophetic speech can be described as performative speech-acts, in that the words are intended to bring about the message in the very speaking of them. But the prophets who often embodied their message were clearly more than orators. Embodiment is shown sometimes in highly provocative performances and often within the prophet's own life experiences." See also Steven Tuell, *Ezekiel*, UBC (Grand Rapids: Baker, 2012), 24–25; 38–39.
3 Ezekiel is himself called a מופת in Ezek 12:6, 11; 24:24, 27.
4 Isaiah and his children are themselves called a sign (אות) in Isa 8:18.
5 Indeed, all of the passages here cited from Exod 4, which use these two terms interchangeably, seem to belong to the same layer of tradition, commonly called J (see Richard Elliott Friedman, *Who Wrote the Bible?* [New York: Harper & Row, 1987], 250).

https://doi.org/10.1515/9783111521015-001

can we generalize meaningfully about the literary form used to report sign-acts. Always, there is a command to perform the sign; however, while that command may be followed by a description of the performance, reaction to the performance, and an interpretation (e.g., Ezek 12:1–16; 24:15–27), often one, or another, or even *all* of these other elements are absent.

Much research into prophetic sign-acts treats them as a rhetorical strategy on the part of the prophet: as non-verbal communication[6] or as performance art.[7] Such approaches can be enlightening and are certainly applicable to those sign-acts that were actually performed by the prophets. However, particularly in the case of Ezekiel, it is apparent that some of his sign-acts (certainly 4:4–8, and probably 37:15–28) were not actually performed – indeed, *could* not have been performed as described. They are features of the book, rather than of the public ministry of the historical prophet. These literary sign-acts call for different interpretive strategies.

1 Ezekiel's Sign-Acts

Arguably, sign-acts play a larger role in Ezekiel than in any other prophetic book. We can identify nine sign-acts in Ezekiel: 4:1–3, 4–8, 9–17; 5:1–17; 12:1–16, 17–20; 21:18–24; 24:15–27; and 37:15–28. The first four come in sequence immediately after the prophet's call vision (1–3).[8] The first sign-act, 4:1–3, is explicitly called

---

6 Friebel, *Sign-Acts*, 40: "The rhetorical (interactive) function of the prophetic sign-acts was a significant part of the whole communication event, for the prophets were not merely trying to disseminate message content didactically but were attempting to persuade their audiences of a different way of viewing their situations and circumstances."

7 Mathews, *Prophets as Performers*, 61: "An important motivation underlying scholarship in this area is the recognition that biblical communities were predominantly oral cultures so that communication events reflected in the Scriptures originally comprised oral performances before audiences. Biblical Performance Criticism thus attempts to get behind the written script to analyze the *whole* performance event and not just the aspects that have been transmitted in written composition."

8 There is no explicit transition between the call report in 1–3 and these first four sign acts. So, Moshe Greenberg included Ezekiel eating the scroll (2:8–3:3) among the sign acts (Greenberg, *Ezekiel 1–20: A New Translation with Introduction and Commentary*, AB 22 [Garden City, NY: Doubleday, 1983], 117) while Margaret Odell incorporates the sign acts into Ezekiel's call to form an extended prophetic initiation (Margaret S. Odell, "You Are What You Eat: Ezekiel and the Scroll," *JBL* 117/2 (1998): 229–37). However, there are good reasons for distinguishing the call narrative from what immediately follows. The report of Ezekiel's call is formally distinct from the commencement of his mission in 4–7, and while there is no clear indication of the ending of one unit and the beginning of another at the juncture of 1–3 and 4–7, the characteristic

"a sign [אוֹת] to the house of Israel" (4:3).[9] Although all are commanded by Yhwh, for none of the four do we have a report of the sign's performance. The prophet's protest at the defilement incurred by the third sign-act (4:14), and Yhwh's permissive alteration of the sign (4:15), suggest that it was in fact performed – although, again, the prophet's reaction is all that we are given, not the response of an audience. An interpretation is provided for the third (4:16–17) and fourth (5:5–17) signs.

Another sequence, of two sign-acts, appears in Ezek 12:1–16 and 17–20. The first of these is fulsomely presented, with a command to perform the sign-act (12:3–6), a report of its performance (12:7), the audience's response (12:9),[10] and the sign's interpretation (12:10–16). At the conclusion of Yhwh's command to perform that first sign, Yhwh informs Ezekiel, "I have made you a sign [מוֹפֵת] for the house of Israel" (12:6). Again, at the beginning of the sign's interpretation, Yhwh commands the prophet, "Say, 'I am a sign [מוֹפֵת] for you: as I have done, so shall it be done to them; they shall go into exile, into captivity'" (12:11). But for the sign-act in 12:17–20, only the command to perform the sign and its interpretation are given.

The seventh sign-act in the book of Ezekiel is in 21:23–29 (18–24); here again only the command to perform the sign-act and its interpretation are presented. However, the next sign-act, 24:15–27, is once more fulsomely presented: we have the command (24:15–17), the performance (24:18), the people's response (24:19), and a dual interpretation of the sign, one for the community (24:20–24), and one for the prophet (24:25–27). Here as well, Ezekiel himself is said to be a מוֹפֵת, in 24:24 and 27: at the end of each of the two interpretations of this sign-act. For the last sign-act in the book, 37:15–28, we are given the command to perform the sign-act, the people's response, and the sign's interpretation; however, nothing is said of its actual performance.

As this swift run-through demonstrates, in by far the majority of Ezekiel's reported sign-acts, nothing is said about the sign actually being performed. For the reader of the book, of course, it does not matter if a sign-act described on the page was performed or not. As we are not part of the prophet's original exilic

---

vocabulary of the first section does not continue into the following. For example, the expression מְרִי בֵית ("rebellious house," 3:27; compare 2:4–7; 3:11) is not found again until 12:2–3. Finally, the visionary character of these first three chapters, and their close relationship to chapters 8–11 and 40–48, clearly set them apart.

9 Unless otherwise indicated, English Bible citations will be from the NRSV.

10 That response, note, is conveyed to the prophet by a word from Yhwh. This is typical of the book's radical theocentricity: everything – even the words of Ezekiel's fellow exiles – is viewed from the Divine perspective.

audience, we have no immediate access to Ezekiel's performances anyway; our access to the prophet's message comes solely through this written text. Then again, one could say that Ezekiel's audience is not merely the small community of exiles physically present before him in Tel-abib. Through this book, the prophet intentionally addresses a far larger audience of *readers*, of which we too are a part.[11]

Concerning not only Ezekiel, but the entire prophetic canon, Martti Nissinen writes:

> Hence, in the biblical context in particular, prophecy *is* literature – not *written* prophecy, that is, prophetic oracles recorded in written form, but distinctly *literary* prophecy, that is, a corpus of written works that, in their present context, are not immediately connected with any flesh–and–blood prophets whose oral performances may or may not loom in the background.[12]

Indeed, some have gone so far as to propose that the prophets in general – and Ezekiel in particular – should best be regarded, not as figures of history, but as literary characters in the books where they appear.[13] Still, others of us do regard at least something of the prophets' pasts, and of their distinctive voices, as recoverable, through close reading and careful historical-critical analysis.[14] For that enterprise, whether a particular sign-act was actually performed *does* matter, for our understanding of the life and message of the historical prophet.

Only two of the sign-acts in Ezekiel make the claim that they actually *were* performed: the fulsomely-described signs of Ezekiel digging through the wall of

---

11 So Robert R. Wilson "Ezekiel," in *Harper's Bible Commentary*, ed. James L. Mays et al. (San Francisco: Harper & Row, 1988), 657. On Ezekiel as an intentional composition, see also Hermann Gunkel, "Die israelitische Literatur," in *Die orientalischen Literaturen*, ed. P. Hinnenberg, Die Kultur der Gegenwart 1/7 (Berlin, 1906), 82; and Rudolf Smend, *Der Prophet Ezechiel*, KeH 8 (Leipzig: S. Hirzel, 1880), xxi: *"man könnte kein Stück herausnehmen, ohne die ganze Ensemble zu zerstören."*

12 Martti Nissinen, *Ancient Prophecy: Near Eastern, Biblical, and Greek Perspectives* (New York: Oxford University Press, 2017), 146.

13 E.g., Mark McEntire, *A Chorus of Prophetic Voices: Introducing the Prophetic Literature of Ancient Israel* (Louisville: Westminster John Knox, 2015), who rejects a reading of prophetic books as "historical biography" (20), and regards the prophets as literary characters. Regarding Ezekiel specifically, see Matthijs J. de Jonge, "Ezekiel as a Literary Figure and the Quest for the Historical Prophet," in *The Book of Ezekiel and Its Influence*, eds. Henk Jan de Jonge and Johannes Tromp (Aldershot, UK/Burlington, VT: Ashgate, 2007), 1–16; and Corrine L. Patton (Carvalho), "Prophet, Priest and Exile: Ezekiel as a Literary Construct," in *Ezekiel's Hierarchical World: Wrestling with a Tiered Reality*, eds Stephen L. Cook and Corrine L. Patton (Carvalho); SBLSS 20 (Atlanta: Society of Biblical Literature, 2004), 73–90.

14 See Stephen L. Cook, John T. Strong, and Steven S. Tuell, *The Prophets: Introducing Israel's Prophetic Literature* (Minneapolis: Fortress, 2022).

his house with a bundle of possessions on his back (12:1–16), and of Yhwh forbidding the prophet to mourn his wife's death publicly (24:15–27). Intriguingly, these are also the two places in the book where, through the performance of a sign-act, Ezekiel himself *becomes* a sign (מופת). Some may find the depiction of Ezekiel digging his way through the wall of his house with his hands less than credible. However, in the refugee settlement at Tel-abib (3:15) where Ezekiel and his fellow exiles lived, walls would have been made of mud brick, and such an action would have been possible.[15] So too, as emotionally wrenching as the sign-act in 24:15–27 plainly must have been, there is nothing physically impossible about wearing festival clothes instead of sackcloth and ashes after a loved one's demise.[16] As Kelvin Friebel notes, "*Difficulty* must be distinguished from *impossibility*, since the former does not obviate actual performance."[17] In short, Ezekiel could have performed both of these sign acts, despite their physical (and emotional) difficulty.

However, the same is clearly true of most of the other sign-acts, even those that are not explicitly said to have been performed. Nothing prevented Ezekiel from, say, carving a map of Jerusalem into a mud brick, and then sitting in the dirt, building little siege ramps and launching an assault on his toy "city" (4:1–3).

---

15 Daniel I. Block, *The Book of Ezekiel, Chapters 1–24*, NICOT (Grand Rapids: Eerdmans, 1977), 370.

16 Many interpreters, such as Walther Zimmerli (*Ezekiel 1*, trans. Ronald E. Clements; Hermeneia [Philadelphia: Fortress, 1979], 29), hold that Ezekiel and the exiles alike are in shock: their inability to mourn is an indication of the depth or extent of their grief (cf. Jer. 16:6–7). Rashi interpreted 24:22 by paraphrasing the prophet's message: "You shall not go into mourning for you shall have no comforters, inasmuch as not one of you but shall be a mourner" (cited by Moshe Greenberg, *Ezekiel 21–37: A New Translation with Introduction and Commentary*, AB 22a [New York: Doubleday, 1997], 515). David J. Halperin, finding here still further evidence of Ezekiel's psychopathology, claims that Ezekiel was *unable* to mourn, because of an ambivalence toward his wife prompted by the prophet's loathing of women (*Seeking Ezekiel: Text and Psychology* [University Park, PA: Pennsylvania State University Press, 1993], 179–81): an assessment irreconcilable with Ezekiel's evident, quiet grief, poignantly described in 24:16–17. In any case, Yhwh does not tell Ezekiel and his audience that they will be *unable* to observe mourning rites; rather, God forbids them to do so. Further, Yhwh instructs Ezekiel and the exiles who follow his example to put on festival garments: fine turbans and sandals. Margaret Odell cites evidence from anthropology and from the Hebrew Bible indicating that a change of clothing, and particularly putting on a turban, is a sign of a change of status (*Ezekiel*, Smyth and Helwys Bible Commentary [Macon, GA: Smyth and Helwys, 2005], 319): "Donning the turban signifies not merely the end of mourning, but the transition to a wholly new identity as the beloved of Yahweh." The fall of Jerusalem is an occasion for rejoicing, not for mourning, for now God is about to do a new thing.

17 Friebel, *Sign-Acts*, 21. As Friebel goes on cogently to observe, "The criterion for actual performance that a behavior must be within a certain range of easiness should be dismissed since an action's higher degree of difficulty may have a correspondingly greater rhetorical impact on the audience" (21).

There is no reason he could not have shaved his head with a sword, divided the hair carefully into thirds, then burned part on his "Jerusalem" brick, hacked at part with his sword, scattered the remains to the wind – and then tied up a few hairs carefully in a corner of his tunic (5:1–4). Given that in most sign-act reports, one or another part of the fulsome form found in Ezek 12:1–16 and 24:15–27 is missing, there seems to be no intrinsic reason to assume that the absence of an explicit statement of performance means that any particular sign-act was *not*, in fact, actually performed.

2 Literary Sign-Acts in Ezekiel

The case of *Ezekiel 4:4–8*, however, is quite different. Here, Ezekiel is commanded to lie on his left side for 390 days, and on his right side for forty days. This would have been extremely difficult, if not physically incapacitating – although, as Friebel notes specifically regarding this sign-act, "difficult" does not mean "impossible."[18] One might ask, though, how Ezekiel was supposed to perform the third and fourth signs while lying on his side? To this Friebel responds that lying on his left or right side "was not a continuously permanent posture, but a position taken in public view only during the time when people were cognizant of the activity."[19] This certainly sounds reasonable; however, it is not what the text *says*.

Another possibility is that Ezekiel literally *could not* move: that he was paralyzed, or catatonic. In 1946, Edwin C. Broome, Jr. offered a confident diagnosis of Ezekiel's disability: based on his catatonic states (Ezek 3:26; 4:4–5, 8),[20] his visions of eyes and of an "influencing machine" (Ezek 1:15–21),[21] and his "Delusions of persecution and grandeur" (Ezek 37:1–14 and 38–39),[22] Ezekiel was suffering from paranoid schizophrenia. As to the actions Ezekiel claims to take in his catatonic state, Broome argues that these are hallucinations experienced during those 430 days.[23] Although rightly rejecting Broome's approach, many interpreters continue to describe Ezekiel as psychologically damaged, based in part on this bizarre sign-act.[24]

---

18 Friebel, *Sign-Acts*, 21.
19 Friebel, *Sign-Acts*, 222.
20 Edwin C. Broome, Jr., "Ezekiel's Abnormal Personality," *JBL* 65 (1946): 279–81.
21 Broome, Jr., "Ezekiel's Abnormal Personality," 284–87.
22 Broome, Jr., "Ezekiel's Abnormal Personality," 291.
23 Broome, Jr., "Ezekiel's Abnormal Personality," 281.
24 Although Zimmerli argues that, given both the later editing and the highly stylized form of Ezekiel's prophecy, we have no immediate access to the prophet's biography (*Ezekiel 1*, 18), he nonetheless says "Ezekiel was a prophet of particular sensitivity and dramatic power, for whom

A close reading of the text of Ezekiel, however, makes it plain that in the final form of the book, the performance of this sign–act is not merely difficult, but impossible. Ezekiel's first vision came in the fourth month on the fifth day of the fifth year of the exile of King Jehoiachin (1:1–2); then, seven days later, Ezekiel was commissioned as a watchman (3:17). Presumably, then, the signs described in 4–5 are understood to have been performed sometime soon after the twelfth day of the fourth month in Jehoiachin's fifth year of exile. The next date in Ezekiel is "the sixth year, in the sixth month, on the fifth day of the month" (8:1) – about 418 days later, at which time the prophet is said to be sitting in his house, with the elders of Judah gathered before him. This is considerably less than the 430 days that, according to the text in its final form, Ezekiel lay on his right or left side, unable to rise (4:8). In short, quite apart from the physical toll this sign-act would have taken on the prophet, or the problem of how to fit in the third and fourth sign-acts, the sign-act in 4:4–8 could not have been performed literally as described. It must be read as a literary feature of Ezekiel's book, not an aspect of his prophetic activity – and certainly not of his psychopathology.

The interpretation of Ezekiel's second sign-act is complicated by three inter-connected problems: the translation of עָוֹן, the referent of the terms "house of Israel" (4:4–5) and "house of Judah" (4:6), and the meaning of the 390 and the forty days. The Hebrew term עָוֹן can denote either a sin (e.g., Exod 20:5) or its penalty (e.g., Gen 4:13). Some interpreters render the term here as "punishment," so that Ezekiel is said to bear the *punishment* of Israel and Judah.[25] However, Yhwh tells Ezekiel, "For I assign to you a number of days, three hundred ninety days, equal to the number of the years of their עָוֹן" (4:5). It is difficult to tell what the significance of 390 years of punishment might be. Note, too, that the LXX has αδικιαν ("guilt" or "violence") for עָוֹן in 4:5. It is better, then, to read with the NIV, and understand Ezekiel, by this sign-act, to be taking upon himself "the *sin* of the house of Israel" (4:4; although, as we will see, the forty years of עָוֹן assigned to Judah call for a different interpretation). This is a priestly act:[26] the priests took

---

a metaphor could become a fully experienced event ... up to the point of actual physical emotion-al participation" (*Ezekiel 1*, 20). Similarly, R. E. Clements (*Ezekiel* [Westminster Bible Companion; Louisville: Westminster John Knox, 1996], 19) writes, "There are several indications in the book that Ezekiel suffered at times from severe nervous and physical disabilities. ... If so, it is a most remarkable testimony to Ezekiel as someone whose work as a prophet absorbed his whole being. Even a seemingly cruel and overpowering disability, which left him without speech or strength to move for long periods, could become part of the message of God to him."

25 So, for example, the NRSV, the NJPS, and Joseph Blenkinsopp, *Ezekiel*, Interpretation (Louis-ville: John Knox, 1990), 36–37.

26 Appropriately so, as Ezekiel was a priest (see Ezek 1:3; Tuell, *Ezekiel*, 9). Cf. Mathews, *Prophets as Performers*, 192: "Ezekiel shares his community's fate, interacts with their God in ways that lead to new outcomes, and is able to articulate new realities. Ezekiel shows us that the performer

the iniquity of their people upon themselves, and so carried away their guilt (Exod 28:38; Num 18:1; regarding the eating of the sin offering, cf. Lev 6:26; 10:17). However, removed from the temple and its system of sacrifices, Ezekiel cannot fully assume this role. While in this sign-act the prophet/priest identifies with his people in their guilt, he has no mechanism to remove it; that guilt still remains.[27]

The difficulty with interpreting the term "house of Israel" also derives from an ambiguity in the term itself. In P (Exod 16:31; Lev. 10:6; Num. 20:29), and particularly in the Holiness Code (Lev 17:3, 8, 10; 22:28), בית ישראל ("house of Israel") refers to the entire nation. However, the term also can refer to the northern kingdom (e.g., Hos 1:4, 6; Mic 1:5). In Ezekiel, where בית ישראל appears eighty-three times (more than in all the other books of the Hebrew Bible combined) the expression is ordinarily used, as in the Holiness Code, for all Israel – or, since with the loss of the northern tribes Judah is all of Israel that remains, for Judah alone.[28] For example, בית ישראל in the first sign-act (4:1–3) must refer to Judah, since it is Jerusalem's imminent destruction that is the point of the sign.

Elsewhere, when Ezekiel is certainly referring to the northern kingdom, he usually does not use the term Israel. So, in 23:4, Samaria, capital of the northern kingdom, is the wicked sister Oholah; and 37:16, the northern kingdom is designated Ephraim and Joseph. Ezekiel 9:9 is the exception that proves the rule: "He said to me, 'The guilt of the house of Israel and Judah is exceedingly great; the land is full of bloodshed and the city full of perversity." The mention of Judah here is unexpected; nothing in the context would lead the reader to assume that בית ישראל means anything other than it usually does in this book – namely, the entire nation, or all of it that remains. With Walther Zimmerli, it seems best to see "Judah" as a later addition to this text,[29] likely by the same hand that in 4:6 added Judah's 40 days/years to the sign concerning Israel's sin.

Still, the use of the contrasting terms "house of Israel" and "house of Judah" in 4:4–8 certainly suggests the northern and southern kingdoms – particularly since the house of Israel is identified with Ezekiel's left side, and the house of Judah with his right (in Hebrew directions, one is assumed to be facing east, so that left means north, and right means south). To solve this mystery, we must first deal with the 390 and forty days/years.

The LXX of 4:5 has not 390, but 190 days. If we subtract from that the forty days/years assigned to Judah, we get 150 for Israel alone – approximately the

---

who is willing to put their body on the line in the service of God's word may make significant contribution to the reshaping of theology and community."

27 Gregory Yuri Glazov, *The Bridling of the Tongue and the Opening of the Mouth in Biblical Prophecy*; JSOTSup 311 (Sheffield: Sheffield Academic Press, 2001), 273.

28 Block, *Ezekiel 1–24*, 176; Friebel, *Sign-Acts*, 216.

29 Walther Zimmerli, "Israel im Buche Ezechiel," *VT* 8 (1958): 82.

number of years from the fall of the northern kingdom to the time of Ezekiel's exile.[30] The LXX translators, then, assumed that "house of Israel" meant the northern kingdom. However, if we stay with the 390 days/years of the MT, and with Ezekiel's typical rendering of "house of Israel" as referring to *all* Israel, then we arrive at another, more probable interpretation. Approximately 390 years before the Babylonian exile, Solomon became king, and the first temple was built.[31] The point of the 390 days, then, would be that the years of the temple are also the years of Israel's עָוֹן (4:5). This harsh assessment is consistent with Ezekiel's statements elsewhere of the radical sin of Jerusalem and of Israel (see Ezek 8; 16; 20). The hopeless corruption of Jerusalem's temple through the long years of Israel's iniquity has led, inevitably, to the city's destruction. Ezekiel 4:4–8, where the prophet lies on his side for 390 days and so takes on himself the sins of his people, is a literary sign-act depicting the years of Jerusalem's temple as the years of its sin.

What do we do, then, with the house of Judah and its forty days? In the description of the third sign-act (4:9–17), the dubious bread is to be eaten "During the number of days that you lie on your side, three hundred ninety days, you shall eat it" (4:9). Only the 390 days are mentioned, not the forty, and nothing further is said of the house of Judah. The most probable explanation is that Judah's forty days are an expansion of the original text of 4:4–8, by Ezekiel's priestly editors. Those first interpreters of Ezekiel understood the house of Israel in the second sign to refer to the northern kingdom; therefore, the representation of Israel's offense had to be counterbalanced by the representation of Judah's.

The forty days assigned to Judah are readily understandable in symbolic terms. Customarily, forty years is the length of a generation. The people of Israel spent forty years in the wilderness so that the entire generation that had rebelled against Yhwh and Moses would die there (cf. Num 14:34, where the correspondence of years to days found in 4:4–8 also appears). Just as Yhwh had decreed that none of the generation that had come out of Egypt would see the land of promise, so none of the generation that went into exile in Babylon would return home. The prophet Jeremiah likewise declared that none of those going into exile would return, though he placed the exile at seventy rather than forty years (see Jer 25:11–12; 29:1–14). Further, 390 + 40 = 430, another important number, as Israel spent 430 years enslaved in Egypt.[32] In regard to Judah, then, עָוֹן *does* mean "punishment." By this expansion to the original text, the focus is further tightened on the people of Judah at the time of the exile. Further, in the final form of the

---

30 Block, *Ezekiel 1–24*, 175–76.
31 Zimmerli, *Ezekiel 1*, 166.
32 Zimmerli, *Ezekiel 1*, 166–68.

book, the addition of Judah's forty days makes the performance of this sign-act impossible, and so renders its literary status absolutely plain. However, the resulting confusion regarding the meaning of the 390 days, the "house of Israel," and the meaning of עוֹן enables us to identify the sign concerning Judah as an expansion.

Note that in this sign-act, Ezekiel has "put the sin of the house of Israel upon [himself]" and, for the duration of this sign, he is said "to bear their sin" (4:4). Ezekiel's sign-act, for all that it is a purely literary sign, is no mere illustration; it accomplishes something. In all his sign-acts, Ezekiel not only witnesses to Yhwh's activity, but also becomes an agent of that activity.

Another problematic sign-act is *37:15–28*. As we have noted, nothing is said of the prophet actually performing this sign. But we do have the command to perform the sign (37:15–17), the people's response (35:18), and the sign-act's interpretation (37:18–28).

Yhwh tells Ezekiel to take one stick (Hebrew עֵץ אֶחָד) and write on it, "For Judah, and the Israelites associated with it," and then take another stick (again, עֵץ אֶחָד) and write on it, "For Joseph (the stick of Ephraim) and all the house of Israel associated with it" (37:16). We might ask how Ezekiel was to write on the sticks, or how an audience could tell what he had written. But the next part of the sign is difficult even to imagine: "Join them together into one stick so that they will become one in your hand" (v. 17). Perhaps Ezekiel places the sticks end to end, hiding the join in his hand, so that they appear as one – though that would be hard to do if the sticks were of any length at all. Or, Ezekiel could have prepared beforehand two interlocking halves of a single stick, which he now rejoins[33] – but that is not what the text says.

The Hebrew term עֵץ means, simply, "wood." It can refer, depending on the context, to a stick, a board, a branch, or even a tree. In *Targum Nebi'im*, עֵץ is translated throughout this passage as לוּחַ, "tablet," suggesting that Ezekiel's "sticks" may have been writing boards. As Daniel Block observes, writing boards coated with colored beeswax and written upon with a pointed stylus are widely attested in the ancient world.[34] If 37:16–17 refers to a writing board, there would be no problem either with the prophet writing on the board, or with the legibility of his message. Finally, writing tablets were often hinged or tied together, so that two could, literally, be brought together as one.[35]

This is a very neat solution, which makes this sign-act certainly doable. Indeed, I earlier advocated for this reading in my commentary.[36] Unfortunately, I

33 Mathews describes this sign-act as "a conjurer's trick" (*Prophets as Performers*, 169).
34 Daniel I. Block, *Ezekiel 25–48*, NICOT (Grand Rapids: Eerdmans, 1998), 400–401.
35 Block, *Ezekiel 25–48*, 405.
36 Tuell, *Ezekiel*, 256.

am now persuaded that it is altogether *too* neat. The Targum is notorious for providing just this sort of solution for difficult texts, and no other ancient version supports its reading. The Vulgate *lignum unum* simply means, like the Hebrew, a piece of wood. But the LXX of 37:16–17 renders עץ as ῥαβδος, which often means "staff" (e.g., Num 17:23, where ῥαβδος translates the Hebrew מטה). In Zechariah 11:7–14, a literary sign-act certainly based on Ezek 37:15–28, the prophet has two staves (שני מקלות; מקל is paralleled with מטה in Jer 48:17), also with symbolic names. In Hebrew, the words מטה and שבט (both meaning "staff") can also mean "tribe" or "clan," since the head of a tribe or clan bears a staff as a symbol of authority (cf. Num 17:1–11). The best reading of Ezek 37:16–17, therefore, is that it refers to two staves, symbolizing rulership over the two kingdoms of Judah and Israel.

As Odell observes, the Black Obelisk of Shalmaneser shows Jehu of Israel bowing to the Assyrian ruler and records in an inscription that he presented to Shalmaneser his ruler's staff, representing his kingdom.[37] So when Ezekiel takes the two staves, he is playing the role of God, who has now assumed rule over all the tribes: "The two 'sticks' thus signify Yahweh's sovereign prerogative to rule and protect these people."[38] This interpretation leaves unexplained both how Ezekiel wrote on the staves, and how he combines the two staves into one; still, as Zimmerli wryly observes, "the argument of clearness of presentation is much less forceful in Ezekiel than with one of the other prophets"![39] Further, that objection vanishes if this is not an actual sign-act, whose performance we must try to visualize, but a purely literary one.

The meaning of the sign-act is certainly obvious. Still, Yhwh says that when Ezekiel's audience asks what all this means (37:18), he is to tell them,

> Thus says the Lord GOD: I will take the people of Israel from the nations among which they have gone, and will gather them from every quarter, and bring them to their own land. I will make them one nation in the land, on the mountains of Israel; and one king shall be king over them all. Never again shall they be two nations, and never again shall they be divided into two kingdoms (Ezek 37:21–22).

The reunification of the tribes into "one nation," signified by the unification of their two staves, will be manifest through one ruler: the line of David will be established once more (37:22–25; cf. 34:23–24). The identification the future Davidic ruler as king (Heb. מלך) in 37:22 and 24 (by contrast 37:25, like 34:24, uses נשיא)

---

37 Odell, *Ezekiel*, 456–57.

38 Odell, *Ezekiel*, 456.

39 Walther Zimmerli, *Ezekiel 2*, trans. J. D. Martin; Hermeneia (Philadelphia: Fortress, 1983), 274.

belongs to the later editing of this book.[40] It is doubtful that Ezekiel, who has been so consistent in his avoidance of the term "king," would change his characteristic usage now.[41]

Once more (37:26; cf. 34:25), Yhwh says "I will make a covenant of peace with them;" although here, that covenant is also called a עולם ברית ("everlasting covenant;" 37:26; cf. 16:60): the term used for God's covenant with all living things following the great flood (Gen 9:16), Yhwh's covenant with Abraham (Gen 17:1–22; see also Ps 105:10//1 Chr 16:17), God's covenant at Sinai (Exod 31:16; Lev 24:8) and the covenant of kingship with David's line (2 Sam 23:5). It is clear that Ezekiel understands none of these covenants as "everlasting" in the sense that they guarantee survival for Israel: indeed, quite to the contrary, as Judah and Jerusalem are doomed. Instead, as in Jeremiah 31:31–34, the promised covenant is implicitly discontinuous with the former, broken one.

The exilic prophets Ezekiel, Jeremiah, and later Second Isaiah understood עולם ברית in new ways. For these prophets of the exile, the focus of the עולם ברית became the *future*, not the past, and would be not be between Yhwh and some exalted individual – Abraham or Moses or David – but between Yhwh and the people. So, in Ezek 37:25–26, while David (implicitly, David's restored lineage cf. 17:22–24) is to be prince forever, God makes the עולם ברית with the people (cf. Jer. 32:40; 50:5; and Isa. 55:3–5).

The one kingdom under one ruler will also have one temple: "I will bless them and multiply them, and will set my sanctuary among them forevermore. My dwelling place shall be with them; and I will be their God, and they shall be my people" (37:26–27). This promise opens up a guarantee of divine presence that brings the book full circle. In chapters 1–3, Ezekiel experienced the Glory in exile, prompting the question: What has become of Jerusalem? In chapters 8–11, the prophet watched in horror as the Glory departed from Jerusalem, abandoning city and temple to their fate. Now Ezekiel promises that, in the future, God will once more establish a dwelling among God's people.

---

40 Walther Eichrodt, *Ezekiel*, trans. Coslett Quin, OTL (Philadelphia: Westminster, 1970), 511–12; Zimmerli, *Ezekiel 2*, 271–72; Ronald M. Hals, *Ezekiel*, FOTL 19 (Grand Rapids: Eerdmans, 1989), 273–74.
41 See Steven Tuell, *The Law of the Temple in Ezekiel 40–48*, HSM 49 (Atlanta: Scholars, 1992), 105–108.

3 Conclusion

The presence of purely literary sign-acts within the book of Ezekiel has both positive and negative implications for the study of the book and the prophet. To take the negative implications first, knowing that 4:4–8 is a literary feature of the book, rather than a bizarre act performed by the prophet, removes a major bit of "evidence" commonly cited for Ezekiel's allegedly broken psyche.[42] Similarly, treating 37:15–28 as a literary sign-act sets the interpreter free to pursue the natural implications of the two staves, without getting lost in the attempt to visualize the sign's performance. Positively, that Ezekiel and his editors were able to transform the sign-act into a literary device provides another example of the way in which this book functions *as* a book – an intentionally shaped literary unity, rather than a collection of performances and pronouncements by the prophet. The evident influence of Ezekiel on the composition and editing of the book of Zechariah also gains further ground. In Zechariah as in Ezekiel, we find sign-acts that are purely literary: Zech 6:9–15 and 11:4–17.[43] The postexilic prophet and his editors have likely learned this tactic from Ezekiel. As effective as the embodiment of Yhwh's message through the performance of a sign-act may be, sometimes it is enough – even necessary – to *tell* rather than to show.

---

42 For a further discussion of this issue, see Steven Tuell, "Should Ezekiel Go To Rehab? The Method to Ezekiel's 'Madness.'" *Perspectives in Religious Studies* 36 (2009): 289–302.

43 While no one would question the characterization of Zech 11:4–17 as a literary sign-act, proposing that 6:9–15 is one also is a bit more controversial. While Zechariah 6:9–15 presents the Lord's command to "Collect silver and gold from the exiles … make a crown [MT "crowns"], and set it on the head of the high priest Joshua" (6:10–11), it describes neither the actual performance of the sign nor the reaction of Zechariah's audience (let alone the reaction of the Persian officials). Both Haggai (1:1–11; 2:2) and Zechariah (1:12; 4:10) stress the limited resources of the *golah* community, making it doubtful that they had any silver and gold to spare. But even assuming that Zechariah could have gathered sufficient silver and gold from these donors to fashion crowns, and assuming that he had the necessary tools and skill to craft crowns from these materials, both making such crowns and using them in the coronation of Jewish officials would have been acts of rebellion against Persia. Neither Haggai nor Zechariah ever call for such a rebellion. Almost certainly, then, Zechariah could not actually have performed this sign-act. But as we have seen with Ezekiel, for the purposes of the prophetic book, the description of the act is enough for the reader to understand the sign-act's meaning: God's blessing upon Joshua the high priest, and upon the Branch (likely, Zerubbabel; 6:12–13).

C. L. Crouch

Jeremiah and Ezekiel's Sign-Acts through the Lens of Trauma

The books of Jeremiah and Ezekiel are replete with sign-acts. Although the parameters of this prophetic genre remain disputed – whether, for example, symbolic actions observed but not performed by the prophet, as in the case of Jeremiah and the potter (Jer 18), are included – it is clear that there are more sign-acts associated with Jeremiah and Ezekiel, respectively, than there are sign-acts involving all the other 'writing' prophets combined.[1]

---

1 Georg Fohrer's classic form-critical analysis identified two sign-acts in Hosea, three in Isaiah, nine in Jeremiah, eleven in Ezekiel, one in Zechariah, and four in 1–2 Kings (*Die symbolischen Handlungen der Propheten*, 2nd edn. [Zurich: Zwingli, 1968]: 1 Kg 11:29–31; 19:19–21; 22:11; 2 Kgs 13:14–19; Isa 7:3; 8:1–4; 20:1–6; Jer 13:1–11; 16:2–4, 5–7, 8–9; 19:1, 2a, 11–11a; 27:1–3, 12b; 28:10–11; 32:1, 7–15; 43:8–13; 51:59–64; Ezek 3:16a with 4:1–3; 3:22–27 with 24:25–27 and 33:21–22; 4:4–8, 9–17; 5:1–17; 12:1–11, 12, 17–20; 21:11–12, 23–29; 24:1–14, 15–24; 37:15–28; Hos 1:2–9; 3:1–5; Zech 6:9–15). He also notes several that fail his form-critical criteria but might otherwise be considered symbolic actions (pp. 71–73). David Stacey, approaching the phenomenon in terms of 'prophetic drama', found three in Hosea, four in Isaiah, one in Micah, two in Zechariah, thirteen in Jeremiah, and sixteen in Ezekiel, plus a further nine in the Deuteronomistic History (*Prophetic Drama in the Old Testament* [London: Epworth, 1990]: 1 Sam 15:27–28; 1 Kgs 11:29–31; 18:20–46; 19:19–20, 21; 22:1–12 [2 Chr 18:1–11]; 2 Kgs 2:12–13; 13:14–17, 18–19; Isa 7:3, 10–17; 8:1–4; 20; Jer 13:1–11; 16:1–4, 5–7, 8–9; 18:1–12; 19:1–13; 25:15–29; 27–28; 32:1–15; 35; 36; 43:8–13; 51:59–64; Ezek 2:8–3:3; 3:22–27, cf. 24:25–27 and 33:21–22; 4:1–3, 4–6, 7, 9–17; 5:1–4; 6:11–14; 12:1–16, 17–20; 21:11–12, 17, 13–22, 23–27, 33–37; 24:1–2, 3–14, 15–24; 37:15–28; Hos 1:2–3, 3–9; 3:1–5; Mic 1:8; Zech 6:9–15; 11:4–17). Deeming the unconventional nature of the act crucial, Åke Viberg drew up a narrower list that nevertheless highlights Jeremiah and Ezekiel: one sign-act in the Deuteronomistic History, one in Isaiah, six in Jeremiah, eleven in Ezekiel, one in Hosea, and one in Zechariah (*Prophets in Action: An Analysis of Prophetic Symbolic Acts in the Old Testament*, ConBOT 55 [Stockholm: Almqvist and Wiksell, 2007]: 1 Kgs 11:29–31; Isa 20; Jer 13:1–11; 19:1–2, 10–11; 27:2–3; 28:10–11; 32:6–15; 43:8–10; 51:59–64; Ezek 4:1–3, 4–8, 9–12; 5:1–4; 12:3–7, 17–20; 21:11–12, 17, 19; 24:15–24; 37:15–22; Hos 1:2–3; 3:1–4; Zech 6:9–15). Counting 'all the nonverbal behaviours (i.e. bodily movements, gestures and paralanguage) whose primary purpose was

---

Note: I am grateful to students in 'Prophetic Responses to Trauma' at Fuller Theological Seminary, in conversation with whom I was first able to explore these ideas. Kiel McFarland provided assistance in navigating the psychological literature and Nicola Patton assisted with the bibliography and references. The essay has also benefitted from the engagement of the Biblical Seminar at Radboud University, attendees at the joint session of the Writing/Reading Jeremiah and the Theological Perspectives on the Book of Ezekiel programme units at the 2021 Annual Meeting of the Society of Biblical Literature in San Antonio, Juliana Claassens, and the editors of this volume. Its weaknesses of course remain my own.

https://doi.org/10.1515/9783111521015-002

This concentration of sign-acts is not coincidental but reflects these traditions' origins in the traumatic experiences of the sixth century BCE. These two books are by now widely recognised as major loci of the traumas associated with the demise of the kingdom of Judah and its capital at Jerusalem, including – though not limited to – widespread death, displacement, and deportation.[2] Contemporary evidence from the social sciences indicates that difficulty with language and the substitution of somatic expression as a means of communication is common among persons who have experienced traumatic events of this kind. Jeremiah and Ezekiel's extensive use of non-verbal, somatic modes of communication is thus in keeping with this wider human proclivity.[3]

Although a handful of trauma-informed biblical scholars have made passing comments linking (particularly Ezekiel's) sign-acts to trauma – thus Smith-Christopher has suggested that 'many of Ezekiel's "bizarre" actions can be seen as modelling the trauma of the fall of Jerusalem',[4] Furman suggests that Ezekiel's 'radical deeds ... show the existence of "national-theological post-trauma"',[5] and Bowen connects Ezekiel's behaviour to trauma re-enactments[6] – no one has yet connected the exceptional preponderance of sign acts in Jeremiah and Ezekiel to the traumatic experiences of the sixth century, or attempted a sustained interpre-

---

communicative and interactive', whilst limiting the list to those that were 'actually performed before audiences', Kelvin Friebel identifies eight sign-acts in Jeremiah and thirteen or fourteen in Ezekiel (*Jeremiah's and Ezekiel's Sign-Acts: Rhetorical Nonverbal Communication*, JSOTSup 283, [Sheffield: Sheffield Academic, 1999], 14, 15: Jer 13:1–11; 16:1–9; 19:1–13; 27–28; 32:1–44; 35:1–19; 43:8–13; 51:59–64a; Ezek 3:22–27 cf. 24:25–27 and 33:21–22; 4–5; 6:11–12; 12:1–16, 17–20; 21:11–29; 24:15–24; 25:15–24; 37:15–28). Whether the sign-acts described in these books were actually performed in public by prophets bearing the names of Jeremiah and Ezekiel is not of primary interest in the present study. Real or imagined, these sign-acts play an outsized role in these two particular books.

2 The secondary literature in this area is growing fast; major works include C. L. Crouch, *Israel and Judah Redefined*, SOTSMS (Cambridge: Cambridge University Press, 2021); Kathleen M. O'Connor, *Jeremiah: Pain and Promise* (Minneapolis, MN: Fortress, 2012); Ruth Poser, *Das Ezechielbuch Als Trauma-Literatur*, VTSup 154 (Leiden: Brill, 2012); Daniel Smith-Christopher, *A Biblical Theology of Exile*, OBT (Minneapolis, MN: Fortress, 2002); Louis Stulman and Hyun Chul Paul Kim, *You Are My People: An Introduction to Prophetic Literature* (Nashville, TN: Abingdon, 2010). For a bibliography of work up to the mid-2010s, see David G. Garber, Jr., "Trauma Theory and Biblical Studies", *CBR* 14/1 (2015): 24–44.

3 Unlike certain older psychological studies of Ezekiel, the following is not an attempt to 'diagnose' Jeremiah or Ezekiel with one or more mental health disorders. Rather, it seeks to observe the ways in which an appropriate sensitivity to the effects of traumatic experience can help make sense of a prominent feature of these traditions.

4 Smith-Christopher, *A Biblical Theology of Exile*, 95.

5 Refael Furman, "Trauma and Post-Trauma in the Book of Ezekiel", *OTE* 33/1 (2020): 32–59, 56.

6 Nancy R. Bowen, *Ezekiel*, AOTC (Nashville, TN: Abingdon, 2010), 28–29.

tation of the sign-act phenomenon in conversation with recent literature from trauma studies. The following seeks to fill that gap.[7]

1 Language

Traumatic experience can prompt a wide variety of atypical behaviours. The type and severity of these vary, depending on the prior mental and physical state of the victim(s), the availability of social and psychological support networks, and local cultural expectations regarding the expression of acute distress. One of the most well-documented difficulties faced by survivors of traumatic experiences concerns language: insofar as trauma stands outside of the normal range of human experience, it is common to find survivors struggling to talk about what has happened to them.[8] Ordinary language proves inadequate to the task of describing extraordinary experience; as a consequence, 'the fragmented, silence-riddled language of the trauma victim' arises in the gap between words and experience.[9]

A growing body of research indicates that these linguistic issues are not purely problems of the mind, but are linked intimately to the effects of trauma on the body. That is, in some physical way, 'trauma disrupts the brain's ability to

---

7 The following discussion contains material that some trauma survivors may find triggering.
8 Note that to describe trauma as outside the range of normal human experience is not the same as saying that it is uncommon. Herman explains: 'Traumatic events are extraordinary, not because they occur rarely, but rather because they overwhelm the ordinary human adaptations to life. Unlike commonplace misfortunes, traumatic events generally involve threats to life or bodily integrity, or a close personal encounter with violence and death. They confront human beings with the extremities of helplessness and terror, and evoke the responses of catastrophe.' Judith L. Herman, *Trauma and Recovery: The Aftermath of Violence – From Domestic Abuse to Political Terror* (New York: BasicBooks, 1993), 33.
9 Constance J. Dalenberg, *Countertransference and the Treatment of Trauma* (Washington, D.C.: American Psychological Association, 2000), 57–68; cf. e.g., Judy K. Eekhoff, 'No Words to Say It: Trauma and Its Aftermath', *American Journal of Psychoanalysis* 81/2 (2021): 186–206; Julia Huemer et al, 'Emotional Expressiveness and Avoidance in Narratives of Unaccompanied Refugee Minors', *European Journal of Psychotraumatology* 7 (2016): 1–9; Lena Jelinek et al, 'Verbal and Nonverbal Memory Functioning in Posttraumatic Stress Disorder (PTSD)', *Journal of Clinical and Experimental Neuropsychology* 28 (2016): 940–948. On the resistance of pain of all kinds to language see also Elaine Scarry, *The Body in Pain: The Making and Unmaking of the World* (Oxford: Oxford University Press, 1985), esp. 4–5. On the manifestation of these language struggles in literature and art, see e.g., Cathy Caruth, 'Recapturing the Past', in *Trauma: Explorations in Memory*, ed. Cathy Caruth (London: Johns Hopkins University Press, 1995), 151–157; Lea Wernick Fridman, *Words and Witness: Narrative and Aesthetic Strategies in the Representation of the Holocaust* (Albany, N.Y.: State University of New York Press, 2000) and below.

linguistically and logically organize experience', as is necessary for the articulation of experience in words.[10] Whatever the precise mechanisms of the phenomenon, it is now widely recognised that a 'common social response to a traumatic past event is silence and inhibition'.[11] This is true across a very wide range of traumatic experiences, including war, natural disasters, and experiences of personal violence such as rape.[12]

1.1 Language in Jeremiah and Ezekiel

Trauma-induced language issues are pervasive in both Jeremiah and Ezekiel. Perhaps the most obvious manifestation of these linguistic inhibitions is the thrice-repeated report of Ezekiel's mutism (Ezek 3:25–27; 24:25–27; 33:21–22). Whatever the practicalities of the prophet's silence – and much ink has been spilt arguing over whether it was absolute or intermittent, whether one or both of the main reports in Ezek 3 and 33 has been temporally displaced for literary reasons, and so on – this declaration that the prophet will be incapable of speech is a prominent and profound acknowledgment of the chasm between his and his community's lived experience of Judah's downfall and the capacity of prophetic language adequately to describe that experience in words. As Ruth Poser puts it, in such circumstances 'silence ... is the only appropriate reaction to the unbearably traumatic events'.[13]

Another indication of that these books reflect a trauma-induced struggle with language is the way that they talk around the prophets' and their communities' experiences, rather than expressing them directly. Ezekiel's opening vision

---

10 Huemer et al, 'Emotional Expressiveness', 3; cf. Bessel A. van der Kolk, *The Body Keeps the Score: Brain, Mind, and Body in the Healing of Trauma* (New York: Penguin, 2014), esp. 39–47; Ruth Kevers et al, 'Remembering Collective Violence: Broadening the Notion of Traumatic Memory in Post-Conflict Rehabilitation', *Culture, Medicine, and Psychiatry: An International Journal of Cross-Cultural Health Research* 40, no. 4 (2016): 620–640; all with further references.
11 Kevers et al, 'Remembering Collective Violence', 627, 630
12 The phenomenon has been especially extensively discussed in relation to the Holocaust; see, e.g., Michael F. Bernard-Donals and Richard R Glejzer, *Witnessing the Disaster: Essays on Representation and the Holocaust* (Madison, WI: University of Wisconsin Press, 2003); Shoshana Felman and Dori Laub, *Testimony: Crises of Witnessing in Literature, Psychoanalysis and History* (Florence: Taylor and Francis, 2013); Geoffrey H. Hartman, *The Longest Shadow: In the Aftermath of the Holocaust* (New York: Palgrave Macmillan, 2002); Lawrence L. Langer, *The Holocaust and the Literary Imagination* (New Haven, CT: Yale University Press, 1975).
13 Ruth Poser, 'No Words: The Book of Ezekiel as Trauma Literature and a Response to Exile', in *Bible Through the Lens of Trauma*, ed. Elizabeth Boase and Christopher G. Frechette (Atlanta, GA: SBL, 2017), 27–48, 38.

offers an immediate example. Struggling to find words adequate to describe his experience, Ezekiel resorts to a litany of similes: he sees 'something *like* gleaming amber ... something *like* four living creatures ... something that looked *like* burning coals of fire ... *like* the gleaming of beryl ... something *like* a dome ... the sound of their wings *like* the sound of mighty waters, *like* the thunder of Shaddai ... something *like* a throne, in appearance *like* sapphire ... something that seemed *like* a human form ... something *like* gleaming amber, something that looked *like* fire' (Ezek 1).[14]

The book thereafter is saturated with allegory and metaphor – artistic circumlocutions that seek to convey traumatic experience by 'telling it slant'.[15] The so-called Song of the Sword (Ezek 21) is famously incomprehensible; commentators have proposed all manner of emendations and reorganisations in their efforts to render it even so much as translatable. Commenting wryly on YHWH's suggestion that Ezekiel is to use plain speech (Ezek 3:4–7), Jacob Myers remarks that in fact 'Ezekiel presents the most *obscure* and *difficult* display of language in all of Scripture.'[16] Ordinary language simply will not do; hunting for words capable of expressing the trauma of defeat and deportation, Ezekiel resorts to Hebrew's furthest reaches.

That Jeremiah also struggles to put these traumatic experiences into words is even more widely recognised than is the case with Ezekiel.[17] From the very first chapter, Jeremiah reveals the disorientating impact of catastrophe – even the book's depiction of the passage of time has been disrupted.[18] Notoriously

---

14 Notably: even as the verbal part of the brain shuts down during traumatic events and their recall, the imaging areas are extremely active (van der Kolk, *The Body Keeps the Score*, 43–44). Ezekiel's visual emphasis is widely noted; this may also reflect the aftermath of trauma.

15 The phrase comes into biblical studies from the poetry of Emily Dickenson via O'Connor, *Jeremiah*, 33. From the psychological perspective, Dalenberg, *Countertransference*, 59–68, who makes special reference to the life and work of Elie Wiesel. On the articulation of traumatic experience through artistic modes of communication, see further below.

16 Jacob D. Myers, 'Obscure Preaching: Postmodern Homiletical Insights from Ezekiel the Prophet', *RevExp* 111/4 (2014): 401–410, 401, 410.

17 O'Connor, *Jeremiah*.

18 Yosefa Raz, 'Jeremiah "Before the Womb": On Fathers, Sons, and the Telos of Redaction in Jeremiah 1', in *Prophecy and Power: Jeremiah in Feminist and Postcolonial Perspective*, ed. Christl M. Maier and Carolyn J. Sharp, LHBOTS 577 (London: Bloomsbury, 2013), 86–100; cf. Bessel A. van der Kolk and Onno van der Hart, 'The Intrusive Past: The Flexibility of Memory and the Engraving of Trauma', in *Trauma: Explorations in Memory*, ed. Cathy Caruth (Baltimore, MD: Johns Hopkins University Press, 1995), 158–182, 177. Fridman, *Words and Witness*, 130 explicitly links the 'unrepresentable' nature of trauma with its defiance of temporality: 'Having fallen out of time, it [trauma] has also fallen out of language'; cf. Cathy Caruth, *Unclaimed Experience: Trauma, Narrative, and History* (Baltimore, MD: Johns Hopkins University Press, 1996), 61; van der Kolk, *The Body Keeps the Score*, 47, 69–73.

repetitive, the body of the book is a frequently frustrating agglomeration of poetry and prose that leaps from topic to topic, and from form to form, with what often seems like the barest semblance of coherence.[19] In several publications, O'Connor has observed the way that, in its efforts to communicate the horror of Jerusalem's destruction, Jeremiah 'searches relentlessly for language ... wanders down many literary avenues', and 'spills worlds of words into the ruptures of communal life'.[20] The book is littered with marginally-coherent exclamations, such as *hôy* and *'ôy*, 'woe' (Jer 4:13, 31; 6:4; 10:19; 13:27; 15:10; 43:3); groans that express a profound loss of hope, purpose, and identity.[21] It is now widely recognised that Jeremiah's 'inconcinnities and disjunctions reflect the *incomprehensibility of trauma* in the human ... and divine realms'.[22]

In fact, both Jeremiah and Ezekiel struggle with words to the point of excess. In its Hebrew form Jeremiah is the longest book in all of the Hebrew Bible; Ezekiel is not far behind. Both outstrip their nearest prophetic competition, Isaiah, by several thousand words, despite Isaiah's century-plus head start. Because Hebrew is typically (notoriously) laconic, these books' surfeit of words is especially striking: as they attempt to describe experiences that are fundamentally indescribable, they spew verbiage in all directions. Trauma creates 'a hole in the fabric of language' that these books are desperately trying to patch over.[23] Both are plagued with textual and transmissional difficulties, from the micro-level to the macro. The climactic chapters at the end of Ezekiel 1–39, for example, are organised differently in P967 than they are in the Masoretic tradition; Jeremiah's oracles against the nations appear variously in the middle or at the end of the book. Both have a fairly high rate of *hapax legomena*.[24] Frequently minor but nevertheless pervasive differences between the Hebrew *Vorlage* of Jeremiah's Greek rendering and the extant Masoretic text further suggest that efforts to convey the incomprehensible events of the kingdom's destruction in (something resembling) comprehensible language continued to demand scribal attention for some time.

---

19 O'Connor and Stulman have undertaken extensive analyses of Jeremiah from the perspective of trauma's effects on language; see, e.g., O'Connor, *Jeremiah*; Louis Stulman, 'Jeremiah as a Polyphonic Response to Suffering', in *Inspired Speech: Prophecy in the Ancient Near East*, ed. John Kaltner and Louis Stulman (London: T&T Clark, 2004), 302–318.
20 O'Connor, *Jeremiah*, 32–33.
21 Samuel Hildebrandt, '"Woe Is Me! The Book of Jeremiah and the Language of Despair', *JBL* 139/3 (2020): 479–497, 482.
22 Louis Stulman, 'Art and Atrocity, and the Book of Jeremiah', in *Jeremiah Invented: Constructions and Deconstructions of Jeremiah*, ed. Else K. Holt and Carolyn J. Sharp, LHBOTS 595 (London: Bloomsbury, 2015), 92–103, 101.
23 Fridman, *Words and Witness*, 79.
24 Job and Psalms, which have been fruitfully examined from a trauma-informed perspective, exhibit similar trends.

These struggles to convey what is happening to the kingdom and its people echo one therapist's description of a traumatised patient's effort to communicate: 'She began to have difficulty completing a sentence. She couldn't speak without stopping, pausing, and starting again, speaking tangentially and then abruptly stopping again ... Her breaks made following her difficult'.[25] As readers of these prophetic books attempt to follow Jeremiah and Ezekiel's stops, starts, and digressions, they will do well to recognise that these strange ways of speaking mirror the extraordinary experiences they seek to describe.

2 Somatisation

If words are an inadequate (or inaccessible) communicative instrument for the trauma survivor – what alternatives are there? 'Trauma' itself suggests one possibility: etymologically, the word originates as the Greek term for a physical wound. In the psychological sciences, the term was taken over in the late nineteenth century to describe the invisible injuries inflicted on the mind by certain kinds of psychologically disturbing experiences. Yet, even as trauma research continues to focus primarily on the psychological effects of traumatic experience, the potential for these experiences to affect other parts of the body is increasingly recognised.

Clinically referred to as 'somatisation', these physical symptoms of trauma – symptoms which cannot be linked clearly to physical injury, or other physical cause – manifest in a variety of ways, including gastrointestinal issues, vomiting, paralysis, amnesia, headaches, double vision, dizziness, fatigue, and muscular or joint pain.[26] The precise manifestation of symptoms, the way they are communicated, and the way they are treated are influenced by a wide range of physical, social, cultural, and psychological factors.[27] Sometimes traumatised persons will even re-enact the traumatic event, usually without being fully aware that what they are doing is a repetition of their earlier experience. One of the most famous of such cases is Pierre Janet's patient Irène, who re-enacted the night her mother

---

25 Eekhoff, 'No Words to Say It', 192.

26 'Physical symptoms are common after severe or recurrent traumatic stress and/or if there were physical sensations at the time of the stressor (for example, rape), irrespective of whether there was permanent tissue damage' (Charles V. Ford, 'Somatic Symptoms, Somatization, and Traumatic Stress: An Overview', *Nordic Journal of Psychiatry* 51/1 [1997]: 5–13, 5).

27 See Charles C. Engel, Jr., 'Somatization and Multiple Idiopathic Physical Symptoms: Relationship to Traumatic Events and Posttraumatic Stress Disorder', in *Trauma and Health: Physical Health Consequence of Exposure to Extreme Stress*, ed. Paula P. Schnurr and Bonnie L. Green (Washington, D.C.: American Psychological Association, 2004), 191–215; van der Kolk, *The Body Keeps the Score*, 186–190.

died for several months before she was able to speak about what had happened and assimilate it into her conscious memory. The phenomenon has been documented many times since then.[28]

Relevant to the sixth century situation is that 'multiple traumas may progressively lower the threshold for the development of [somatic] symptoms'.[29] The years surrounding the kingdom's collapse were rife with potentially traumatising events: Jerusalem's eventual surrender was the culmination of decades of political instability, accompanied by an array of national security threats. These years saw multiple sieges – one of which lasted for more than a year, resulting in widespread starvation and death, and both of which resulted in the forced deportation of significant numbers of people. The homeland saw widespread internal displacement and refugee movements, as families sought to evade first the incoming army and then the consequences of imperial rule. The sacred precincts were invaded and plundered, and much of the city went up in flames. Though the picture is sketched by the biblical texts only in its broad and largely communal outlines, it depicts a generation repeatedly exposed to opportunities for trauma.

Somatic symptoms appear remarkably consistently in the wake of war and violent trauma of this kind. Perhaps especially striking is the marked association between the development of somatic symptoms and experiences of dead body handling.[30] Although the exact numbers are unknown, the death toll of Jerusalem's successive sieges and forced deportations would have been significant (Lam 2:21; 4:5; etc.). Estimates of death rates during Middle Eastern involuntary migrations in the eighteenth and nineteenth centuries CE range from twenty to fifty per cent.[31] Interaction with corpses may have been especially traumatic for those with priestly connections, as both Ezekiel and Jeremiah profess to have,

---

28 See van der Kolk, *The Body Keeps the Score*, 31–33, 181–185 for this and other examples.

29 Ford, 'Somatic Symptoms', 9. Jeremiah and Ezekiel undoubtedly underwent long periods of expansion and revision (see above), but the events of the sixth century are their consistent frame of reference.

30 Engel, Jr., 'Somatization and Multiple Idiopathic Physical Symptoms', 201–203; Ford, 'Somatic Symptoms', 10 for discussion and references. On the sheer volume of bodies in Jeremiah and Ezekiel see below.

31 Dawn Chatty, *Displacement and Dispossession in the Modern Middle East* (Cambridge: Cambridge University Press, 2010), 94, 96, 102. Note that somatic post-traumatic symptoms are attested in other literature of the ancient world (Carol S. North, 'Somatization in Survivors of Catastrophic Trauma: A Methodological Review', *Environmental Health Perspectives* 110/4 [2002]: 637–640, 637; David B. Mumford, 'Somatization: A Transcultural Perspective', *International Review of Psychiatry* 5 [1993]: 231–242); somatic language is also frequently used in connection with emotional states in the Hebrew Bible, indicating an awareness of the emotional significance of physical symptoms (David B. Mumford, 'Emotional Distress in the Hebrew Bible: Somatic or Psychological?', *British Journal of Psychiatry* 160 [1992]: 92–97).

because dead bodies rendered those in contact with them ritually unclean (Jer 1:1; Ezek 1:3 cf. Lev 21:1–4; Num 19:11–18). Somatic manifestations of trauma also appear to be more prevalent among refugees than non-refugees, likely as a result of the traumatic nature of the experiences that drive persons to flee their home-land.[32] Both books attest to repeated involuntary migration in the run-up to and aftermath of Jerusalem's destruction.

Why traumatic experience can affect the body in this way is still not very well understood, though recent research in this area has made some helpful suggestions.[33] One explanation connects somatisation to the language problems discussed above, suggesting that memories of traumatic events are laid down in the body, precisely because they cannot be processed in the mind via language. That is, when trauma leaves an individual 'in a state of "speechless terror" in which words fail to describe what has happened ... [their traumatic memories are] stored as sensory perceptions, obsessional ruminations, or as behavioral re-enactments'. [34] Indeed, a person's 'memories of trauma may have no verbal (ex-plicit) component whatsoever', at least in the first instance; rather, they are 're-membered' in the form of somatosensory flashbacks, in a variety of modalities (e.g., visual, olfactory, affective, auditory or kinesthetic).[35] This is the memory of a rape victim who flinches from a lover's touch; the memory of a combat veteran who dives for cover at the sound of a car backfiring. Not words but rather sensa-tion triggers a re-living of the original traumatic experience.

Another explanation of traumatic somatisation relates to the way that the body responds to the kind of extreme conditions that give rise to trauma, suggest-ing that somatic symptoms 'may derive from a permanent state of arousal' in the

---

32 Hans G. Rohlof, Jeroen W. Knipscheer, and Rolf Kleber, 'Somatization in Refugees: A Review', *Social Psychiatry and Psychiatric Epidemiology* 49 (2014): 1793–1804.

33 For an accessible discussion of research on trauma's effects on the body, see van der Kolk, *The Body Keeps the Score*, esp. 49–104.

34 Bessel A. van der Kolk, 'Trauma and Memory', *Psychiatry and Clinical Neurosciences* 52 (1998): 552–564; cf. Herman, *Trauma and Recovery*, 37–42.

35 van der Kolk, 'Trauma and Memory', n.p. He reports that, 'when asked about the traumatic memory, all of these subjects reported that they initially had no narrative memory of the event; they could not tell a story about what had happened, regardless of whether they always knew that the trauma had happened, or whether they retrieved memories of the trauma at a later date. All these subjects, regardless of the age at which the trauma occurred, claimed that they initially 'remembered' the trauma in the form of somatosensory flashback experiences. These flashbacks occurred in a variety of modalities: visual, olfactory, affective, auditory and kinesthet-ic, but initially these sensory modalities did not occur together. As the trauma came into con-sciousness with greater intensity, more sensory modalities were activated, and a capacity to tell themselves and others what had happened emerged over time.'

autonomic nervous system.[36] This is the system responsible for the existential 'fight or flight' response, which in trauma survivors fails to shut down even after the danger is past. It is responsible for trauma survivors' characteristic hyper-reactivity to non-threatening situations, and the exhaustion that its constant flood of hormones and chemicals produces in the body has been proposed as a possible source of the body's subsequent symptoms: the body, incapable of relaxing its hyper-vigilant state, simply exhausts itself.

In its most extreme form, the body's defensive response to danger is to freeze (tonic immobility): feigning death in hope that the source of the threat might lose interest and go away. This is especially well-documented in animals, but has also been observed among humans, where it is primarily associated with severely traumatised persons, those for whom escape during the traumatising event was either impossible or unsuccessful.[37] Perhaps the most well-known example among humans is the rape victim who recalls being unable to move or fight back during the assault. Notably, immobilisation at the time of the original trauma is associated with particularly strong psychological consequences thereafter, including feelings of shame, contempt for self, and self-blaming; a similar, involuntary immobility may also be re-triggered by later reminders of the original traumatic situation.[38] Perhaps most striking are cases in which traumatised persons, under threat of additional trauma, withdraw from the world entirely, progressing from reduced speech and loss of appetite to complete or near-complete unresponsiveness.[39]

---

36 Rohlof, Knipscheer, and Kleber, 'Somatization in Refugees', 1794; cf. van der Kolk, *The Body Keeps the Score*, 45–47; Herman, *Trauma and Recovery*, 35–36.

37 Frank M. Corrigan, 'Defense Responses: Frozen, Suppressed, Truncated, Obstructed, and Malfunctioning', in *Neurobiology and Treatment of Traumatic Dissociation: Toward an Embodied Self*, ed. Ulrich F. Lanius, Sandra Paulsen, and Frank M. Corrigan (New York: Springer, 2014), 131–152; Pat Ogden and Janina Fisher, 'Integrating Body and Mind: Sensorimotor Psychotherapy and Treatment of Dissociation, Defense, and Dysregulation', in *Neurobiology and Treatment of Traumatic Dissociation*, 399–422; Engel, Jr., 'Somatization and Multiple Idiopathic Physical Symptoms'; Herman, *Trauma and Recovery*, 42–47. Note that 'trauma-related disorders have long been characterized by a vacillation between intrusive reliving of past trauma, accompanied by dysregulated autonomic arousal and animal defences, and numb avoidance of traumatic reminders, accompanied by constriction, loss of energy, and diminished pleasure' (Ogden and Fisher, 'Integrating Body and Mind', 399). That is, trauma originates with and is subsequently characterised by extremes of human experience; both acute sensitivity/hyper-reactivity and complete numbness/inactivity are equally possible outworkings of trauma.

38 Corrigan, 'Defense Responses', 131–137, 143–149; Ogden and Fisher, 'Integrating Body and Mind', 405, 416.

39 Although best-known today in connection with migrant children in Sweden and Australia, the phenomenon was described by psychiatrists as early as the 1950s (see Anne-Liis von Knorring and Elisabeth Hultcrantz, 'Asylum-Seeking Children with Resignation Syndrome: Catatonia or Traumat-

2.1 Somatisation in Jeremiah and Ezekiel

The fact that traumatic experiences can manifest themselves somatically, especially in the aftermath of war and involuntary flight, sheds light on a number of aspects of Jeremiah and Ezekiel's efforts to communicate.

At the broadest level, trauma-induced somatisation explains the sheer volume of bodily language in these two books – there is more of it here, with greater intensity, than anywhere else in the prophetic literature.[40] In addition to the material typically considered sign-acts, the somatisation of the prophets' and the people's traumatic experiences is remarkably pervasive – and remarkably explicit. Ezekiel resorts to intense, physically graphic allegories as it attempts to describe what has happened and what will happen to Jerusalem (Ezek 16; 23). Ezekiel 22 'deal[s] with the physical experiences of violence, suffering and pain by those under siege in Jerusalem and by the exiles in Babylon' and describes the consequences of the bloodshed in explicitly bodily terms (Ezek 22:13).[41] Corpses pile up (Ezek 6:4–13; 9:7; 11:6–7; 37:1–2, 9), past transgressions are failures of the body (Ezek 3:7; 11:21; 16:30, etc.), and the future depends on an organ transplant (Ezek 11:19; 36:26). Likewise in Jeremiah, bodies are everywhere: dead (Jer 7:33; 9:1, 22; 16:4; 18:21; 19:7; 25:33; 26:23; 28:16; 31:40; 33:5; 34:20; 36:30; 51:49), diseased (Jer 16:4), leaking (Jer 9:1, 18; 13:17; 14:17; 31:16), and bloody (Jer 2:34; 19:4; 22:17; 51:35).

These books also focus on the prophetic personae in a way that other prophetic books do not – a fact that has stood out for many of Jeremiah's and Ezekiel's interpreters. Jeremiah scholars, in particular, have focused on the way that Jeremiah's life and physical person are used to communicate suffering.[42] Some

---

ic Withdrawal Syndrome?', *European Child & Adolescent Psychiatry* 29 [2020]: 1103–1109; cf. Giuseppe Sarli et al, 'COVID-19 Related Lockdown: A Trigger from the Pre-Melancholic Phase to Catatonia and Depression, a Case Report of a 59 Year Old Man', *BMC Psychiatry* 20 [2020]: n.p.).

40 Yvonne Sherwood, 'Prophetic Scatology: Prophecy and the Art of Sensation', in *Biblical Blaspheming: Trials of the Sacred for a Secular Age* (Cambridge: Cambridge University Press, 2012), 129–175, 148: 'More than any other prophetic book, Ezekiel exhibits the divine habit of writing on the body or expressing messages on male and female flesh at its most visible and lurid'. Somatic language is also especially prominent in Lamentations – which is likewise a product of acute trauma. Boase highlights its extensive use of bodily metaphors, arguing that they somatise trauma in order to 'embod[y] the trauma in a way that gives voice to the unutterable' (Elizabeth Boase, 'The Traumatized Body: Communal Trauma and Somatization in Lamentations', in *Jeremiah Invented*, 193–209, 194). A similar phenomenon – the inadequacy of speech resulting in an effort to communicate via the body – appears to be at work in Jeremiah and Ezekiel.

41 Dorothea Erbele-Küster, 'Eat This Scroll (Ezekiel 3): Reading as Eating with Special Reference to "Niddah" (Menstruation)', *Canon and Culture* 2 (2009): 5–26, 18–19.

42 See especially O'Connor, *Jeremiah*. On Ezekiel, see Rhiannon Graybill, *Are We Not Men? Unstable Masculinity in the Prophets* (Oxford: Oxford University Press, 2017), 97–120.

of this material is conventionally considered part of the sign-act genre, though not all. Jeremiah remains unmarried and childless, as a sign of the destruction of the kingdom's families (Jer 16:1–4). He buys a field in Anathoth, as a promise that 'houses and fields and vineyards shall again be bought' by the people (Jer 32:6–15). He is imprisoned in a pit from which he is unable to escape, just as the people are trapped in the city by the Babylonian siege (Jer 32:1–5, etc.). Later he is taken out of the country by force, just as many of his compatriots had been (Jer 43:5–6).[43] As Corrine Carvalho memorably described it: Jeremiah's 'body is the stage on which [Jerusalem's] urban disaster is enacted'.[44]

Ezekiel, for his part, bears the horrors of Jerusalem's siege in his person: day after day after day (Ezek 4:4–8).[45] His hair goes the way of Jerusalem's inhabitants: scattered and destroyed (Ezek 5:1–4). He crawls through a wall, enacting the frantic flight of Jerusalem's past and future refugees (Ezek 12:1–16). The dismant-

---

43 On Jeremiah as an involuntary migrant, see David J. Reimer, 'There – But Not Back Again: Forced Migration and the End of Jeremiah', *HeBAI* 7/3 (2018): 359–375; Crouch, *Israel and Judah Redefined*, 115–146.

44 Corrine L. Carvalho, 'Drunkenness, Tattoos, and Dirty Underwear: Jeremiah as a Modern Masculine Metaphor', *CBQ* 80 (2018): 597–618, 597; cf. J. Lindblom's description of the sign-acts as '*verbum visibile*, a visible word' (*Prophecy in Ancient Israel* [Oxford: Basil Blackwell, 1973], 172).

45 Furman has highlighted this episode as potentially symptomatic of trauma (Ezek 4:4–8) ('Trauma and Post-Trauma', 56; he also refers to the 'ecstasies of sexual abasement' in Ezek 16; 23 and to Ezekiel's passivity, cf. Ellen F. Davis, *Swallowing the Scroll: Textuality and the Dynamics of Discourse in Ezekiel's Prophecy*, JSOTSup 78 / BLS 21 [Sheffield: Almond, 1989], 52). A common interpretive concern here is the purported impossibility of the sign-act's execution, due to its duration and physical toll on the prophet's body. One of the characteristics of traumatic memory, however, is that it 'takes too long' – far, far longer than it would take to convey the same information in speech. Janet's patient Irène took three to four hours to tell her story in traumatic re-enactments; 'when she was finally able to tell her tale [verbally], it took her only half a minute' (van der Kolk and van der Hart, 'The Intrusive Past', 163; for a longer description of this and other traumatic re-enactments see van der Kolk, *The Body Keeps the Score*, 181–182). Trauma survivors may also suffer from extended periods of immobility. Responsiveness in such states varies; it has been observed especially among survivors of violent conflict and among refugees, and appears to be linked to a fear that the traumatic experience will repeat itself (Engel, Jr., 'Somatization and Multiple Idiopathic Physical Symptoms', 201–203; Knorring and Hultcrantz, 'Asylum-Seeking Children'; Sarli et al 'COVID-19 Related Lockdown'). The majority of Jeremiah's and Ezekiel's sign-acts are located narratively between the first and second sieges of Jerusalem – when one massive trauma had been survived, but safety was nowhere in sight. A sense of safety has been widely identified as a critical prerequisite for recovery from trauma; living in a state of continuous threat – either in Jerusalem, where the kingdom was in a constant state of political turmoil (Jeremiah), or in Babylonia, where the deportees were facing the complete unknown (Ezekiel) – is prone to exacerbate traumatic symptoms (Herman, *Trauma and Recovery*, 155–174). Ezekiel, in particular, is clearly convinced that the earlier traumas of Jerusalem were but a foreshadowing of the horrors to come.

ling of Ezekiel's priestly identity in Ezek 4–5 mirrors the dismantling of his fellow deportees' identities; they have survived the disaster, but not (yet) resolved its consequences into a coherent account of the self.[46] Both men are forbidden from mourning – especially striking, given that a failure to grieve appropriately is one of the things that inhibits the resolution of trauma (Jer 16:5–7; Ezek 24:15–24).[47]

These books' exceptionally intense focus on the body as an instrument of prophetic communication makes sense from the perspective of somatised trauma: struggling to find words capable of communicating the trauma of the kingdom's collapse, the prophets resort to the communicative capacity of their physical bodies.

Both books overtly acknowledge that they resort to embodied forms of communication as a result of words' failure. Jeremiah and Ezekiel are each described as consuming the Word they are given from YHWH, transferring the (unspeakable) divine words concerning the kingdom's doom directly into the prophets' bodies, from which and through which they can subsequently be expressed (Jer 15:16–18; Ezek 2:8–3:3). In the topsy-turvy world of trauma, words enter the body instead of leave it, until finally 'the body of the prophet literally reflects the cultural traumatic experiences the people have undergone'.[48] Jeremiah's recollection of eating the divine word appears alongside an anguished query, linking his consumption of the communicative content to his unrelenting physical and psychological distress: 'Why is my pain unceasing, my wound incurable?' (Jer 15:16–18).[49] These images of prophets ingesting YHWH's words echo what trauma researchers already know: language and the body are deeply interrelated.

The prophetic sign-acts of Jeremiah and Ezekiel are one aspect of this wider somatic symptomology. The bodies of the prophets become the surfaces on which these books' messages are written because, in the face of traumatic experience,

---

46 Ezekiel 4–5 is frequently discussed as a prolonged transformation of Ezekiel's identity, in which elements of his previous identity are erased or dissolved in favour of aspects demanded by his new situation; see Margaret Odell, 'You Are What You Eat: Ezekiel and the Scroll', *JBL* 117/2 (1998): 229–248, 234–236; Guy Darshan, 'The Meaning of ברב (Ez 21,24) and the Prophecy concerning Nebuchadnezzar at the Crossroads (Ez 21,23–29 [18–24]'. *ZAW* 128/1 (2016): 83–95, 93; and Christoph Uehlinger, 'Virtual Vision vs. Actual Show: Strategies of Visualization in the Book of Ezekiel', *WO* 45 (2015): 62–84, 72, 82, who describes the Ezek 4–5 sign-acts as 'openly transgressive'. Contra R. Andrew Compton, 'The Sign-Acts of Ezekiel 3:22–5:17: Formative Rituals of Priestly Identity', *Mid-America Journal of Theology* 29 (2018): 47–80, who contends that Ezekiel retains his priestly identity throughout. Lapsley contends that it is less Ezekiel's priestly identity than it is Ezekiel's priestly *body* that is altered (Jacqueline Lapsley, 'Body Piercings: The Priestly Body and the "Body" of the Temple in Ezekiel', *HeBAI* 1 [2012]: 231–245).
47 Herman, *Trauma and Recovery*, 69–71, 188–195.
48 Erbele-Küster, 'Eat This Scroll', 6, 7; cf. Graybill, *Are We Not Men?*, 102.
49 NRSV's translation prioritises physical injury, but the Hebrew phrasing covers both psychological and physical elements; see HALOT II: 455, 579.

ordinary language simply fails: 'there are no words' that can convey the horror of what has occurred.[50] The body is pressed into service as a communicative instrument that requires 'no words'; it functions as a 'mediating symbolic device', which stands in the breach where words cannot go.[51] Through the body, in lieu of words, the prophet is able to 'press[] against the limits of discourse';[52] through the body he is able to 'convey a message beyond the semiological capacity of words alone'.[53] Jeremiah and Ezekiel so characteristically communicate the traumas of the kingdom's demise through their bodies because language proves – despite their long-winded efforts – an inadequate means of communicating the horror of what has and what will befall Jerusalem and its people. That the body enters where words cannot is a sign and a symptom of these books' traumatic background.

2.2 Trauma, Somatisation, and the Arts

The nature and purpose of this embodied prophetic communication may be further illuminated by the use of the body in artistic and performance contexts – specifically, those in which individuals and communities seek to communicate and process traumatic experience. For those who find the horror of traumatic experience impossible to put into words, the material and the dramatic arts have proven effective mediating modes of communication.[54] Noting this, Louis Stulman suggests that the prophetic books work in a similar way to more recent attempts to articulate and process trauma through art.[55] Like modern trauma literature, art, and theatre, these works are not 'art for art's sake', but rather 'grow out of

---

50 Eekhoff, 'No Words to Say It', 190.

51 Katherine Low, 'Implications Surrounding Girding the Loins in Light of Gender, Body, and Power', *JSOT* 36/1 (2011): 3–30. Recognising the way that these sign-acts 'disrupt the social normative' (see below), Hornsby describes them as a 'withdrawal from the linguistic' (Teresa Hornsby, 'Ezekiel Off-Broadway', *The Bible and Critical Theory* 2/1 (2006): 1–8, 02.7).

52 Myers, 'Obscure Preaching', 410.

53 Corrine L. Carvalho and Paul Niskanen, *Ezekiel, Daniel*, New Collegeville Bible Commentary: Old Testament 16 (Collegeville, MN: Liturgical, 2012), 18, as paraphrased by Myers, 410.

54 There is extensive literature on the use of various forms of art therapy with trauma victims; for a somatically-orientated discussion of theatre's use in this way, see van der Kolk, *The Body Keeps the Score*, 332–348; for a case study involving refugees, see C. A. Strine, 'The Catalytic Image: Migration, Image, and the Exegetical Imagination in the Jacob Narrative (Genesis 25–33)', in *Image as Theology: The Power of Art in Shaping Christian Thought, Devotion, and Imagination*, ed. C. A. Strine, M. McInroy, and A. Torrance (Turnhout: Brepols, 2022), 125–142.

55 Picasso's *Guernica* is frequently cited in these discussions, with its broken, disordered attempt to communicate the unspeakable horror of war.

atrocity: they absorb it, interpret it, and survive it'.[56] Mark McEntire evokes the therapist's office stocked with art supplies when he comments that 'modern readers might envision something like Tinker Toys or Lego when they imagine Ezekiel building little war machines to attack the city' (Ezek 4:1–3).[57]

With an awareness of the way that trauma can be somatically expressed, it is not surprising that a number of scholars have profitably approached the sign-acts with reference to modern performance art – a genre in which the artist's body is a key site of communication.[58] Jeanette Mathews, for example, has argued that performance art is a useful lens through which to view the sign-acts, because 'the biblical script focuses our attention on the body of the prophet as a vehicle for transmitting the message he is asked to present to his audience'; thus, like performance artists, the prophet 'privileges the body', then uses ordinary objects and actions to provoke the audience.[59]

Although not all of the prophetic sign-acts in Jeremiah and Ezekiel are explicitly said to have occurred in the presence of an audience, many of them are obviously performances or performance-like. Jeremiah's encounter with the rival prophet Hananiah, complete with the bearing and breaking of symbolic yokes, is highly public (Jer 27–28). He invites Rechabites to drink wine in a public test of their resolve (Jer 35). Jeremiah himself traipses around the nations, getting them drunk on a cup of wrath-filled wine (Jer 25:15–29); though the mechanics of such a sign-act are baffling, the drama is effectively staged. The peripatetic wanderings of the scroll in Jer 36 draw attention, in their own distinct way, to the instability

---

56 Louis Stulman, 'Reading the Bible through the Lens of Trauma and Art', in *Trauma and Traumatization in Individual and Collective Dimensions: Insights from Biblical Studies and Beyond*, ed. Eve-Marie Becker, Jan Dochhorn, and Else K. Holt, Studia Aarhusiana Neotestamentica 2 (Göttingen: Vandenhoeck and Ruprecht, 2014), 177–192, 182; Stulman, 'Art and Atrocity', 92; cf. Jacqueline Lapsley, 'Body Piercings Revisited: Piercings and Profanations of "Bodies" and the Character of God in Ezekiel', in *The Unrelenting God: God's Action in Scripture*, ed. David J. Downs and Matthew L. Skinner (Grand Rapids, Mich.: Eerdmans, 2013), 1–14.

57 Mark McEntire, 'From Bound and Gagged to Swimming in the Water of Life: How God Breaks and Heals Ezekiel', *RevExp* 111/4 (2014): 329–336, 333.

58 Johanna Erzberger, 'Prophetic Sign Acts as Performances', in *Jeremiah Invented*, 104–116; Hornsby, 'Ezekiel Off-Broadway'; Jutta Krispenz, 'Leben als Zeichen: Performancekunst als Deutungsmodell für prophetische Zeichenhandlungen im Alten Testament', *EvT* 64/1 (2004): 51–64; Jeanette Mathews, *Prophets As Performers: Biblical Performance Criticism and Israel's Prophets* (Eugene, OR: Cascade, 2020). Krispenz helpfully observes that, whilst the prophets were not artists in the sense that the term is generally used today, the prophets' social function has shifted in the present to artists ('Leben als Zeichen', 63). In terms of communicative art, then, the analogy is a useful one – though, as with all analogies, there is an eventual limit to the comparison.

59 Mathews, *Prophets as Performers*, 170, 159.

and uncertain reliability of words.[60] Ezekiel is out on the (imaginary) highways and byways as Nebuchadnezzar's approach looms (Ezek 21:23–25); his baffled audience asks what he is doing when he sighs and moans over Jerusalem's imminent demise (Ezek 21:11–12). He is explicitly likened to a public performer – albeit one whose performance is not well received (Ezek 33:32). Like performance artists, the prophets also make frequent use of ordinary objects; Jeremiah has a fondness for pots (Jer 19:1–13) and potters' workshops (Jer 18:1–12), whilst Ezekiel uses a number of common items to attract attention and convey his message – from pots and pans to bricks, swords, and sticks (Ezek 4:1–3; 21:6–22; 24:3–14; 37:15–28).

Trauma is also 'an affliction of the powerless', and it is therefore significant that performance art 'hold[s] a privileged place in the arsenal of those who battle power from below': they use it to 'disrupt or threaten to destabilize the orderliness of societal norms (maintained by language)'.[61] A number of modern protest movements make this connection between public performance and the communication of trauma especially apparent. Massive protests over Vietnam in the 1960s and 1970s – many involving veterans suffering with PTSD – ultimately changed public attitudes to and national policy concerning the war. In the 1980s and 1990s, Act Up staged dramatic, public acts of protest in an ultimately successful attempt to pressure the government into taking action against AIDS. More recently, the migrant-justice group RAICES took to the streets of New York with child-sized mannequins in dog kennels, accompanied by audio recordings of real children crying in detention centres. Similar performance art pieces cropped up across the country between 2018 and 2021, drawing public attention to a national moral failure whose victims could not speak for themselves.

The last few years have seen public witness to the traumas endured by Black Americans in the form of mass street protests, marches, and performance art – from choreographed 'die-ins' to the formation of human chains that block freeways and city streets.[62] Like the prophets' sign-acts, such events communicate the existence and the meaning of trauma through the bodies of the traumatised.

---

60 Mark Brummitt and Yvonne Sherwood, 'The Fear of Loss Inherent in Writing: Jeremiah 36 as the Story of a Self-Conscious Scroll', in *Jeremiah (Dis)Placed: New Directions in Writing/Reading Jeremiah*, ed. A. R. Pete Diamond and Louis Stulman, LHBOTS 529 (London: T&T Clark, 2011), 47–66.
61 Herman, *Trauma and Recovery*, 33; Hornsby, 'Ezekiel Off-Broadway', 02.1, 5. Hornsby is explicitly discussing Ezekiel's 'prophetic performances' here.
62 See already Carolina A. Miranda, '"It Hasn't Left Me": How Black Lives Matter Used Performance to Create Unforgettable 2016 Moments', *Los Angeles Times*, December 15, 2016. Many of these actions are rooted in the traditions of the civil rights movement, which staged lunch counter sit-ins and marches across the American South to force public attention on the traumas inflicted on Black Americans by segregation and related expressions of white supremacy.

Describing the significance of these bodily forms of communication, Black Lives Matter co-founder Patrisse Cullors has emphasised the importance of conveying the harm experienced by herself and other Black Americans 'without having to say it, but to show it.'[63] In words that might as well be Jeremiah's or Ezekiel's, she responded to a query about how it felt to engage in these acts of public witness by saying that it was 'Painful. Literally, physically painful. Also really transformative, powerful and necessary.' In such acts those whose voices have been silenced witness with bodies instead of words; they place their bodies in the public sphere as a means of communicating other-wise.[64]

Several scholars have recently sought to analyse this intersection between performance, protest, and trauma with particular attention to traumatic somatisation. In a study of Latin American protest groups, Diana Taylor has proposed that protest-performances constitute public, bodily expressions of trauma; moreover, because trauma so often 'expresses itself viscerally through bodily symptoms, re-enactments, and repeats', trauma is – by its very nature – 'performatic'.[65] Taylor also suggests that these trauma-driven performances seek to 'channel [performers'] own terrible loss into productive social action', attempting to change public behaviour in a way that limits the recurrence of similar traumas in future.[66] Here

---

[63] Quoted in Reed Dunlea, 'Black Lives Matter Co-Founder on Building a Movement through Art', *Rolling Stone*, June 23, 2020 (italics added). With Ezekiel's displaced community in mind, her comment that 'For black people living in this country, this place has not felt like home for really, forever' is especially striking.

[64] On the communicative capacity of the body as distinct from that of the voice, see Judith Butler, *Notes toward a Performative Theory of Assembly* (Cambridge, MA: Harvard University Press, 2015).

[65] Diana Taylor, 'Trauma and Performance: Lessons from Latin America', *Proceedings of the Modern Language Association* 121/5 (2006): 1674–1677, 1675.

[66] Taylor, 'Trauma and Performance', 1676. See also Nelson Arteaga Botello, '"It Was the State": The Trauma of Enforced Disappearance of Students in Mexico', *International Journal of Politics, Culture, and Society* 32/3 (2019): 337–355, who discusses protests in the wake of the disappearance of 43 students in Mexico as 'symbolic representations and discourses signifying ... events that cause suffering and pain' (p. 341); and Thomas Riccio, 'Shadows in the Sun: Context, Process, and Performance in Ethiopia', *New Theatre Quarterly* 28/3 (2012): 272–295, who describes the way that 'performance provides a forum for revealing social, political, and cultural trauma' with reference to a theatre project in Ethiopia (p. 272). Martínez Ruiz likewise suggests that public political activism can function therapeutically for survivors of trauma (Rosaura Martínez Ruiz, 'Overcoming Psychic Trauma and Hate Speech: On Performativity and Its Healing Power', *Journal of Theoretical and Philosophical Psychology* 41/3 (2021): 174–186); recent research further suggests that, in a mirrored image of the way that trauma manifests itself in the body, therapies that support re-engagement with the body can be effective in helping trauma survivors to process their traumatic experiences, and sometimes to be able to articulate those experiences in language (van der Kolk, *The Body Keeps the Score*, 215–219, 265–278, 298–310, 332–348).

Ezekiel's anxious obsession with the avoidance of future trauma is especially reso-nant; the prophet repeatedly berates his audience for their misdeeds, seeking to correct their behaviour so that it does not provoke further punishment.[67]

In a similar vein, Jan-Dirk Döhling has argued that the prophetic sign-acts are confrontational by nature; they use the prophet's body in ways that defy ancient expectations of bodily conformity, and thereby draw the audience's atten-tion to the ways in which present reality fails to conform to the expectations of the old.[68] This echoes Helena Buffery's analysis of theatre representations of the Spanish Civil War, in which she observes 'the ways in which living bodies con-tinue to be marked by and transmit the impact' of past traumas, and the way that the inescapably bodily nature of performance 'draws attention to and trans-mits the immediate effects of violent acts on the body, and confronts us with a body as embodied witness'.[69]

3 Conclusion

The bodies of Jeremiah and Ezekiel, as depicted in the books that bear their names, are embodied witnesses to the lasting consequences of traumatic violence. The sign-acts with which they are associated represent remarkable efforts to com-municate in a world beyond the capacity of ordinary vocabulary to describe. In the face of words' failure, the communicative potential of the *soma* comes to the fore; the traumas that cannot be expressed in words are expressed instead through the body.

Although a few scholars have suggested a connection between the prophetic sign-acts and trauma, none have suggested that the particular prevalence of sign-acts in Jeremiah and Ezekiel should be linked to the traumatic aftermath of the kingdom's demise. This essay has sought to make explicit and to clarify the connec-

67 Crouch, *Israel and Judah Redefined*, 49–90, esp. 56–70.
68 Jan-Dirk Döhling, 'Prophetic Körper: Ein exegetisch-soziologisches Plädoyer zu einer vernach-lässigten Dimension der sog. "prophetischen Zeichenhandlungen"', *BZ* 57/2 (2013): 244–271, 259, 266; cf. Kathleen Blee and Amy McDowell, 'Social Movement Audiences', *Sociological Forum* 27, no. 1 (2012): 1–20. Compare Hornsby, who juxtaposes the bodily communication of performance art with the linguistic communication favoured by the status quo ('Ezekiel Off-Broadway'); also Joseph Blenkinsopp's observation that the author of Ezekiel is trying to address the simultaneous and interrelated breakdown of communication and community (*Ezekiel*, Interpretation [Louis-ville: John Knox, 1990], 25).
69 Helena Buffery, 'Bodies of Evidence, Resistance and Protest: Embodying the Spanish Civil War on the Contemporary Spanish Stage', *Bulletin of Hispanic Studies* 94/8 (2017): 863–882, 863, 878.

tion among traumatic experience, linguistic inhibition, and overtly bodily forms of communication, arguing that the unusual prominence of sign-acts and other somatic phenomena in these two books may be traced to the language difficulties characteristic of trauma survivors and the development of somatic phenomena as an alternative means of communication.

Brad E. Kelle

Ezekiel 3:24–27 and Prophetic Moral Injury: Trauma and the Interdisciplinary Study of Ezekiel's Sign-Acts

The sign-acts in the book of Ezekiel are well-suited for interdisciplinary study. They depict embodied performances that reflect communal experiences involving physical, mental, psychological, and social dimensions, especially personal and communal fear, pain, upheaval, disaster, and the attempts to come to grips with those experiences. They invite engagement with approaches shaped by sociology, psychology, trauma, disaster studies, performance theory, and gender criticism. Additionally, the book's sign-acts are literary constructions (regardless of particular historical realities "behind the text"), and thus invite consideration of their rhetorical formulations and effects, and the ways that meaning emerges through dialogue with diverse contexts, audiences, and experiences.

This study offers an interdisciplinary exploration of Ezek 3:24–27 in the context of the book's sign-acts that builds upon the use of trauma hermeneutics for reading Ezekiel and considers how the emerging concept of "moral injury" might illuminate the text's rhetorical elements and function. The divine instructions given to the prophet generate many interpretive questions, and commentators disagree over whether 3:24–27 should be considered a prophetic sign-act. The discussion that follows first examines the nature of Ezek 3:24–27 as a sign-act. I then explore how insights from trauma theory have illuminated the text and how the notion of moral injury foregrounds the elements of isolation, loss of social trust, and inability to speak openly that appear in Ezekiel's sign-act. These elements signal moral disjuncture and distress stemming from a sense of betrayal or the violation of long-held beliefs about God and the world.

1 Ezekiel 3:24–27 as a Prophetic Sign-Act

Ezekiel 3:24–27 may be translated as follows:

> (3:24) And [the] spirit entered into me and caused me to stand on my feet. And he spoke with me and said to me, "Go, shut yourself/be shut[1] inside your house. (3:25) And you,

---

[1] The verb (niphal imperative m. sg.) can be rendered as passive or reflexive. The immediately preceding imperative ("Go!") suggests the reflexive meaning for this form.

https://doi.org/10.1515/9783111521015-003

mortal, behold, they will put cords/cords will be put upon you and they will bind you/you will be bound[2] with them, so that you will not go out in their midst. (3:26) And I will make your tongue stick to your palate so you will be unable to speak. And you will not be for them an arbitrator,[3] for they are a rebellious house. (3:27) But when/whenever I speak with you, I will open your mouth and you will say to them, 'Thus says the Lord Yhwh.' The one who would hear may hear, and the one who would refuse may refuse; for they are a rebellious house."[4]

Should Ezek 3:24–27 be considered a prophetic sign-act and, if so, what significance follows from that identification? Although there is ongoing debate over their definition, nature, and function, sign-acts (or symbolic actions) are probably best understood as performed prophecies – non-verbal, action-based means of communicating a message to an audience through a symbolic and visual representation. Discussion of the initial sequence of sign-acts in Ezekiel is usually limited to those in 4:1–5:17. On form-critical grounds, one may object that 3:24–27 lacks the expected public setting and the report of the act's performance, or has an unusual focus on the prophet himself – even on his own body – as the site of meaning.[5] The verses also appear in a visionary context (see 3:22–24), which is not typical for sign-acts.

The depiction in 3:24–27, however, aligns with the book of Ezekiel's proclivity for departing from the typical form of the sign-act.[6] The text fits with the book's emphasis on the first-person reporting of Yhwh's words, and thus resembles the other sign-acts in the book, which give only Yhwh's command and rarely a report of the performance or the audience's reaction.[7] The prescribed actions, while set in the prophet's home, include plural forms (see v. 25) that suggest an audience who at least observes and perhaps participates. Ezekiel here also represents a larger group (the exiles), an element that is typical for many sign-acts. Additionally, the book's other divinely commanded act concerning losing and regaining

---

2 The verbs (both qal perfects) can be translated as active or passive. The LXX and Vulgate both presuppose the passive niphal verb forms.
3 A hiphil participle m.sg.
4 For the translation of the final sentence, see Leslie C. Allen, *Ezekiel 1–19*, WBC 28 (Dallas: Word, 1994), 47.
5 See Ronald M. Hals, *Ezekiel*, FOTL 19 (Grand Rapids: Eerdmans, 1989), 25–26, 30–31.
6 See Brad E. Kelle, *Ezekiel: A Commentary in the Wesleyan Tradition*, New Beacon Bible Commentary (Kansas City: Beacon Hill, 2013), 42; Kelvin G. Friebel, *Jeremiah's and Ezekiel's Sign-Acts*, JSOTSup 283 (Sheffield: Sheffield Academic, 1999), 24.
7 Kelvin G. Friebel ("Sign Acts," in *Dictionary of the Old Testament Prophets*, eds., Mark J. Boda and J. Gordon McConville [Downer's Grove, IL: IVP Academic, 2012], 708) identifies only the divine command and its interpretation as the defining elements of the genre.

speech in 33:22 also involves a vision.[8] And more than one sign-act in Ezekiel focuses not on the act but on the prophet's person – and even body – as the carrier of the message (e.g., 4:4–8; 5:1–4; 12:17–20).

On the whole, then, Ezek 3:24–27 fits the genre of a prophetic sign-act with allowances for the book's unique rhetorical characteristics. Several commentators identify 3:24–27 in this way and connect the passage structurally and thematically to the series of sign-acts in 4:1–5:17.[9] These views often relate the sign-acts to Ezekiel's personal experiences in the Babylonian exile, albeit in different ways.[10] But the sign-acts that begin in 3:24–27 are also an extension of the prophet's commissioning in chs. 1–3.[11] So these acts connect Ezekiel's commissioning explicitly to the context of the exile. Seen in this way, the sign-act in 3:24–27 is what Friebel calls a "representational" or "iconic" sign-act – that is, one in which the act itself represents what it signifies (in this case, the difficult experiences of exile).[12] Ezekiel's actions are reported in a setting of loss, destruction, and exile

---

8 In both cases, the visions precede the prophet's acts and are not their context. See Friebel, *Jeremiah's and Ezekiel's Sign-Acts*, 32. Note also that a later reference to Ezekiel's release from speechlessness (24:25–27) is explicitly labeled a "sign" (Heb. מופת v. 27).

9 Walther Zimmerli (*Ezekiel 1*, Hermeneia [Philadelphia: Fortress, 1979] 147; 154), for example, sees a single textual unit spanning 3:16–5:17, although he posits a great deal of redactional complexity. For others who identify Ezek 3:22–27 as a sign-act, see Moshe Greenberg, *Ezekiel 1–20: A New Translation with Introduction and Commentary*, AB 22 (Garden City, NY: Doubleday, 1983), 117; Margaret S. Odell, *Ezekiel*, Smyth and Helwys Biblical Commentary (Macon, GA: Smyth and Helwys, 2005), 54; Katheryn Pfisterer Darr, "The Book of Ezekiel," in *The New Interpreter's Bible Volume 6*, 12 vols. (Nashville: Abingdon, 2001), 1136; Allen, *Ezekiel 1–19*, 55.

10 Some see here an initiation into Ezekiel's role as prophet (e.g., Odell, *Ezekiel*, 55). Others see "formative rituals" giving the prophet a more priestly identity (e.g., R. Andrew Compton, "The Sign-Acts of Ezekiel 3:22–5:17: Formative Rituals of Priestly Identity," *Mid-America Journal of Theology* 29 [2018]: 47–80; quote on p. 47). Daniel I. Block (*The Book of Ezekiel Chapters 1–24*, NICOT [Grand Rapids: Eerdmans, 1997], 153; 159–60) sees a ritual initiation into the prophetic office, but he does not view 3:22–27 as a sign-act by genre.

11 Note the literary boundaries around 3:16–5:17 that are established by the divine word formula ("the word of Yhwh came to me") in 3:16 and 6:1 (Compton, "Sign-Acts," 59).

12 Friebel, "Sign Acts," 710. As a sign-act, Ezek 3:24–27 is non-verbal rhetoric (rather than quasi-magical efficacy) designed to persuade an audience in relationship to particular social, historical, and theological exigencies. For associations with magical rites or views of sign-acts as singularly efficacious, see Georg Fohrer, *Die Symbolischen Handlungen der Propheten*, 2d ed.; ATANT 54 (Stuttgart/Zurich: Zwingli, 1968); Zimmerli, *Ezekiel 1*, 28–29; Hals, *Ezekiel*, 34. For critiques, see Friebel, *Jeremiah's and Ezekiel's Sign-Acts*, 61, 466–67; Johanna Erzberger, "Prophetic Sign Acts as Performances," in *Jeremiah Invented: Constructions and Deconstructions of Jeremiah*, eds. Else K. Holt and Carolyn J. Sharp, LHBOTS 595 (London: T&T Clark, 2015), 104–16; Block, *The Book of Ezekiel Chapters 1–24*, 165.

shared with his audience, with the apparent goal of getting them to acknowledge the reality and meaning of their circumstances.[13]

2 Ezekiel and the Representation of Trauma

Modern interpreters have struggled to explain the details of Yhwh's instructions to Ezekiel in 3:24–27 and to reconcile those details with other portrayals throughout the book. Is Ezekiel's divinely commanded silence literal or symbolic? Is it temporary or permanent? What exactly does Yhwh forbid him from doing in v. 26? How does Ezekiel's confinement square with his apparent movement and actions throughout chs. 4–7?[14]

An analysis of these questions goes beyond the scope of this article. But one way that recent interpreters have tried to engage Ezek 3:24–27 is through interdisciplinary insights from trauma hermeneutics. The use of trauma theory has become a staple of today's Ezekiel scholarship.[15] This way of reading draws upon sociological and psychological research related to the human experiences involved in war, disaster, and forced migration, and connects those insights to the traumatic nature of the experiences suffered by Ezekiel and his audience in the sixth century BCE. The use of trauma hermeneutics has led to proposals that the book of Ezekiel may be trauma and survival literature – a literary effort to testify to the reality and implications of that which was too overwhelming for the exilic

---

13 Erzberger ("Prophetic Sign Acts as Performances," 104–16) compares biblical sign-acts to modern performance art. Both create meaning by establishing a relationship between the actor and the audience and by pointing beyond themselves and their immediate circumstances.

14 For redactional explanations, see Hals, *Ezekiel*, 25–26; Allen, *Ezekiel 1–19*, 56–57; Zimmerli, *Ezekiel 1*, 161; Greenberg, *Ezekiel 1–20*, 120.

15 See Refael Furman, "Trauma and Post-Trauma in the Book of Ezekiel," *OTE* 33 (2020): 32–59; Ruth Poser, *Das Ezechielbuch als Trauma-Literatur*, VTSup 154 (Leiden: Brill, 2012); Kelle, *Ezekiel*; Nancy R. Bowen, *Ezekiel*, AOTC (Nashville: Abingdon, 2010); Daniel L. Smith-Christopher, "Ezekiel on Fanon's Couch: A Postcolonialist Dialogue with David Halperin's *Seeking Ezekiel*," in *Peace and Justice Shall Embrace: Power and Theopolitics in the Bible*, eds. Ted Grimsrud and Loren L. Johns (Telford, PA.: Pandora, 1999), 108–44; David G. Garber, Jr., "Traumatizing Ezekiel, the Exilic Prophet," in *Psychology and the Bible: A New Way to Read the Scriptures Volume 2: From Genesis to Apocalyptic Vision*, eds. J. Harold Ellens and Wayne G. Rollins, Praeger Perspectives: Psychology, Religion, and Spirituality (Westport, CT: Praeger, 2004), 215–35. More generally, see David M. Carr, *Holy Resilience: The Bible's Traumatic Origins* (New Haven: Yale University Press, 2014); Elizabeth Boase and Christopher G. Frechette (eds.), *Bible Through the Lens of Trauma*, Semeia Studies 86 (Atlanta: SBL, 2016); David Janzen, "Claimed and Unclaimed Experience: Problematic Readings of Trauma in the Hebrew Bible," *BibInt* 27.2 (2019): 163–85.

community to fully apprehend.[16] The focus is on literary devices and rhetorical features (word play, repetition, puns, sign-acts, gendered and violent imagery) that express the overwhelming nature of the traumatic events.

Specifically concerning Ezekiel's sign-acts, trauma interpretation has emphasized that sign-acts in the Hebrew Bible are literary phenomena.[17] Thus, consideration of sign-acts includes not only how they might have functioned in the prophets' social and historical circumstances, but also what and how the sign-acts as literary elements communicate to a particular book's readers. Ezekiel's sign-acts (especially in chs. 4–5) are part of the book's literary symbols that communicate some of harshest realities of the community's trauma of destruction and exile. The sign-acts create meanings that transcend their contexts, involve claims about worldviews and values more general in nature, and invite readers to ask what larger ways of thinking about or seeing the world are evident in the text's portrayals. Simultaneously, however, trauma theory has emphasized that Ezekiel's sign-acts are embodied representations of the social and historical trauma of destruction and exile, a perspective that connects to the so-called somatic turn in trauma study.[18] Alongside the cognitive and literary approaches to trauma, this turn emphasizes how bodies and physicality are involved in both trauma and its healing. The body itself remembers the trauma, so expressions of trauma manifest in physical ways, and recovery must involve bodily practices. Ezekiel's sign-acts are neither magic rites nor mere ornamentation; they are ways the prophet "enacts in his body the symptomatology of trauma."[19]

From this starting point, interpreters have applied insights from trauma hermeneutics to the details of Ezek 3:24–27 as one of the book's "literary traumatic expressions".[20] The instructions that Yhwh gives Ezekiel are a strange way to commence a prophetic ministry, since Ezekiel is to be secluded, bound, and speechless. Trauma interpretations understand these things as embodied symbols of the traumatic calamities experienced by Ezekiel and his fellow exiles that cannot be fully grasped or expressed verbally.

---

16 See Poser, *Ezechielbuch als Trauma-Literatur*; Garber, "Traumatizing Ezekiel;" Kelle, *Ezekiel*, 30–31, 49–61. This literary perspective is relevant for Ezekiel in particular, as several elements suggest the book is more explicitly (and perhaps originally) literary in character than other prophetic books. See Ellen F. Davis, *Swallowing the Scroll: Textuality and the Dynamics of Discourse in Ezekiel's Prophecy*, Bible and Literature Series 21 (Sheffield: Almond, 1989).

17 Friebel, *Jeremiah's and Ezekiel's Sign-Acts*, 20–34; Hals, *Ezekiel*, 354–55.

18 Shelly Rambo, *Spirit and Trauma: A Theology of Remaining* (Louisville: Westminster John Knox, 2010); Bessel van der Kolk, *The Body Keeps the Score: Brain, Mind, and Body in the Healing of Trauma* (New York: Penguin, 2015).

19 Bowen, *Ezekiel*, 18.

20 Furman, "Trauma and Post-Trauma," 32. See especially Bowen, *Ezekiel*, 13–19 and Kelle, *Ezekiel*, 79–84.

For example, much of the trauma interpretation of 3:24–27 centers on the individual divine commands, especially whether they should be rendered in active or passive voice. The first command seems more straightforward than the others. The form of the verb (niphal imperative) in Yhwh's command for Ezekiel's seclusion in v. 24 likely carries a reflexive ("shut yourself in") rather than passive ("be shut in") meaning, since it is preceded by an active imperative ("Go!") directed to Ezekiel. The first commanded action is something Ezekiel is to do for himself. As we will see with regard to later commands, the self-imposed seclusion commanded here probably does not indicate a complete restriction on public ministry (see 4:12; 12:1–16; 37:20).

The actions commanded in vv. 25–26, however, are not actions that Ezekiel does to himself. Verse 25 describes Ezekiel being bound with cords so that he is unable to move about freely in public. Both of the verbs involved can be rendered as active or passive. Many commentators take the verbs in an active sense ("they will put cords upon you ... they will bind you") and understand this action as a symbol of the exiles' opposition to Ezekiel's message, whether the action be literal or only metaphorical.[21] Trauma interpretation, however, seizes upon the possible passive translation (implying that Yhwh should be seen as the agent of binding).[22] Seen in this way, the prophet's confinement and binding become embodied symbols of the traumatic experiences of siege, defeat, and deportation known by Ezekiel and his fellow exiles in the first Babylonian capture of Jerusalem and signs of the experiences to come for those who remained in the land.[23] The sign-acts find parallels in references to confinement and binding in the book of Lamentations, which shares the context of Jerusalem's destruction and exile.[24] Ezekiel is a "communal representative" whose symbolic acts express solidarity with his audience's experiences.[25] The reference to "cords" (Heb. עבותים) in v. 25 provides an example of the links to trauma, as this term appears in the Samson narratives (Judg 15:13–14) and various psalms (e.g., Pss 2:3; 129:4) in relation to bondage and

---

21 E.g., Friebel, *Jeremiah's and Ezekiel's Sign-Acts*, 175 n. 219, 220; Allen, *Ezekiel 1–19*, 47, 61. Some scholars render the verbs as past tense (Greenberg, *Ezekiel 1–20*, 98, 120; Block, *The Book of Ezekiel Chapters 1–24*, 151).
22 See Zimmerli, *Ezekiel*, 147; Paul M. Joyce, *Ezekiel: A Commentary*, LHBOTS 482 (New York: T&T Clark, 2007), 82; Darr, "The Book of Ezekiel," 1137; Smith-Christopher, "Ezekiel on Fanon's Couch," 139; Kelle, *Ezekiel*, 81.
23 Kelle, *Ezekiel*, 81; Bowen, *Ezekiel*, 13–19; Bernhard Lang, *Ezechiel: Der Prophet und das Buch*, ErFor 153 (Darmstadt: Wissenschaftliche Buchgesellschaft, 1981), 66–74.
24 E.g., Lam 3:7–9. See Smith-Christopher, "Ezekiel on Fanon's Couch," 139–43.
25 Odell, *Ezekiel*, 54–57. Odell renders the verbs as active but notes parallels to the binding of enemy kings in Assyrian annals (p. 57).

oppression.[26] More commonly, however, the term appears in priestly material as the gold cords that bind the high priest's ephod and breastplate (e.g., Exod 28:14, 22, 24, 25; 39:15, 17, 18).[27] Hence, a trauma perspective notes that in this text the calamities of exile and destruction transform the formerly priestly cords known from the life of the temple into cords of bondage known in the realities of Babylon. A trauma interpretation sees in the prophet's actions a symbol of the physical disconnection, social isolation, and emotional withdrawal experienced by exiles.[28]

The language in v. 26 indicates that the third symbolic action will be done to Ezekiel by Yhwh ("I will make your tongue stick to your palate") with the result that the prophet will be unable to speak to (or perhaps for) the exiles. Interpreters have struggled with how Ezekiel could be rendered mute in light of his preceding commissioning (2:3–7; 3:11) and the subsequent portrayals of his public ministry (throughout chs. 4–33).[29] Scholars have suggested nearly innumerable proposals, some of which depend upon redactional hypotheses and others upon differing understandings of the nature of Ezekiel's speechlessness.[30] Discussion has revolved around whether the muteness should be understood as literal or symbolic. If literal, was Ezekiel incapable of speech or voluntarily mute and, in either case, was his speechlessness continuous or only intermittent? If symbolic, was the silence a metaphor for Ezekiel's restriction to speaking solely oracles of judgment, his inability to be understood, his use of private correspondence only, or the singularly divine origin of his messages as one who speaks only when Yhwh provides the words?[31]

Verse 26 also states the reason for Ezekiel's speechless, as Yhwh declares that the prophet "will not be for them an arbitrator." This phrase has likewise received extensive scholarly attention, especially the Hebrew term מוכיח ("arbitrator, reprover, intercessor, mediator"). The participle is from the verbal root meaning

---

26 Zimmerli, *Ezekiel*, 160.

27 Odell, *Ezekiel*, 57; Compton, "Sign-Acts," 63.

28 Bowen, *Ezekiel*, 18.

29 According to the book's chronology, Ezekiel was mute for seven and a half years, from the twelfth day of Tammuz 593 BCE (see 1:1–2; 3:16) until the fifth day of Tevet 585 BCE (see 33:21–22).

30 This text stands as one of three passages in Ezekiel concerning the prophet's loss and recovery of speech (3:26–27; 24:25–27; 33:21–22).

31 For a survey of proposals, see Friebel, *Jeremiah's and Ezekiel's Sign-Acts*, 169–88. The question of whether Ezekiel's speechlessness was continuous connects to v. 27, especially the translation of the temporal infinitive at the beginning of the verse. If taken as iterative ("whenever I speak") rather than durative ("the next time I speak"), the infinitive suggests Ezekiel's silence will be only intermittent and will be broken whenever Yhwh gives him a word to say (see Greenberg, *Ezekiel 1–20*, 103; Friebel, *Jeremiah's and Ezekiel's Sign-Acts*, 183).

"to decide, judge, prove," and the discussion of its understanding has largely involved whether the root's meaning here reflects its use in didactic/wisdom contexts or judicial/legal contexts.[32] In the former, the root denotes the activity of one like a parent or teacher who reproves in order to cause change (e.g., Prov 9:7–8; 24:25; 25:12). Seen in this way, Yhwh prohibits Ezekiel from serving as an intercessor who would reproach the exiles with a call to change. After the fall of Jerusalem the time for intercession will return, but for now the prophet may only declare the judgment that is sure to come.[33] In judicial/legal contexts, however, the term denotes an arbitrator – a neutral, third-person legal mediator between the plaintiff and defendant who renders a decision (e.g., Gen 31:37; Job 9:33). Seen in this way, Yhwh declares that Ezekiel can no longer serve as a legal umpire who allows both parties to have their say and mediates a decision because the time for adjudication is over. The exiles' guilt is firmly established and henceforth Ezekiel will only speak for God *to* the exiles.[34]

As with the symbolic actions in v. 25, trauma interpretation has offered new insights into Ezekiel's divinely mandated muteness in v. 26. From this perspective, Ezekiel's silence is a recognizable reaction to traumatic experiences. As modern Post-Traumatic Stress Disorder (PTSD) reveals, traumatic events can be "missed" as victims are often unable to fully grasp or verbally articulate their experiences, being physically unable to speak about them. In Ezekiel's case, the trauma of destruction and exile overwhelms him in way that he is "unable to express his anxieties and fears."[35] The Hebrew root (אלם, Niphal), which yields the translation "you will be unable to speak", appears in the Hebrew Bible as a reference to the physical incapability of speaking (e.g., Exod 4:11), but it is also used to denote being unwilling, unable, or not allowed to speak due to one's circumstances.[36]

---

32 See Darr, "The Book of Ezekiel," 1137–39.

33 So Greenberg, *Ezekiel 1–20*, 102; Furman, "Trauma and Post-Trauma," 51.

34 See Darr, "The Book of Ezekiel," 1138–39; Robert R. Wilson, "An Interpretation of Ezekiel's Dumbness," *VT* 22 (1972): 91–104; Block, *The Book of Ezekiel Chapters 1–24*, 156–57; Friebel, *Jeremiah's and Ezekiel's Sign-Acts*, 187; Joyce, *Ezekiel*, 82.

35 Bowen, *Ezekiel*, 18. See also Friebel, *Jeremiah's and Ezekiel's Sign-Acts*, 177; Ruth Poser, "No Words: The Book of Ezekiel as Trauma Literature and a Response to Exile," in *Bible Through the Lens of Trauma*, eds. Elizabeth Boase and Christopher G. Frechette; Semeia Studies 86 (Atlanta: SBL, 2010), 38; Kelle, *Ezekiel*, 79–84.

36 For example, the term describes the poor or afflicted who are unable to defend themselves in a trial or those who have been rendered speechless by their circumstances (e.g., Ps 31:19[MT]; 38:14[MT]; Prov 31:8; Isa 53:7). See Block, *The Book of Ezekiel Chapters 1–24*, 155; Friebel, *Jeremiah's and Ezekiel's Sign-Acts*, 178–79. Block (p. 159) notes parallels to Ezekiel's binding and muteness in ancient Akkadian medical incantation texts in which the afflicted expresses feeling bound in his limbs and mouth.

These insights from trauma theory have opened new interpretive dimensions for Ezekiel's initial sign-act in 3:24–27. The prophet's isolation and muteness represent the "loss of self" that can accompany the experience of trauma – the loss of a clear sense of identity (is Ezekiel now a priest or a prophet?) and a feeling of being overwhelmed and unable to speak forthrightly about what has occurred.[37] This emphasis on the deleterious effects of trauma on one's sense of self and of the moral character of one's community and world connects to the emerging notion of moral injury. This notion highlights how isolation, loss of social trust, and inability to speak openly can emerge not only from traumatic events but also from the experience of moral dissonance and disjuncture associated with a sense of betrayal or the violation of long-held beliefs about God and the world.

3 Ezekiel 3:24–27 and Prophetic Moral Injury

To conclude my analysis, I propose briefly here that the notion of moral injury might extend the interdisciplinary, trauma-informed hermeneutic for Ezekiel's sign-act in 3:24–27. Moral injury has emerged in earnest since 2009 within clinical psychology, veterans care, and related fields to refer to a non-physical wound (psychological and emotional pain and its effects) that results from the violation (by oneself or others) of a person's core moral beliefs (about oneself, others, or the world). Originally developed for the moral effects of war and violence, moral injury initially referred more technically to the deleterious effects of war participation on moral conscience and ethical conception – the wrecking of a person's fundamental assumptions about "what's right" and how things should work in the world that may result from a sense of having violated one's core moral identity and the loss of any reliable, meaningful world in which to live.[38] Moral injury today remains a developing concept, but the starting point has been the conviction that although the label is recent, the experience is ancient. And now, reli-

---

37 David G. Garber Jr., "Trauma, History, and Survival in Ezekiel 1–24" (Ph.D. diss., Emory University, 2005), 64.

38 See Rita Nakashima Brock and Gabriella Lettini, *Soul Repair: Recovering from Moral Injury after War* (Boston: Beacon, 2012); Nancy Sherman, *Afterwar: Healing the Moral Wounds of Our Soldiers* (Oxford: Oxford University Press, 2015); Brad E. Kelle, *The Bible and Moral Injury: Reading Scripture Alongside War's Unseen Wounds* (Nashville: Abingdon, 2020); Brad E. Kelle, "Moral Injury and Biblical Studies: An Early Sampling of Research and Emerging Trends," *CBR* 19.2 (2021): 121–44.

gious, pastoral, theological, and biblical studies have engaged moral injury direct-ly, as well.[39]

The significance of moral injury for my purposes is its recognition that the dangers and damages of war and violence are not limited to physical or psycho-logical injuries but may also involve moral and ethical dimensions. Much of the discussion of moral injury, for example, has been linked to PTSD – a psychological disorder featuring a fear-based response in the victim – and the question of whether that accounts sufficiently for aspects of war's aftermath that go beyond emotional wounds and adjustment disorders to include moral and ethical sensi-bilities. Although moral injury traditionally focused on the consequences of per-petrating or inflicting harm on others, it adds a moral dimension to thinking about all personal and communal traumas. In the case of Ezekiel and his audi-ence, for instance, how would the traumatic events of destruction and exile dis-turb and possibly alter their sense of the moral goodness and stability of them-selves, the world, and even their God? And what kinds of physical, psychological, and emotional reactions would that moral disjuncture produce?

There is currently no single, agreed-upon definition of moral injury, nor of the precise experiences that cause it, the effects that result from it, or the best strategies to overcome it.[40] But elements within moral injury's two most founda-tional definitions open the way for its connection to Ezekiel. The first definition emphasizes that a person can experience moral injury not only by perpetrating acts that violate one's sense of morality and goodness (for themselves or the world) but also by failing to prevent or even simply witnessing acts that trans-gress their deeply held moral convictions and expectations.[41] The second under-standing notes that moral injury can result from the experience of betrayal – a sense that those in authority have betrayed what is right in a critical situation.[42] Regardless of an individual's actions, moral dissonance and distress may result

39 E.g., Larry Kent Graham, *Moral Injury: Restoring Wounded Souls* (Nashville: Abingdon, 2017); Joseph McDonald (ed.), *Exploring Moral Injury in Sacred Texts*, Studies in Religion and Theology (London: Jessica Kingsley, 2017); Nancy J. Ramsay and Carrie Doehring (eds.), *Military Moral Injury and Spiritual Care: A Resource for Religious Leaders and Professional Caregivers* (St. Louis: Chalice, 2019); Zachary Moon, *Warriors Between Worlds: Moral Injury and Identities in Crisis*, Emerging Perspectives in Pastoral Theology and Care (Lanham, MD: Lexington Books, 2019); Brad E. Kelle (ed.), *Moral Injury: A Guidebook for Understanding and Engagement* (Lanham, MD: Lexington Books, 2020).
40 Kelle, *The Bible and Moral Injury*, 183–85 lists sixteen definitions offered in current literature.
41 Brett T. Litz et al., "Moral Injury and Moral Repair in War Veterans: A Preliminary Model and Intervention Strategy," *Clinical Psychology Review* 29 (2009): 695–706.
42 Jonathan Shay, *Achilles in Vietnam: Combat Trauma and the Undoing of Character* (New York: Touchstone, 1994), 208.

when someone with legitimate authority betrays those less powerful by acting immorally or unethically, and perhaps causing the less powerful to do the same. From these potential causes, moral injury's effects can take many forms, some internal (distorted values, self-condemnation, shame, guilt) and some external (lost sense of an ordered and just world, loss of social relationships). And these effects may be emotional, psychological, spiritual, and social.[43] Of particular import for considering Ezek 3:24–27, researchers have noted how these internal and external effects often manifest in self-isolation, loss of social trust, and reticence to speak openly about the sense of moral despair and the events that caused it.[44]

How, then, might moral injury extend the interdisciplinary consideration of Ezek 3:24–27 suggested by trauma hermeneutics? Most basically, this perspective emphasizes that the experiences reflected by Ezekiel's sign-act, and indeed the symbolic actions themselves, have a moral dimension. The experiences of loss, destruction, and exile entailed a sense of moral disjuncture and despair for the prophet and his audience that may have included a sense of betrayal or the violation of long-held beliefs about God and the world.

Moral injury invites readers to consider why and how the traumatic events experienced by Ezekiel and his audience would have affected their moral and ethical visions of themselves, others, and the world. Clearly, the context is right for moral injury. Babylonian military conquest and exile provided the war-making and violent setting with which moral distress is associated. As the basic definitions of moral injury note, a sense of moral disjuncture and the loss of a reliable moral world can come from simply witnessing acts that transgress strong beliefs about persons and the world. The experiences of the initial Babylonian capture of Jerusalem and deportation confronted Ezekiel and his audience with killing, forced migration, and other acts of cruelty that they were powerless to stop and that violated many of their long-held moral convictions. Such powerlessness and violation can lead to a despairing of self and the world, the wrecking of fundamental assumptions about the presence of goodness in the world and how things should rightly work. And from this moral despair can come shame and guilt, alongside self-condemnation, reduced trust, and loss of spirituality. The oracles in the book of Ezekiel attest to the collapse of confidence in the pillars of orthodox Yahwism in the aftermath of exile (Israel's choseness, covenant, the promise of

---

43 Clinical research has produced matrices for identifying specific effects of moral injury. See Joseph M. Currier et al., "Development and Evaluation of the Expressions of Moral Injury Scale – Military Version," *Clinical Psychology and Psychotherapy* 25 (2017): 474–88; Harold G. Koenig et al., "The Moral Injury Symptom Scale – Military Version," *Journal of Religion and Health* 57 (2018): 249–65.
44 See Kelle, *The Bible and Moral Injury*, 29–36.

land, a perpetual Davidic dynasty, divine presence in the temple).[45] The prophet gives voice to despair over the present and future (e.g., 7:1–27; 9:8–10; 13:13) as well as the experiences of guilt and shame (6:1–7; 16:53–54, 63; 20:43; 36:31–32). All of these aspects represent moral dimensions that go beyond the physical and psychological wounds of trauma.

Additionally, as noted above, moral injury may also result from a sense of betrayal – the feeling that those in authority betrayed their commitments and acted in unethical ways that resulted in the suffering of others. For Ezekiel, Judah's political leaders abandoned obedience to Yhwh, pursued their own selfish ambitions, and brought divine judgment upon the people. The book contains numerous condemnations of Judah's kings and ruling elite, many expressing a sense of betrayal (e.g., 11:1–13; 12:8–16; 17:1–21; 34:1–10). But recent moral injury work related to the experience of religious persons in modern armies has also noted that moral injury can involve a sense of divine betrayal – an experience in which violence, unethical leadership, and morally suspect circumstances and actions lead to the feeling that God is unjust, has been overcome by evil, or simply does not exist.[46] The presence and voice of Yhwh plays a central role in the book of Ezekiel, and the words of both the prophet and the exiles at times express doubt about the divine actions and intentions (e.g., 9:8–10; 11:13; 12:14–15; 18:1–29). The idea of divine betrayal as part of moral injury may provide a new lens onto the book's central theme of reestablishing the knowledge of Yhwh's name, character, reputation, and holiness in the face of destruction and exile.[47]

Insights from moral injury may also provide new perspectives on the specific actions depicted in Ezek 3:24–27. Readers may reconsider the prophet's actions here not simply as expressions of traumatic events endured by the exiles, but also as symbols of the experience of moral injury and its effects. For instance, Ezekiel's confinement within his home and inability to be among the people (vv. 24–25) resemble the self-isolation and loss of social trust and relationships that often accompany the collapse of moral confidence in oneself, others, and the world. The prophet's withdrawal, seclusion, and alienation may symbolize not only the rejection of his message or the captivity associated with being taken into exile, but also an emotional detachment and loss of trust in interpersonal and communal relationships that reflects a deep uncertainty and disillusionment with the moral goodness of one's community and world. And if, as some have suggest-

---

45 Block, *The Book of Ezekiel Chapters 1–24*, 7–8; Kelle, *Ezekiel*, 51–55.
46 See Joseph M. Currier, J. D. Foster, and S. L. Isaak, "Moral Injury and Spiritual Struggles in Military Veterans: A Latent Profile Analysis," *Journal of Traumatic Stress* (March 12): https://doi.org/10.1002/jts.22378.
47 See Kelle, *Ezekiel*, 55–61.

ed, Ezekiel's house confinement was forced upon him by his own exilic community, the circumstances symbolize the rejection often felt by those who have known the moral ambiguities and violations of war but find no welcome for the acknowledgment of such things in their own communities.[48] For some today, the very presence of the veteran in their midst represents the moral discomfort associated with war that they would just as soon not face directly, and thus leads to an avoidance or exclusion of the veteran from the community's embrace.

Moral injury also adds another dimension to Ezekiel's symbolic speechlessness (vv. 26–27). Just as trauma can render a victim unable to speak about what they have experienced, the morally injured (especially soldiers returning from combat) often struggle to find opportunities and encouragement to speak honestly about their experiences, to give candid expression to things they have done, witnessed, or felt.[49] Ezekiel's attempt to speak about the causes, nature, and meaning of exile and the people's future required uninhibited truth-telling about particular events and broader realities for the sake of new moral understanding and transformation. However, because such honest speech involves expression of pain, betrayal, guilt, shame, and disillusionment, it is often met with resistance by the very communities that need to hear it. The morally injured may feel incapable of testifying (rendered mute) because their truth simply would not be received. What is most needed for those in moral distress is exactly the opposite of what Ezekiel's muteness symbolizes: communities should serve as faithful hearers who receive the testimony of the morally wounded as witnesses. The hearers should validate their truth-telling and acknowledge the whole community's complicity in the morally injurious events, sharing the responsibility, and bearing the burdens of moral agency and suffering.

4 Conclusion

Questions concerning Ezekiel's divinely commanded actions in 3:24–27 will continue to abound. And there is much to consider from the perspectives of redaction analysis, ritual and performance studies, and literary and text-critical insights. As with many of the sign-acts in the book, however, Ezek 3:24–27 presents an embodied performance that bears a special relationship to the context of war, destruc-

---

48 See Brock and Lettini, *Soul Repair*; Sherman, *Afterwar*.
49 See Nancy J. Ramsay, "Moral Injury as Loss and Grief with Attention to Ritual Resources for Care," *Pastoral Psychology* (December 2018), doi: https://doi.org/10.1007/s11089-018-0854-9; Kelle, *The Bible and Moral Injury*, 104–10; 135–36; Brock and Lettini, *Soul Repair*, 81.

tion, and exile, and thus reflects personal and communal fear, pain, upheaval, disaster, and the attempts to come to grips with those experiences. Interdisciplinary perspectives drawn from trauma theory illuminate the text's rhetorical elements, context, and function in new ways, especially by highlighting how the prophet's actions symbolize both the physical experiences of trauma through violence and exile and the emotional and psychological struggles involved in expressing and surviving that trauma. There is, however, also a moral dimension to the loss, destruction, and exile experienced by Ezekiel and his audience. The emerging notion of moral injury – born out of the moral and ethical struggles of combat veterans – highlights how the prophet's symbolic actions reflect a sense of moral disjuncture, distress, and despair. Moral injury provides another interdisciplinary lens onto Ezekiel's sign-acts and points interpreters toward consideration of how the book engages the moral and ethical aspects of a message about Israel's judgment and Yhwh's holiness. The combination of trauma study and moral injury invites readers of Ezekiel to take up larger questions about the morality of self, others, God, and the world, and the ways those perceptions are affected by the experiences of suffering, violence, disaster, and death.

Rosanne Liebermann

Ezekiel's Confinement: From the Sublime to the Conspicuous

In Ezekiel 3:22–27, Yhwh summons Ezekiel out onto an open plain, only to command him: "Come, be confined inside your house. As for you, son of man, they have placed cords upon you and bound you with them, and you will not go out among them" (vv. 24b–25).[1] Ezekiel is also rendered speechless except for the purpose of conveying Yhwh's words to the "rebellious house" around him (vv. 26–27). This thorough shutting-up of the prophet comes as an unexpected anti-climax at the end of the book's dramatic first three chapters, in which Yhwh, enthroned above heavenly creatures, appears to Ezekiel (1:1–28) and repeatedly instructs him to speak to "the house of Israel" despite their unyielding hostility (2:1–7, 3:4–11, 17–21). The restrictions placed on Ezekiel in 3:24b–27 appear to conflict with this commission.

The spatial element of Ezekiel's constraints is this chapter's primary focus, although the selective silencing of the prophet is an interrelated aspect of his isolation from the rest of society. Ezekiel's confinement to his house is usually omitted from commentators' lists of his sign-acts.[2] Moreover, it is nearly always treated either as an element of his prevention from speaking on his own prerogative (3:26–27)[3] or as an anticipatory detail of his symbolic enactment of the

---

1 All translations are my own. The identity of those who will place cords upon Ezekiel is not stated, but the result that Ezekiel will be unable to "go out among them" suggests that "they" are members of the community around him. Some commentators, however, interpret the verbs as passives as a reflection of their missing subject (e.g. Robert R. Wilson, "An Interpretation of Ezekiel's Dumbness," *VT* 22 (1972): 91–104 [98]; R. Andrew Compton, "Sign-Acts of Ezekiel 3:22–5:17: Formative Rituals of Priestly Identity," *Mid-American Journal of Theology* 29 (2018): 47–80 [61]).
2 Wilson, "Ezekiel's Dumbness," 92; Moshe Greenberg, *Ezekiel 1–20: A New Translation with Introduction and Commentary*, AB 22 (Garden City, NY: Doubleday, 1983) 120–122; Daniel I. Block, *The Book of Ezekiel 1–24*, NICOT (Grand Rapids, MI: William B. Eerdmans, 1997), 150–162; Kelvin Friebel, "A Hermeneutical Paradigm for Interpreting Prophetic Sign-Actions," *Didaskalia* 12/2 (2001): 29–38 [25]; Margaret S. Odell, *Ezekiel*, (Macon, GA: Smyth & Helwys, 2005), 54. Walther Zimmerli (*Ezekiel 1: A Commentary on the Book of the Prophet Ezekiel, Chapters 1–24*, trans. Ronald E. Clements, Hermeneia [Philadelphia: Fortress Press, 1979], 159) represents an exception.
3 Hans Ferdinand Fuhs, *Ezechiel 1–24*, (Würzburg: Echter Verlag, 1986), 31; Wilson, "Ezekiel's Dumbness," 91; Greenberg, *Ezekiel 1–20*, 120; David Stacey, *Prophetic Drama in the Old Testament* (London: Epworth Press, 1990), 176; Block, *The Book of Ezekiel 1–24*, 153–160; Odell, *Ezekiel*, 57–58.

https://doi.org/10.1515/9783111521015-004

siege of Jerusalem (4:1–3).[4] Neither of these interpretations accounts for the specific circumstance of Ezekiel being confined to his house – ostensibly for seven years! – in 3:24b.[5]

Since Ezekiel's lengthy confinement to his house is not a necessary condition either for his silence or for his symbolic besieging of Jerusalem, it merits consideration in its own right. There is nothing in the book of Ezekiel to suggest that Ezekiel's confinement lasts any less time than his enforced silence: from his prophetic commission in the fifth year of his displacement to Babylonia until the destruction of the temple in the twelfth year, according to the book's chronology (1:1–2; 24:25–27; 33:21–22).[6] During this period, elders from Ezekiel's community visit him at home (8:1; 14:1; 20:1; 33:30–32) and all of his prophetic activity could plausibly take place inside the house (4:1–5:4; 12:1–20; 24:15–24),[7] with the exception of escaping out through the house's walls in 12:6 (discussed below). Ezekiel's confinement adds a strange and unexpected facet to his identity as a divine messenger, the meaning of which has not been fully explored.

The present chapter argues that Ezekiel's isolation in his house secludes him from the perceived impurity of his foreign surroundings, mirroring the sublime isolation of Yhwh in the innermost part of his temple. Both Yhwh's idealized sanctuary in Ezekiel's vision of chapters 40–48 and Ezekiel's house form interior, removed spaces in the midst of a select "in-group" of Judeans. This concentric spatial model reveals how the book of Ezekiel uses the concept of purity to define the boundaries and hierarchies of those inside Yhwh's covenant group, placing its eponymous prophet in the centre with Yhwh. By setting up the confined pro-

---

4 Zimmerli, *Ezekiel 1*, 159; G. A. Cooke, *A Critical and Exegetical Commentary on the Book of Ezekiel*, ICC (Edinburgh: T&T Clark, 1936), 47.

5 Exceptions include a few imaginative interpretations, such as that Ezekiel's confinement was an imprisonment imposed by his enemies, or that Yhwh commanded Ezekiel to stay home as a protective measure against those who would otherwise cause him harm (Zimmerli, *Ezekiel 1*, 158–159 includes a thorough history of scholarship). Yet there is no indication in the narrative that Ezekiel had begun speaking to the people at the time of his confinement or that their opposition to him ever amounted to anything more than disbelief.

6 Wilson, "Ezekiel's Dumbness," 92–93; Zimmerli, *Ezekiel 1*, 159; Greenberg, *Ezekiel 1–20*, 120. Ezekiel's apparently lengthy confinement also undermines the argument made by some that Ezekiel 3:22–27, or some part of it, originally belonged later in the book, e.g. Cooke, *The Book of Ezekiel*, 46.

7 Kelvin Friebel posits a public arena for Ezekiel's sign-acts based on the presence of witnesses suggested by 3:25; 4:12; 12:3–6 (*Jeremiah's and Ezekiel's Sign-Acts: Rhetorical Nonverbal Communication* [Sheffield: Sheffield Academic Press, 1999], 26), but as the text attests to community members visiting Ezekiel's house, there is no need to posit that the presence of spectators renders the setting in Ezekiel's home impossible.

phet in migration[8] as the one who both envisions and models the new, pure temple space occupied by Yhwh, the book of Ezekiel demonstrates that the most interior space – that is, the centre – of Judean religion is no longer located inside the land of Judah. It has moved outside the borders of the land along with the Judeans displaced to Babylonia in 597 BCE. Ezekiel's conspicuous confinement also draws attention to the prophet's unique access to Yhwh's inner sanctum, portraying him as a singular kind of religious leader: a high priest for the migration. His positioning as such functions as a sign-act indicating that Yhwh's presence is exclusively with the Judeans who are outside of Judah. Ezekiel's confinement therefore holds great significance for the book's interpretation of the Babylonian exile and for its portrayal of the prophet. It is a multivalent sign-act that is both about the prophet's identity as a religious leader and about the religious standing of Judeans in migration.

1 The Sign-Acts in Ezekiel 3:22–5:17

Traditionally, commentators have interpreted Ezekiel 3:22–5:17 as narrating a series of prophetic sign-acts (sometimes referred to as sign actions, symbolic actions, or symbolic acts[9]) beginning with Ezekiel's mutism in 3:26[10] or his enactment of the siege of Jerusalem in 4:1–3.[11] They usually base this classification either explicitly or implicitly on the definition of sign-acts as non-verbal communications of a divine message to an audience, often via actions that bear resemblance to what they depict.[12] Scholars who accept this communication-focused

---

8 I use the term "migration" to reflect that although the book of Ezekiel claims its origins in the Judean displacement to Babylonia in the sixth century BCE, its message would have had as much relevance for the descendants of this group (who likely edited the book) and the numerous other Judeans who found themselves outside of Judah, whether by force or choice, in the centuries that followed.

9 Friebel (*Jeremiah's and Ezekiel's Sign-Acts*, 38; "A Hermeneutical Paradigm," 26–27) makes a good case for the use of "sign" over "symbol," pointing out that in semiotics, "symbol" indicates a subset of encoded meanings in which there is no semblance between the sign and the referent. Since the opposite is usually true of prophetic actions, the more general term "sign" is preferable.

10 Friebel, "A Hermeneutical Paradigm," 25; Friebel, *Jeremiah's and Ezekiel's Sign-Acts*, 169.

11 Greenberg, *Ezekiel 1–20*, 98; William H. Brownlee, *Ezekiel 1–19*, WBC 28 (Waco, TX: Word Books, 1986), 60; Fuhs, *Ezechiel 1–24*, 32; Block, *Ezekiel 1–24*, 162; Odell, *Ezekiel*, 54.

12 This definition is broadly (though not uncritically) influenced by Georg Fohrer's identification of prophetic sign-acts as a distinct literary genre (*Die symbolischen Handlungen der Propheten*, 2. Auflage [Zürich: Zwingli Verlag, 1968], 17–19), e.g. Bernhard Lang, *Monotheism and the Prophetic Minority* (Sheffield: The Almond Press, 1983), 80–82; Greenberg, *Ezekiel 1–20*, 122; Friebel, *Jeremiah's and Ezekiel's Sign-Acts*, 11–14; Friebel, "A Hermeneutical Paradigm," 25 n.1, 27–28, 30,

definition tend to evoke the confrontational aspect of sign-acts: that they attract an audience's attention and demand a response.[13] Ezekiel's confinement does not comfortably fit this description, which may explain its frequent exclusion from scholarly discussions of his sign-acts. Yet by this same logic, Ezekiel's long period of isolation should also disqualify nearly all of his following actions from being sign-acts, since it places them inside his home, away from the public eye. Thus, a broader understanding of sign-acts is required if Ezekiel's actions in 3:22–5:17 are to be identified as such and his confinement taken into account.

Some have questioned whether Ezekiel's behaviour in 3:22–5:17 should be classified as sign-acts in the sense of public communication, recognizing that this section of the book focuses more on establishing the prophet's identity in seclusion than it does on narrating how he conveys divine messages to an immediately present audience. For example, Margaret Odell identifies Ezekiel's actions in 3:22–5:17 as a series of experiences that strip him of his previous identity, initiating him in his new role as prophet.[14] Meanwhile, Andrew Compton argues that Ezekiel's sign-acts in this section have the ritual function of establishing Ezekiel as a priest, rather than the more commonly understood communicative function.[15]

The recognition that Ezekiel's actions in 3:22–5:17 convey as much information about the prophet's vocational identity as they do about external matters is key to understanding a section of the book in which Ezekiel's body is so much in focus. Moreover, both Odell and Compton recognize that sign-acts can be multivalent. Compton claims that "in *addition* to their communicative value, the details point towards these initial sign-acts as serving as formative-rituals in Ezekiel's commission,"[16] while Odell argues that Ezekiel's actions "serve a dual function,"

35; Block, *Ezekiel 1–24*, 166; Johanna Erzberger, "Prophetic Sign Acts as Performances," in *Jeremiah Invented: Constructions and Deconstructions of Jeremiah*, ed. Else Kragelund Holt and Carolyn J. Sharp (London: Bloomsbury T&T Clark, 2015), 104–116 (108, 110–111); Barbara Green, "Genre Criticism and the Prophets," in *The Oxford Handbook of the Prophets*, ed. Carolyn J. Sharp (Oxford: Oxford University Press, 2016), 258–276 (273). Alternative definitions have been proposed; for example, David Stacey (*Prophetic Drama*, 264–268, 277–282) argues that the primary function of "prophetic drama" (his preferred term) is to express Yhwh's intention, whether or not an audience is present.

13 Bernhard Lang, *Monotheism and the Prophetic Minority*, 80; Erzberger, "Prophetic Sign Acts," 110–111.

14 Margaret S. Odell, "You Are What You Eat: Ezekiel and the Scroll," *JBL* 117/2 (1998): 229–48; Odell, *Ezekiel*, 53–57.

15 Compton, "Sign Acts of Ezekiel 3:22–5:17," 60–62.

16 Compton, "Sign-Acts of Ezekiel 3:22–5:17," 47 (emphasis mine). Despite this statement, Compton primarily dedicates his article to proving why Ezekiel's sign-acts have a ritual function and *not* a communicative one.

simultaneously preparing Ezekiel for his role and disclosing Yhwh's message concerning the fate of Jerusalem.[17] In the case of Ezekiel's confinement, this action reveals the identity of the prophet as a divine representative with special access to Yhwh, which in itself conveys Yhwh's presence among the Judean community in migration.[18] It can be defined as a sign-act in the sense of using a non-verbal method to communicate a divine message: a message that is both about the vocational identity of the messenger and about what that identity means for Judeans in migration.

The issue of whether Ezekiel's confinement had any significant audience is rendered void by focusing on his actions as described in the text, which is the only way we have access to them.[19] The relationship between the final form of the book of Ezekiel and any historical prophet Ezekiel who may have lived in the sixth century BCE, not to mention any sign-acts or other activities he may have conducted during his lifetime, is too obscure to attempt reconstruction. Therefore, the present chapter focuses on the account of Ezekiel's actions as part of a text crafted with the purpose of conveying information to readers beyond the immediate context in which it was written.[20] Understood this way, the sign-act of Ezekiel's confinement to his house has no less of an audience than any other prophetic sign-act in the Hebrew Bible. The text describes the body of the prophet Ezekiel as being hidden from public view, but his body is not hidden from the reader. Rather, its suddenly limited location strikes the reader for being so seemingly incongruous, so inconvenient with regard to the prophet's mission. Trapped within four walls, unable to move or speak except by Yhwh's decree, the body of this divine vessel demands all of the reader-audience's attention.

---

17 Odell, *Ezekiel*, 56.

18 David Stacey's interpretation of "prophetic drama" supports this interpretation, as he writes: "The prophet was *himself* a symbol. By his very presence in society he represented the immanence, the power, and the unpredictability of the divine word" (Stacey, *Prophetic Drama*, 61).

19 Odell, *Ezekiel*, 55; Richard Benton, "Narrator, Audience, and the Sign-Acts of Ezekiel 3–5," in *Festschrift in Honor of Professor Paul Nadim Tarazi*, ed. Nicolae Roddy, Bible in the Christian Orthodox Tradition 3 (New York: Peter Lang, 2013), 135–40, 162–64 (135–136).

20 This also negates the (largely discredited) psychoanalytical approaches to the prophet Ezekiel, whereby his actions have been interpreted as a reaction to the traumatic experience of forced migration (e.g. Edwin C. Broome, "Ezekiel's Abnormal Personality," *JBL* 65/3 [1946]: 277–92; David J. Halperin, *Seeking Ezekiel: Text and Psychology* [University Park, PA: Penn State University Press, 1993]). If the text is viewed as an edited product, it may attest to the prophet's trauma (although the extent of this is irrecoverable), but it cannot itself be seen as an individual's uncontrollable response to the Babylonian exile.

2 Sublime Confinement

The location of Ezekiel's body is of the utmost importance for the book: both its immediate location inside the prophet's house and its broader setting in the Babylonian exile. The described context of the book of Ezekiel – the 597 BCE displacement of a group of Jerusalem elites, including the eponymous prophet – shapes the entire text. This is not to say that the book was necessarily finalized in sixth-century BCE Babylonia, but that it presents itself as a Judean response to being outside of the land of Judah. As this was a phenomenon experienced by an increasing proportion of the Judean population from the early sixth century BCE onwards, the book of Ezekiel's relevance for these communities across numerous time periods is clear.

One of the challenges often faced by forced migrant communities is anxiety surrounding religious purity concerns. Mary Douglas demonstrated how a society's conceptualization of clean and unclean displays the symbolic patterns of their religion, including how they organize people and things into hierarchies.[21] When members of a society feel that this structure is destabilized, fears of pollution are at their most acute.[22] Forced migration presents an example of a situation where the normative boundaries between insiders and outsiders as well as hierarchies of status are disrupted, challenging previous conceptions of clean and unclean.[23] Daniel Smith-Christopher examined this phenomenon in texts he dates to the period of the Babylonian exile, especially the priestly literature of the Hebrew Bible. Smith-Christopher suggests that the discomfort and insecurity of being forced to live in a foreign land led the priestly writers to develop an increased interest in purity issues as a way of gaining at least ideological control over the chaos enacted on their religious structures. As a minority group in foreign empires, the ability of Judean migrants to reconceptualize the boundaries of clean and unclean, inside and outside, was vital to their religious survival.[24]

The book of Ezekiel likewise exhibits anxieties about the threat of impurity in a migratory setting.[25] For example, Ezekiel 4:13 claims that bread consumed

---

21 Mary Douglas, *Purity and Danger: An Analysis of Concepts of Pollution and Taboo*, Mary Douglas Collected Works Volume II (London: Routledge, 2003), 2–4.
22 Douglas, *Purity and Danger,* 105.
23 Daniel L. Smith-Christopher, *The Religion of the Landless: The Social Context of the Babylonian Exile* (Eugene, OR: Wipf and Stock, 2015), 50–58, 84.
24 Smith-Christopher, *The Religion of the Landless,* 139–151.
25 Ezekiel's links to priestly concerns are evident both in the prophet's stated identity as a priest (1:3) and in the text's well-documented linguistic and thematic similarities with the priestly literature of the Hebrew Bible (e.g. Menahem Haran, "The Law Code of Ezekiel XL–XLVIII and its Relation to the Priestly School," *HUCA* 50 (1979): 45–71; Menahem Haran, "Ezekiel, P, and the

"among the nations" where Judeans will be scattered will be as "unclean" (טָמֵא) as bread baked over human faeces.[26] Meanwhile, Ezekiel 44:6–7 attests to the potential of uncircumcised people groups to defile (חלל) merely by proximity (cf. Ezek 32:18–30). Ezekiel 16 and 23 describe the danger of impurity inherent in Jerusalem's contact with foreign nations, which Ezekiel characterizes as egregious sexual promiscuity (16:26–29; 23:5–47). Using a different metaphor motif, Ezekiel portrays foreign nations, including Egypt and the ambiguous "Gog of Magog," as monstrous animals who will experience deaths that are both horrifying and unclean (23:20; 29:3–5; 32:2–8; 38:4–6). These descriptions of non-Judeans evoke a sense of disgust concerning their mere physical presence. The book of Ezekiel uses this as a means of creating strong boundaries between its identified in-group and the outsiders who defile.[27]

The prophet Ezekiel's confinement to his house removes his body from the polluting milieu that the book depicts as lurking outside of his doorstep. By avoiding defilement to the greatest extent possible, Ezekiel expresses the continued religious status afforded by his identity as a priest (established in 1:3), since temple priests were required to maintain a higher standard of purity than lay people (Lev 21:1–22:16; Ezek 44:15–27).

There has been a great deal of discussion regarding the significance of Ezekiel's priestly background. Most agree that Ezekiel's priestly vocation, though somewhat frustrated in migration, continues to inform his role and ideology.[28]

Priestly School," *VT* 58 (2008): 211–218; Risa Levitt Kohn, *A New Heart and a New Soul: Ezekiel, the Exile, and the Torah,* JSOTSup 358 (Sheffield: Sheffield Academic Press, 2002), 30–85). The present chapter does not seek to assert that the priestly literature and/or the book of Ezekiel were necessarily composed during the Babylonian exile, but that they share a preoccupation with purity concerns (and a way of resolving them) that likely attests to a desire to construct clear boundaries around a particular in-group.

26 Hosea 9:3 likewise refers to the Israelite exiles eating unclean (טָמֵא) food in Assyria.

27 C. L. Crouch has shown how biblical writers, including Ezekiel, use impurity language (specifically the term תּוֹעֵבָה) to evoke an emotion of disgust that is particularly effective for creating ethnic boundaries (C. L. Crouch, "What Makes a Thing Abominable? Observations on the Language of Boundaries and Identity Formation from a Social Scientific Perspective," *VT* 65 [2015]: 516–541).

28 E.g. Jan William Tarlin, "Utopia and Pornography: Violence, Hope, and the Shattered Male Subject," in *Reading Bibles, Writing Bodies: Identity and the Book,* ed. Timothy K. Beal and David M. Gunn (London: Routledge, 1997), 175–183 (180–182); Compton, "The Sign-Acts of Ezekiel 3:22–5:17"; Marvin A. Sweeney, *Form and Intertextuality in Prophetic and Apocalyptic Literature* (Tübingen: Mohr Siebeck, 2005), 125–43; Andrew Mein, *Ezekiel and the Ethics of Exile* (Oxford: Oxford University Press: 2001), 137. One exception is Margaret Odell, who argues that Ezekiel is unable to enact his priestly identity without access to the Jerusalem temple, so it is stripped away from him during his initiation as a prophet (Odell, "You Are What You Eat," 237; Odell, *Ezekiel,* 53, 55–56). In Odell's view, Ezekiel's prophetic role requires that all aspects of his previous priestly

The book of Ezekiel adapts priestly purity laws for a migration setting, allowing Ezekiel to maintain a higher standard of purity than non-priestly Judeans, even in an impure environment. This is evident, for example, when it comes to the issue of eating. When Yhwh commands Ezekiel to eat the bread baked over human faeces as a sign of the impurities to be suffered in migration, Ezekiel begs Yhwh to spare him such defilement, and Yhwh concedes (4:14–15).[29] Although some lessening of purity standards may be inevitable outside of the land of Judah, the book of Ezekiel is careful to shelter its protagonist from the effects of this circumstance as much as possible, including by keeping him physically secluded from the foreign world he inhabits. The priestly use of confinement to divide between purity and impurity also appears in Leviticus 13:3–5, in which a priest can shut in (הִסְגִּיר) someone with an unclean (טָמֵא) skin disease for seven days to keep them from contaminating the rest of the community. Another example, in which the impurity is shut *out*, occurs in Numbers 12:14–15, where Miriam is excluded (תִּסָּגֵר) from the camp for seven days while she has a skin disease. Both the use of the verb סגר to indicate the purity-based restriction and the number seven as defining the required time period for purification provide parallels to Ezekiel's confinement.

The book of Ezekiel's regard for purity is also linked to another issue of great theological concern for Judean migrants. In the covenantal traditions, the occupation of the divinely promised land of Israel is dependent upon following Yhwh's laws, including maintaining purity in the ways those laws dictate. Expulsion from the land is the punishment for failing to uphold this requirement (Lev 18:24–30; 20:22–26; Deut 4:25–28; 28:36, 64). The book of Ezekiel is aware of these traditions, revealing that those who remained in Jerusalem made use of them to argue that the Judeans in migration were the ones singled out for punishment (11:15; 33:24).[30] For example, Ezekiel 11:15–16 records that the residents of Jerusalem were telling the migrants, "Distance yourselves from Yhwh: the land has been given to *us* as a possession" (15b). Ezekiel deals with this unfavourable view of the migrants by having Yhwh retort, "I have made them distant among

---

status are done away with so that he can identify wholly with his community, even though she concedes that Ezekiel's isolation represents a continued priestly level of "separation for the sake of service" (Odell, *Ezekiel,* 58).

29 Zimmerli, *Ezekiel 1,* 171. Meindert Dijkstra sees this as an early example of halakhic discussion about preparing and eating kosher food ("The Valley of Dry Bones: Coping with the Reality of the Exile in the Book of Ezekiel," in *The Crisis of Israelite Religion: Transformation of Religious Tradition in Exilic and Post-Exilic Times,* ed. Bob Becking and Marjo C. A. Korpel [Leiden: Brill, 1999], 114–33 [132]).

30 Dalit Rom-Shiloni, *Exclusive Inclusivity: Identity Conflicts Between the Exiles and the People Who Remained (6th–5th Centuries BCE),* LHBOTS 543 (London: Bloomsbury, 2013), 145–156.

the nations and I have scattered them among the lands, but I am a small sanctuary for them in the lands where they have come" (16b). Yhwh then describes how he will gather the Judeans who have been scattered among other nations and give *them* the land of Israel. They will be endowed with "one heart and a new spirit" (11:19; cf. 18:31; 36:26), turning their bodies into divinely-altered ones incapable of rebelling against Yhwh (11:20). But first, the land will require cleansing from the disgusting things (שִׁקּוּצִים) and abominations (תּוֹעֲבוֹת) that the Judeans who had temporarily remained in it put there (11:18). They are revealed to be the perpetrators who will bear the ultimate punishment for their defiling actions (11:21).

Thus, the book of Ezekiel seeks to demonstrate that the Judeans living *outside* of Judah are the ones set aside to continue *inside* the covenant relationship with Yhwh; that is, to continue upholding Yhwh's requisite standard of purity inasmuch as it is possible in migration. Because of this, Ezekiel has to invert the competing Judean model that equates being *inside* Yhwh's covenant group with being *inside* the borders of the land promised in the covenant, where the Jerusalem temple is located as the purest space of all. The book of Ezekiel describes and delineates spatiality in ways that illustrate its concepts of inclusion and exclusion. It uses the prophet's body and the spaces that body occupies to communicate to its readers that what is most pure is most interior, furthest away from the uncleanness of the outside world; but also, crucially, that the location of the most interior place in reference to Yahwism has moved outside of Judah.[31]

The prophet's secluded body parallels the secluded body of Yhwh in Ezekiel's temple vision of chapters 40–48. That Ezekiel's concept of Yhwh includes the deity having a physical presence with a body resembling a human being's is established in Ezekiel's first vision in chapter 1 and continues throughout the book (3:22; 10:1–22; 11:22–23; 43:4, 7).[32] In Ezekiel's idealized depiction of Yhwh's dwelling place, the deity occupies the innermost part of the sanctuary, which is the most secluded from anything that could have the potential to defile (41:3–4; 43:1–5; 44:4).[33] Ezekiel here evokes a similar model to the Jerusalem temple, but Ezekiel's parallel vision of that sanctuary in chapter 8 serves as a warning regard-

---

31 On the prophet's body and its spatial locations as means of expressing Ezekiel's interpretation of Judean religion in the context of migration, see Mary E. Mills, *Alterity, Pain, and Suffering in Isaiah, Jeremiah, and Ezekiel*, LHBOTS 479 (London: T&T Clark, 2007), 10 and Dale F. Launderville, *Spirit and Reason: The Embodied Character of Ezekiel's Symbolic Thinking* (Waco, TX: Baylor University Press, 2007), 1 (cf. Douglas, *Purity and Danger*, 116).

32 Robin C. McCall, "The Body and Being of God," *RevExp* 111/4 (2014): 376–389 (378–388).

33 Casey A. Strine, "Theological Anthropology and Anthropological Theology in the Book of Ezekiel," in *Das Buch Ezechiel: Komposition, Redaktion und Rezeption*, ed. Jan Christian Gertz, Corinna Körting, and Markus Witte (Berlin: De Gruyter, 2020), 233–254 (249–250).

ing what can happen if Yhwh's holy place is contaminated. In this earlier vision, Ezekiel details the thorough desecration of the Jerusalem temple from its outside to its innermost space due to the worship of other gods and other illicit ritual activities. Yhwh cannot remain in such an impure space and thus departs the temple in Jerusalem in preparation for its destruction (11:23; 43:8).

In order to avoid the risk of such a catastrophe occurring again, Ezekiel's vision of the new, idealized temple has Yhwh protected from potential contamination through his seclusion in a pure space with preventative measures in place to minimize his contact with the profane. An outer wall separates the temple precinct from the impure world outside (Ezek 42:20), including all foreigners (44:6–9). Only the Levites may serve in the inner court and gates of the temple (44:11–14), while access to the nave of the sanctuary is restricted to Zadokite priests who have ritually prepared their bodies to enter (44:15–27). Meanwhile, the prince and the rest of the people of Israel have severely restricted access limited to certain times, entryways, and routes through the temple's inner court (46:1–10).[34]

By contrast, the prophet Ezekiel is fit to enter Yhwh's sanctuary as he envisions it in migration because the prophet has been secluded from contamination to the greatest extent possible. In Ezekiel 41:1–4, Ezekiel stands in the main room (הֵיכָל) of the temple and, although he does not enter the inner sanctuary (פְּנִימָה) in this instance, he gains access to it visually by learning its measurements. Therefore, in the Yahwism that the book of Ezekiel constructs for the migrant Judeans, the prophet Ezekiel is the only human who has access to the purest, most interior space – that is, to Yhwh – both via his vision and by modelling the purity of confinement in his own house. By making this space accessible to his audience through the reports he is repeatedly commanded to make (40:4; 43:10; 44:5–6), the prophet acts as the channel between divine and human. This role is especially evident in 14:1–5. Elders from the prophet's community come to Ezekiel's house seeking a message from Yhwh, but instead of giving them one, Ezekiel condemns them for asking while they bear the impurity of idol worship (14:3). The prophet is the ultimate access point to Yhwh, but, as with Ezekiel's muteness in 3:26, Yhwh can turn the prophet's body into a boundary between himself and the Judeans when it meets with impurity.

---

34 Note that protection is also required *from* Yhwh's purity by those who occupy the profane world. In Ezekiel 44:17–19, priests must change their clothes before they leave the temple precinct as well as before they enter it. If they exit the sacred precinct wearing the purified clothes they have worn to serve Yhwh, the garments pose a danger to the public, who are not ritually prepared to come into contact with the purified clothing.

Yet the boundaries Ezekiel constructs are not simply dichotomies between inside and outside, pure and impure. Rather, these qualities exist in a hierarchy, from the most pure and interior going outwards to what is most impure and exterior. Ezekiel thus envisions Yhwh's ideal temple in a concentric model whose centre is the purest space. This centre – Yhwh's inner sanctuary – exists inside of the temple, often simply called the "house" (בַּיִת, e.g. 40:5, 47–48; 41:5, 7–8, 13; 43:4–6). In migration, Yhwh's inner sanctuary can only be accessed via the prophet, who is likewise enclosed within his own בַּיִת (3:24). That Ezekiel's house acts as a model of the בֵּית־יהוה is especially evident in the parallel descriptions of the boundaries of these two houses and how they are transgressed. In his vision of Jerusalem, the prophet Ezekiel has to dig (חתר) into the wall (קִיר) of the temple in order to view the defiling actions taking place inside (8:7–8). Then, once Yhwh has finished demonstrating why he is leaving his former sanctuary, he has Ezekiel dig (חתר) himself out of the wall (קִיר) of his own house to demonstrate the forthcoming destruction of the Jerusalem temple (12:5). The walls of Ezekiel's house and of the Jerusalem temple had both served as boundaries between pure and impure. By creating a disordered breech in those boundaries, Ezekiel demonstrates that the pure and impure have become chaotically mixed. When the בֵּית־יהוה in Jerusalem comes to an end, so too do the restrictions placed upon the prophet Ezekiel (24:27; 33:22). The new temple he envisages for Yhwh is then the *only* temple, and its boundaries are secure (40:5; 42:20).

Ezekiel's בַּיִת and Yhwh's בַּיִת both also exist inside a wider boundary. This outer ring of the concentric model consists of lay people who do not uphold a priestly level of purity but do belong to a select community that is purer than those outside of it. In the book of Ezekiel, this group of insiders consists of Judeans who are outside of the land of Judah and who choose to remain part of Yhwh's covenant group by turning away from their former transgressions and avoiding further impurity (Ezek 11:17–20; 18:30–32; 20:33–38; 33:18–20). Ezekiel's preferred term for the book's stated audience is בֵּית־יִשְׂרָאֵל (house of Israel) or occasionally בֵּית מְרִי (rebellious house). Carly Crouch has demonstrated that Ezekiel's use of בֵּית־יִשְׂרָאֵל refers to those who live or used to live in Jerusalem,[35] further suggesting that Ezekiel's attention is focused on the old and new centres of Judean religion. In the same chapter in which Ezekiel is confined to his בַּיִת, the word בַּיִת is also used ten times to refer to the community he addresses (3:1, 4, 5, 7, 9, 27; cf. 12:2). This creates a concentric image of Ezekiel's בַּיִת as located inside a wider בַּיִת. Similarly, Ezekiel's vision of the idealized temple places the בֵּית־יהוה in the centre of the idealized בֵּית־יִשְׂרָאֵל (45:1–8; 47:13–35). Outside the

---

35 C. L. Crouch, "Ezekiel's Immobility and the Meaning of 'The House of Judah' in Ezekiel 4," *JSOT* 44/1 (2019): 182–197 (184).

borders of this renewed and purified בֵּית־יִשְׂרָאֵל are foreigners and the Judeans who had remained in Judah and rejected Yhwh. They define what is impure, excluded from Yhwh's community.

3 Conspicuous Confinement

This definitive distinction between those who are outside of Yhwh's covenant and those who have the potential to be inside pivots around the location of the prophet Ezekiel. Ezekiel's long confinement to his house is conspicuous not only for its mirroring of Yhwh's confinement in the temple but also for its extremity as a sign-act. Throughout the book, Ezekiel's status as a true prophet is repeatedly demonstrated through the dedication of his entire person to the task of being Yhwh's representative at great personal cost. This is conducted through sign-acts that are both physically painful, such as lying bound on one side for 390 days (4:9), and socially damaging, such as being unable to mourn the death of his wife (24:16–18). Further, the book seeks to portray Ezekiel as Yhwh's *only* representative in his generation. Ezekiel 12:21–13:23 and 22:25 condemn other prophets for being false, and in 22:30, Yhwh proclaims that there is not a single person in Jerusalem who can "stand in the breach" to advocate for the city's survival. The prophet Ezekiel is therefore established as the single point of contact between Yhwh and his people,[36] and that point of contact is located outside of Judah.

In this manner, the book of Ezekiel portrays its protagonist as the one human being uniquely suited to interpret and instate a renewed Yahwism in migration. Not only is Ezekiel the single true prophet of the exilic generation: he is also identified as the founder of the idealized cult of Yhwh in migration. In Ezekiel 43:18–27, Yhwh instructs Ezekiel that on the day the temple is rebuilt, Ezekiel must purify its altar with the blood of a bull sacrificed as the sin offering, assisted by the newly installed Zadokite priesthood. This ritual of consecration is similar to the one Moses conducts as part of the ordination of the high priest Aaron and his sons (Exod 29:12, 35–37; Lev 8:15). For the inauguration of Yhwh's new temple in migration, Ezekiel undertakes his own ordination ritual, establishing himself as the leader of the cult under the direct authority of Yhwh.

Despite its detailed focus on the organization and tasks of the priesthood, the book of Ezekiel never explicitly mentions a high priest. This is one of the ways it diverges from the priestly source and holiness code, which pay a great deal of attention to the high priest's special clothing, purity restrictions, and duties

---

36 Strine, "Theological Anthropology," 243.

(Exod 28; 39:1–31; Lev 8:7–12; 16:3–23; 21:10–15).[37] The main distinction the high priest holds above all other priests and lay people is that he enters Yhwh's inner sanctuary, coming into the most direct contact with Yhwh that any human can achieve without dying (Exod 28:29, 35; 39:1, 41; Lev 16:3–23). His ability to do so is dependent upon his maintenance of a higher standard of purity than the other priests, such as being unable to touch even his closest relatives when they die, or to marry a widowed woman (Lev 21:11, 13–15). The book of Ezekiel suggests that Ezekiel bears several of the identity markers of the high priest, especially in association with his confinement. It does not mention a high priest because it holds Ezekiel himself ready to fulfil the role when Yhwh's new temple is actualized.

Margaret Odell has already noted that the term for the cords (עֲבוֹתִים) that bind Ezekiel in his house in 3:25 and on his side in 4:8 is also used for the gold cords that bind the ephod and breast piece to the high priest in the priestly literature (Exod 28:14, 22, 24–25; 39:15, 17–18).[38] The ephod is set with onyx stones engraved with the names of the sons of Israel (Exod 28:9–12; 39:6–7), while the breast piece includes twelve precious stones representing the twelve tribes of Israel (Exod 28:17–21; 39:10–14). When these are bound to the high priest with עֲבוֹתִים, the high priest becomes a representative for the people of Israel, bringing them to remembrance before Yhwh (Exod 28:29). While some have argued that the prophet Ezekiel is presented in the model of a divine statue, channeling Yhwh's presence,[39] his wearing of עֲבוֹתִים may indicate that he also represents the migrant Judeans and their experiences. Ezekiel's dual role is most evident in his sign-acts, where he symbolizes Yhwh one moment (for example, besieging Jerusalem in 4:1–3) and his people the next (such as bearing their punishment in 4:4–8). This further confirms Ezekiel's (high) priestly identity, since the role of priests was to represent both Yhwh to the people and the people to Yhwh.[40] Although most of the luxurious items worn by the high priest in the priestly tradition (such as gold, precious stones, and a blue robe) would have been inaccessible in migration, Ezekiel maintains what markers of this identity he can: not only the עֲבוֹתִים, but also a turban (פְּאֵר; 24:17), the headwear of temple priests according to his own vision (44:18) and of Aaron and his sons in Exodus 39:28 (cf. Isa-

---

37 Haran, "The Law Code of Ezekiel XL–XLVIII," 17; Haran, "Ezekiel, P, and the Priestly School," 212.
38 Odell, "You Are What You Eat," 246; Odell, *Ezekiel*, 57–58.
39 Block, *Ezekiel 1–24*, 162; Casey A. Strine, "Ezekiel's Image Problem: The Mesopotamian Cult Statue Induction Ritual and the Imago Dei Anthropology in the Book of Ezekiel," *CBQ* 76 (2014): 252–272; Strine, "Theological Anthropology," 240–243.
40 Compton, "The Sign-Acts of Ezekiel 3:22–5:17," 64, 69–70. Odell (*Ezekiel*, 54) agrees that Ezekiel identifies with both Yhwh and the people, but on account of his prophetic, not priestly, role.

iah 61:10).[41] Additionally, he avoids contact with his wife's dead body (Ezek 24:17) in accordance with the purity requirement for priests in Ezekiel 44:25 and Leviticus 21:1–5.[42]

Other aspects of Ezekiel's sign-acts likewise support his identity as a high priest for the Judean migration. Andrew Compton and Marvin Sweeney have suggested that Ezekiel's silence in 3:26 may indicate his preparedness to be in contact with Yhwh, since Yhwh's sacred spaces and times are described as being silent in several places in the Hebrew Bible (Hab 2:20; Neh 8:11; Zeph 1:7; Zech 2:17 [Heb.]).[43] There is also no description of there being any sound of prayer or song in Yhwh's temple in either Ezekiel's temple vision or the descriptions in the priestly literature.[44] Therefore, Ezekiel's lack of open speech is appropriate for the pure space he occupies while in communication with Yhwh.[45] Further evidence of his continued association with temple ritual is provided by Ezekiel lying on his left and right sides in 4:4–8 to bear (נשא) the guilt (עָוֹן) of Israel and Judah.[46] Although the language of bearing guilt (נֹשֵׂא עָוֹן) is used in a variety of contexts in the Hebrew Bible, it is associated with the high priest Aaron in significant ways. Exodus 28:38 says that when entering Yhwh's sanctuary, Aaron bears guilt (נֹשֵׂא עָוֹן) on behalf of the Israelites, while in the Day of Atonement ritual described in Leviticus 16:21–22, Aaron transfers their guilt (עָוֹן) to the scapegoat so that the animal bears (נשא) it instead. In migration, Ezekiel is the one who bears the people's guilt, indicating its extent via his sign-act. Yet he is not able to resolve their guilt in the manner of Aaron conducting atonement for Israel in the priestly

---

41 In many places, Ezekiel condemns luxurious clothing and adornment, including those associated with the high priest (blue fabric, precious stones, and gold). The book uses these as symbols of the ignorant pride of foreigners (Ezek 23:5–6; 27:7; 28:13) and of the Judeans remaining in Judah (7:19; 16:13) in the face of their imminent demise. By contrast, the Judeans in migration would likely have lost their generational wealth and would have had (at least initially) less access to such goods.

42 Sweeney, *Form and Intertextuality*, 139.

43 Sweeney, *Form and Intertextuality*, 133; Compton, "The Sign Acts of Ezekiel 3:22–5:17," 64.

44 Yehezkel Kaufmann, *The Religion of Israel: From its Beginnings to the Babylonian Exile*, trans. Moshe Greenberg (London: George Allen & Unwin), 303–4; Israel Knohl, *The Sanctuary of Silence: The Priestly Torah and the Holiness School* (Minneapolis: Fortress Press, 1995), 148–152.

45 Wilson has demonstrated that Ezekiel's silence prevented him from being a mediator (מוֹכִיחַ) on behalf of the people in Yhwh's dispute with them (Wilson, "Ezekiel's Dumbness," 98–102). While this silence temporarily curtails part of Ezekiel's prophetic role, it expresses his continued priestly identity. Odell's suggestion that Ezekiel's prohibition from being a מוֹכִיחַ is connected to the loss of his priestly identity (Odell, *Ezekiel*, 58) cannot be supported, as neither the term מוֹכִיחַ nor the verb יכח are used in relation to priests in the Hebrew Bible.

46 Friebel, *Jeremiah's and Ezekiel's Sign Acts*, 220; Block, *Ezekiel 1–24*, 176–79; Compton, "The Sign-Acts of Ezekiel 3:22–5:17," 67–69.

literature.[47] The new and fully functional temple has not yet been realized, and the people have not yet accepted Ezekiel as their high priest who operates within it. Ezekiel's actions indicate that he is poised to take up his position as leader of the restored cult; yet in migration, full restoration exists only in visionary form.

For this reason, Ezekiel's maintenance of a high-priestly level of purity is by no means perfect. For example, he has to shave his hair (5:1), which is forbidden for priests in his temple vision (44:20). A shaved head may reflect one of the humiliating circumstances of forced migration, similar to what is dictated for female prisoners of war in Deuteronomy 21:12. Additionally, Ezekiel cannot eat the priestly portion from the temple offerings as priests in Jerusalem would have, but instead has to eat meagre rations cooked over dung (4:9–15).[48] However, the text takes care in numerous places to demonstrate that Ezekiel adapted and maintained elements of (high) priestly identity for a migration setting, establishing him as the religious leader of the migration. The fullest extent of his role as cult leader is anticipated for a moment, always in an unspecified future, when the temple would be restored in reality and not only in Ezekiel's vision.

By setting up Ezekiel's role in this way, the book validates its interpretation of the centre of Yahwism moving outside of Judah. It demonstrates that Yhwh's presence in migration is entirely mediated through his earthly representative: his prophet and new high priest, Ezekiel. Thus, it may even be said that the small (or temporary) sanctuary, מְקְדָּשׁ מְעַט, that Yhwh claims to have been for the migrants (11:16) is, in fact, the cloistered body of Ezekiel himself.[49] By placing Yhwh's point of contact with humanity in a migratory setting, the book of Ezekiel demonstrates to its audience that Judeans in migration are the ones who have access to Yhwh. They are not distant from him, as those in Jerusalem may claim (11:15). On the contrary, the centre of his earthly presence is in their midst.

4 Conclusions

Ezekiel's confinement therefore functions as a sign-act that reveals information about the role of the prophet and the god he represents. It communicates to a

---

47 Most agree that Ezekiel's expiatory act cannot be fully effective in the setting of the Babylonian exile, meaning that the people must suffer Yhwh's punishment (e.g. Block, *Ezekiel 1–24*, 177; Odell, "You are what you eat," 247; Sweeney, *Form and Intertextuality*, 133; Odell, *Ezekiel*, 63–64).
48 Sweeney, *Form and Intertextuality*, 133.
49 Stefano Salemi has also suggested this in *A Linguistic-Theological Exegesis of Ezekiel as Môphēt – "I have made you a sign" (Ezekiel 12:6)*, Studia Semitica Neerlandica 76 (Leiden: Brill, 2024) and in "Ezekiel's wife's death: Femicide, 'divine election,' metaphor, or mimic?" in this volume.

wide audience of Judean migrants, who needed a new religious paradigm in order to interpret their situation. The book of Ezekiel's presentation of the prophet and of Yhwh provides the basis for its guidelines concerning the continued existence of a Judean community in migration. If the displaced Judeans want access to Yhwh in his (new) sublime isolation, they must be careful to maintain their purity where those in Jerusalem have failed. This means refusing to integrate with the impure nations surrounding them and eschewing the types of religious syncretism that caused Yhwh to abandon his temple in Jerusalem. In the context of a dispute with those in Judah concerning which group represents the continuation of the covenant, the book of Ezekiel makes the startling claim that Yhwh's sanctuary has moved indefinitely into migration. It demonstrates that Yhwh has chosen to be present with those in migration because they represent the only hope for his covenant people. The prophet's confined body is, literarily, a conspicuous sign-act that confronts its migrant audience with the message that its deity is present within their group. In sublime isolation, he awaits their response.

Karin Schöpflin

Predicting Jerusalem's Siege and Fall through Sign-Acts: Actual Performance or Literary Fiction in Ezekiel 4:1–5:4?

Sign-acts are an important feature within the Book of Ezekiel, because they are fairly numerous all over Ezek 4–37, and draw the reader's special attention to them due to their somewhat strange, even bizarre character. As compared with sign-acts in other prophetic writings we find a special trait in Ezek 4:1–5:4: there are a number of different sign-acts forming a small series intending to illustrate and predict the siege and fall of Jerusalem in 587 BCE, and its immediate consequences, as it stands including an additional outlook on exilic conditions. This article will interpret this sign-acts collection, which offers a number of puzzling elements, especially some inconsistencies and details that are obscure and need interpretation; at the same time, we find interrelations among the different parts of the unit as well. Both aspects attest to the fact that Ezek 4:1–5:4 gradually developed to its present state through redactors' activities. Apart from a historical-critical analysis and interpretation, the article will discuss the nature of every single sign-act, namely whether it was originally actually performed by the prophet or rather composed by some scribe. This issue used to be closely connected with the question of whether magic is involved in the performance of a sign-act or not.[1] In order to deal initially with these problems, there will be a short investigation into two sign-acts in the Book of Jeremiah (Jer 19 and 13) because these are representative for two different models of sign-acts within the writing prophets and helpful for presenting some criteria concerning sign-acts.

1 Two Representative Sign-Acts in Jeremiah

The two sign-acts were picked out because Jer 19 appears as an exemplary model of the genre 'sign-act'. There is little discussion about this instance, whereas Jer 13:1–11 is one of the most disputed passages in the book of Jeremiah due to problems that for the most part arise from its nature as a sign-act.[2]

---

1 The debate was kindled by Georg Fohrer, *Die symbolischen Handlungen der Propheten*, 2nd ed., ATANT 54 (Zürich: Zwingli-Verlag, 1968), and his article "Prophetie und Magie", *ZAW* 78/1 (1966): 25–47.
2 See Winfried Thiel, *Die deuteronomistische Redaktion von Jeremia 1–25* (Neukirchen: Neukirchener Verlag, 1973), 169; according to Franz D. Hubmann, "Jeremia 13,1–11", in *Ein Gott – eine*

https://doi.org/10.1515/9783111521015-005

1.1 The Broken Jug (Jer 19:1–13)

Commentators agree that the passage combines a sign-act with a sermon. As the so-called "Tophet-sermon" is characterized by Deuteronomic language and concepts,[3] one can easily isolate the basic layer, namely the sign-act given in Jer 19:1–2a, 10–11a. It consists of YHWH's commands (1–2a, 10) and a short interpretation (11a). God instructs Jeremiah to buy a ceramic vessel at a potter's – a flask or jug – and to invite a number of persons who represent secular and cultic authority – namely elders and priests – to accompany him (19:1).[4] Later on, these will be witnesses to Jeremiah's action and addressees of his words. Jeremiah is to leave the city with them and to enter the valley Ben-Hinnom at the Potshed Gate (19:2), a place that served apparently as Jerusalem's garbage dump (note the telling name of the gate). Before the witnessing elders and priests, Jeremiah shall smash the vessel (19:10). As it is a ceramic one it will, of course, break, and it goes without saying that it cannot be mended. Then Jeremiah will proclaim God's comment on what the elders and priests have seen. They learn that the vessel is intended as an equivalent to Jerusalem and her inhabitants; these will be destroyed at YHWH's hands (*"I* will break"). The metaphorical breaking of the vessel illustrates that destruction is complete and irrevocable. As with most sign-acts, it is taken for granted that the prophet will do as he is told – Jer 19 does not offer an account of the procedure, let alone of the observers' reaction. The sign-act involves an everyday utensil which is handled by the prophet and it includes an interpretation that explicitly says what the object represents and what the action means. The sign-act makes even more sense as it is enacted before an audience: 19:1b introduces the future spectators, and 19:10 (לעיני האנשים) refers to them once more. Any reader can imagine what is going on and understand its symbolic meaning because of the short explanation.

Maybe there is even more to the sign-act since it probably refers to a traditional ritual which was practiced in Israel's environment. There is archaeological evidence from Mesopotamia and Egypt for magic ceremonies intended to harm se-

---

Offenbarung. Beiträge zur biblischen Exegese, Theologie und Spiritualität. Festschrift für Notker Füglister zum 60. Geburtstag, ed. Friedrich V. Reiterer (Würzburg: Echter Verlag, 1991), 103–125 (108 n27), in fact Cornill was the first to state this.

3 See Thiel's analysis in *Die deuteronomistische Redaktion*, to which most commentators after him refer.

4 Robert P. Carroll, *Jeremiah: A Commentary*, OTL (London: SCM, 1986), 387, thinks that Jeremiah himself is an authority at the time, as he can command the elders and priest to accompany him. Carroll finds an alternative concept of the prophet's position here that differs from the concept of the suffering, persecuted Jeremiah as it is found in the biographical accounts and the so-called 'confessions'.

lected persons or even nations.[5] Incantation specialists employed pottery for these rituals; the names of the persons they wanted to harm were written or engraved on the vessel which was broken in the course of the ritual accompanied by spells. Egyptians and Mesopotamians believed that the magic ceremony would affect the respective persons with damage or even death and destruction. Now, did the elders and priests expect something like this when Jeremiah invited them with a jug in his hands to accompany him? This would qualify them as adherents of magic procedures that are – at least from a Deuteronomic point of view – considered illegitimate for persons worshipping Yʜᴡʜ. But an even more important aspect is that they would expect that Jeremiah is going to perform a ceremony cursing an enemy. In the political context of the time, the adversary is Babylonia. To these witnesses who took it for granted that Yʜᴡʜ's presence in the Temple on Mount Zion guarantees Jerusalem's safety and invincibility, the interpretation of the broken jug as a reference to their own country comes as a shock, even a scandal. Adding insult to injury, it is God himself who is going to destroy Jerusalem irreversibly. The words God puts into Jeremiah's mouth thus pervert a traditional ceremony practiced in Israel's environment (and maybe in Israel as well?) with an unexpected turn and add an ironic touch to it.

Most critics do not doubt that Jeremiah factually did perform this sign-act. Indeed, this seems rather probable. A point open to discussion is the problem of whether or not the action is to be qualified as magic in the sense that its performance causes the event to happen that it is prefiguring.[6] Considering the view presented in the previous paragraph, the jug incident is not a magic ceremony because it perverts such a practice. Jeremiah has not the power to harm the Babylonians by incantation as the witnesses might expect or even hope; God, however, shows them in advance through a symbolic action what he is about to make happen.

1.2 The Linen Loincloth or Girdle (Jer 13:1–11)

Exegetic dispute about this passage is concerned with two problems: What does the account mean, and does it describe a factual performance? A specific topic is connected to the latter question, namely whether the Hebrew פרת "Euphrates"

---

5 Katrin Ott, *Die prophetischen Analogiehandlungen im Alten Testament*, BWANT 185 (Stuttgart: W. Kohlhammer Verlag, 2009), 137–145, offers a variety of material.
6 Werner H. Schmidt, *Das Buch Jeremia. Kapitel 1–20*, ATD 20 (Göttingen: Vandenhoeck & Ruprecht, 2008), 328, for instance, denies any magic function because God alone brings about future events.

(13:4) should be emended to 'Parah' as it is found in Aquila's Greek translation, naming a town in Benjaminite territory.

Jeremiah 13:1–7 is a first-person narrative by the prophet. It is structured by three stereotypical formulae found in Jer, Ezek and the Former Prophets,[7] which indicate the beginning of divine speech. For a start, the citation formula (13:1) introduces a divine order that Jeremiah is to buy a loin-cloth or rather a girdle,[8] to wear it and not to wash it. After the revelation formula (13:3) Jeremiah is told to go, while wearing the girdle, to the Euphrates and to hide it in a cleft of a rock there (13:4). The formula (ויאמר אלי 13:6b) precedes the third instruction that occurs after many days (13:6a). Jeremiah is to return to the hiding place by the Euphrates and to take out the girdle. The three orders to Jeremiah alternate with his short accounts that he acted according to God's orders:[9] he bought and wore the girdle (13:2), he took it with him to the Euphrates and hid it there (13:5), he returned to the hiding place (13:7a). Then he says that he found the girdle had rotted (13:7b). There are three commands and three accounts of obeying them with a surplus in the end, namely the observation that the girdle is ruined.

The revelation formula introduces the second part of the section (13:8), followed by the citation formula (13:9a). The divine speech is apparently intended as an explanation of the previous actions. According to 13:9b, the girdle's rotten condition illustrates the destruction of the people, that is, the result of God's judgement. Jeremiah 13:10 has an obvious Deuteronomic ring; now the people are rotten because they used to practice idolatry, so that the ruined girdle illustrates their iniquity and implies an accusation. Jeremiah 13:11b adds the Deuteronomic idea that the Israelites refused to listen to God's words. In between, Jer 13:11a explains the very first action: wearing the girdle symbolizes the close relationship between YHWH and Israel. Thus, Jer 13:9b and 13:10, 11b offer two different meanings of the action as a result of a redactional process, of course.[10] There is an exegetical controversy as to which verse might be the original interpretation.[11] To identify one precise meaning of the entire unit seems impossible. It remains ambiguous just when

---

7 See Karin Schöpflin, *Theologie als Biographie im Ezechielbuch*, FAT 36 (Tübingen: Mohr Siebeck, 2002), 56–99.

8 The loincloth is underwear, a garment worn close to the body, not visible to others, whereas a girdle is worn visibly around the garment. Therefore, the latter meaning of אזור is preferable here.

9 Cf. כדבר יהוה in 13:2a, and כאשר צוה ההוה אותי in 13:5.

10 The discrepancy of two interpretations made Hubmann argue that the passage consists of two originally separate sign-acts, namely 13:1–2, 11* and 13:3–10*. The first one is an encouraging announcement reflecting God's intact close relation with the people, the second is an extension with a negative ring; 13:10a is connecting the two. See Hubmann, "Jeremia 13,1–11", 117–120.

11 Is it just 13:9, or 10a*,b, or 11? For this see Hubmann's summary, "Jeremia 13,1–11", 109–111.

one considers the two interpretations of the girdle's rottenness reflected in the explanation: It may refer to the people's misbehaviour (cf. 13:9; in another sense 13:10a), or to its future state which is a result of God's punishing them (cf. 13:10b).

But what about the probability that the passage is describing a series of actually performed sign-acts? That Jeremiah has to travel twice to the Euphrates is a severe problem, because the journey covers a great distance and would take several months; in addition, there is an indefinite period of time passing between the two journeys ("many days", 13:6). The enormous distance and the long period of total time – at least more than a year – make the performance quite improbable.[12] This made Aquila's Greek translation attractive for exegetes because there Jeremiah's destination is Parah, a small town quite close to Jerusalem,[13] since this would reduce the journey's time and space.[14] However, this does not solve the problem that the passage does not include any witnesses who would observe Jeremiah's actions. Even if you took these for granted – would they accompany Jeremiah even over the shorter distance to Parah? And would they go with him twice? Taken realistically, the series of sign-acts would only make sense to an audience if Jeremiah told them about wearing, hiding and finding the girdle, then showed them the rotten garment and proclaimed God's interpretation. But the unit does not offer an order to commit the message to the people.[15] Therefore, these sign-acts were never performed;[16] Jer 13:1–11 is clearly a literary text appealing to readers' imagination. It is they who will associate the keyword 'Euphrates' with Babylonia, the power that is going to ruin Jerusalem and be the scene of the exile. It appears most probable that Jer 13:1–11 is a piece of information formally given to the prophet as a personal experience in order to reassure him of his message and his task. What the writer-redactor stylized as Jeremiah's account is in fact a fictitious report intended to appeal to readers of the book.

Bearing these observations in mind, we will turn to Ezekiel's first sign-acts now.

---

12 Schmidt, *Jeremia*, 250, comments: "Das doppelte Hin und Her ist nicht schlechthin unmöglich, aber wenig wahrscheinlich".

13 Did Aquila, the only one to offer this name, deliberately change Parah for Euphrates then? Josef Schreiner, *Jeremia 1–25,14*, 3rd ed., NEB 3 (Würzburg: Echter Verlag, 1993), 88, solved the problem by suggesting that the name "Euphrates" is an addition.

14 See Schmidt, *Jeremia*, 251 (he sees the advantage of the shorter distance that there could be witnesses included then).

15 See Ott, *Analogiehandlungen*, 47.

16 See Ott, *Analogiehandlungen*, 46. The discussion about the genre of the passage reflects exegetes' feeling that the actions were not performed. Jer 13:1–11 was qualified as an imaginary journey, a dream, a vision, or a parable (see Carroll, *Jeremiah*, 295). Carroll, *Jeremiah*, 297, thinks that Jeremiah marked out the Euphrates on the ground and enacted a parable. Maybe this assumption was inspired by Ezek 4:1–2?

2 Context and Structure of Ezek 4:1–5:4

The series of sign-acts is not introduced by one of the (stereo)typical formulae prevailing in the Book of Ezekiel. Therefore it has to be taken either as part of the unit beginning with the revelation formula in Ezek 3:16b,[17] or – as Zimmerli holds[18] – in 3:24b where God confines Ezekiel to his house, or even as part of the book's extensive visionary introduction comprising chapters 1:4–5:17 as a whole;[19] in the latter perspective then, the series of sign-acts in Ezek 4:1–5:4 programmatically sums up and illustrates the prophet's message of doom that will be delivered in detail in a number of oracles as well as sign-acts given in Ezek 6–24. In any case, the chapters as we now have them reveal several hands at work in the production of the text.[20] The two previous passages definitely appear to be redactional insertions: 3:17–21 – where God defines Ezekiel's task as a watchman and admonitor – is clearly borrowed from the original in Ezek 33:1–9. Ezek 3:22–27 combines different aspects also found elsewhere in the book. 3:22–24 renews the visionary quality of the following (after the interruptive lines 3:17–21).[21] Then God tells Ezekiel that he will be fastened by cords so that he cannot leave his house (3:25) – the motif of restricting cords returns in 4:8. Ezek 3:26–27 imparts the motif of Ezekiel's temporary dumbness which is found again in 24:27 and 33:22; as a redactional element it contributes to the marking of the book's macro-structure.

The citation formula (5:5) opening Yнwн's speech, clearly indicates the end of the series of sign-acts. Quite a number of commentators say that the words in Ezek 5:5–17 offer an interpretation of the sign-acts.[22]

---

17 See Leslie C. Allen, *Ezekiel 1–19*, WBC 28 (Dallas: Word, 1994), 55.

18 Walther Zimmerli, *Ezechiel 1–24*, 2nd ed., BK XII/1, (Neukirchen-Vluyn: Neukirchener Verlag, 1979), 108. It follows that the performance takes place in Ezekiel's house situated in Babylonia by the river Chebar.

19 See Schöpflin, *Theologie*, 199.

20 For this and the following see Schöpflin, *Theologie*, 199–215.

21 We find a combination of "the hand of the Lord" (3:22, cf. 1:3), the glory (3:23, cf. 1:28; 3:12) situated by the river of Chebar (3:23, 1:3; 3:15), Ezekiel's falling on his face (3:23, cf. 1:28b), God's command to rise (3:22, cf. 2:1), the spirit entering the prophet so that he stands up (3:24a, cf. 2:2).

22 G. A. Cooke, *A Critical and Exegetical Commentary on the Book of Ezekiel*, ICC (Edinburgh: T&T Clark, 1936), 58; Allen, *Ezekiel*; Daniel I. Block, *Ezekiel 1–24*, NICOT (Grand Rapids: Eerdmans, 1977); Kelvin G. Friebel, *Jeremiah's and Ezekiel's Sign-Acts: Rhetorical Nonverbal Communication*, JSOTSup 283 (Sheffield: Sheffield Academic, 1999), 202–233, take the verses from 5:5–17 as an explanation to the sections in 4:1–5:4. The latest investigation on the sign-acts, Hei Yin Yip, *Ezekiel's Message of Hope and Restoration: Redaction-Critical Study of Ezekiel 1–7*, BZAW 532 (Berlin/ Boston: De Gruyter, 2021), 108, agrees with them. Moshe Greenberg, *Ezekiel 1–20: A New*

The most obvious formal criterion for subdividing Ezek 4:1–5:4 is the second person singular pronoun addressed to the prophet (וְאַתָּה 4:1; 4:3; 4:4; 4:9; 5:1). In 4:1 and 5:1 – that is with the first and the last divine order – God addresses Ezekiel as 'mortal' as he is wont to do throughout the book. This extended address is obviously intended to serve as a frame for the series as a whole. In addition, the introductory formula "he said to me" (וַיֹּאמֶר אֵלַי 4:13; 4:15; 4:16) occurs exclusively in the subsections 4:13–15 and 4:16–17; as it is a characteristic element in the previous section describing Ezekiel's call (2:1–3:11), this irregularity may be a clue to some redactor's hand.

Another characteristic of the passage is the imperative mood as God is uttering commands addressed to the prophet. The series of imperatives is sometimes interrupted by divine comments (4:3bβ; 4:5; 4:8; 4:13), a short dialogue (4:14–15) provoked by 4:12, and an oracle-like outlook (4:16–17). It is remarkable that the imperative קַח־לְךָ ('take') occurs repeatedly (4:1; 4:3; 4:9; 5:1). This already led Hölscher to the idea to isolate a basic tripartite section consisting of 4:1–2; 9a, 10–11; 5:1–2, an assumption basically adopted by Zimmerli as well.[23]

How many sign-acts are eventually found in this section? To answer this question, most critics take into account the contents to establish subsegments.[24] The number of sign-acts found in the text as we have it covers a range from four[25] to nine,[26] a fact that indicates the complex nature of the passage and the difficulties in interpreting it.

Translation with Introduction and Commentary, AB 22 (Garden City, NY: Doubleday, 1983), 123 calls the unit the "script of the accompanying prophecy".

23 Zimmerli, *Ezechiel 1–24*, 101.

24 Note the Massoretic division 4:1–3; 4:4–12; 4:13–14; 4:15–17; 5:1–4; 5:5–6.

25 E.g. Paul M. Joyce, *Ezekiel: A Commentary*, LHBOTS 482 (New York: T&T Clark, 2007), 84–87: 4:1–3; 4:4–8; 4:9–17; 5:1–4. Allen, *Ezekiel 1–20*, 55, also includes 3:24b-27, making it five actions in the series. Karl-Friedrich Pohlmann, *Der Prophet Hesekiel/Ezechiel 1–19*, ATD 22,1 (Göttingen: Vandenhoeck & Ruprecht, 1996), 81, also finds five sign-acts, namely the following: 4:1–3, 7–8; 4:4–6; 4:9–11, 16–17; 4:12–15; 5:1–4.

26 Block, *Ezekiel 1–24*: 4:1–2; 4:3; 4:4–6; 4:7; 4:8; 4:9–11; 4:12, 14–15; 5:1–2; 5:3–4.

3 An Analysis and Interpretation of the Sign-Acts

3.1 Ezek 4:1–3

YHWH addresses the prophet and tells him to take a brick and to engrave on it an outline[27] of a city which is identified as Jerusalem by the last word of 4:1,[28] a hint intended for readers as people watching Ezekiel's activity would recognize Jerusalem in the engraving. After this Ezekiel is told to construct miniature siege-work[29] and to place it around the brick which represents Jerusalem (4:2).[30]

As the brick consisting of baked clay is building material characteristic of Babylonian architecture it fits in with Ezekiel living as an exiled priest among his people in the Diaspora (Ezek 1:3). The miniature arrangement reminds readers of modern models of landscapes as potential battlegrounds and positions of troops in it which are used by military leaders to plan a battle.

The meaning of the first action YHWH imposes on Ezekiel would be quite clear for anyone among the exiled witnessing it when Ezekiel would actually have performed it. The sign-act's meaning is self-evident for Israelite readers as well, as they are familiar with the history of their own people, especially with the disaster that happened in 588/587 BCE, and 4:1 has informed them that the city depicted on the brick is Jerusalem. The first sign-act thus foreshadows the fact that the Babylonian army will lay siege to Jerusalem.

The address through the pronoun in the beginning of Ezek 4:3 indicates a fresh start. The imperative קח־לך from Ezek 4:1 turns up again. This time Ezekiel

---

27 This might refer either to a map (see Zimmerli, *Ezechiel 1–24*, 112) or to a characteristic silhouette of the city (see Christoph Uehlinger, "'Zeichne eine Stadt ... und belagere sie'. Bild und Wort in einer Zeichenhandlung Ezechiels gegen Jerusalem (Ez 4 f.)", in *Jerusalem. Texte – Bilder – Steine*, ed. Max Küchler and Christoph Uehlinger, NTOA 6 [Fribourg/Göttingen: Vandenhoeck & Ruprecht, 1987], 111–200 [141–149], and the illustration p.153; Joyce, *Ezekiel*, 84, refers to reliefs depicting the siege of Lachish). There is archaeological evidence for both, see the material given in Uehlinger, "Zeichne".

28 There is no evidence in manuscripts which would justify omitting את־ירושלם. Zimmerli, *Ezechiel 1–24*, 112, thinks it is a gloss anticipating 5:5. Note that Zimmerli takes the perspective of observers of Ezekiel's factual performance, not of readers who would need this "gloss". Friebel, *Sign-Acts*, 203 with note 279, argues against a gloss.

29 Note that the vocabulary describing the elements of the siege-work is found again in Ezek 21:27, dealing with Nebuchadnezzar on his march towards Jerusalem.

30 Some critics, e.g. Cooke, *Ezekiel*, 50, think that the siege-work is to be engraved as well. As a piece of evidence they refer to Assyrian and Babylonian art. However, it is improbable that there would be room enough for this on the brick (see Greenberg, *Ezekiel 1–20*, 103; Allen, *Ezekiel 1–19*, 64; Block, *Ezekiel 1–24*, 171).

is told to take an iron plate[31] and to place it as an iron wall between the city (i.e. the brick) and himself. Here and in the following instructions Ezekiel gets personally involved in the sign-act's performance. The setting of his face against someone expresses a hostile orientation[32] towards that someone; it is one of the stereotypical phrases in the book. However, as a rule the verb in this phrase is שׂים,[33] not כון *hiphil*, as it is here, and elsewhere the phrase serves as an introduction to a spoken oracle. In Ezek 4:3, it is just a threatening gesture not to be accompanied by words. YHWH goes on to say that the city will be besieged, and that the prophet is to function as her besieger. Now, what is Ezekiel intended to do exactly? For a start, he is looking aggressively at the brick-city as his face probably also bears a hostile expression. Obviously, Ezekiel shall somehow enact a rigorous siege. Is he going to use the iron plate to illustrate this by moving it closer to the brick? The text does not tell us.

Indeed, the iron plate which is intended to represent an iron wall is the first problem with the interpretation. Critics discuss the function of this plate. Does it indicate the severity of the siege by showing that there is no way out for Jerusalem's inhabitants?[34] Is it a symbol of the people's sins?[35] Does it imply that God and the people are strictly separated?[36] The discussion is affected by a second problem, namely whom does the prophet represent? Does he play the part of the Babylonian army, of its commander Nebuchadnezzar? Or is he YHWH's representative? Or is he a fusion of both, as Babylonia is YHWH's instrument? These manifold options show that the interpretation of Ezek 4:3 is by no means clear, since the text does not offer any hints to a solution. Unlike Ezek 4:1–2, Ezek 4:3 needs an explanation because Ezekiel's action as it stands remains obscure. Very

---

31 Zimmerli, *Ezechiel 1–24*, identifies this griddle as an everyday household utensil of the time which could also be made of hardened clay.

32 Block, *Ezekiel 1–24*, 34, calls it "hostile orientation formula".

33 Ezek 6:2; 13:17; 21:2, 7; 25:2; 28:21; 29:2; 35:2; 38:2. In 14:8 and 15:7 God is the subject and the verb is נתן.

34 See Uehlinger, "Zeichne", 180. Considering Jer 1:18 and 15:20 as a background and foil Siegfried Herrmann, "Die Herkunft der „ehernen Mauer". Eine Miszelle zu Jeremia 1,18 und 15,20" in *Altes Testament und christliche Verkündigung*, ed. Manfred Oeming and Axel Graupner, (Stuttgart: Kohlhammer, 1987), 344–352, stated that originally an iron wall has a protective function which is perverted in Ezek 4:3. Zimmerli, *Ezechiel 1–24*, 114, confirms this, saying that the defensive aspect in Jer turns aggressive in Ezekiel.

35 See Uehlinger, "Zeichne", 179, note 263. Åke Viberg, *Prophets in Action: An Analysis of Prophetic Symbolic Acts in the Old Testament*, ConBOT 55 (Stockholm: Almqvist & Wiksell, 2007), 186, says that this was common in part of the Jewish tradition whose argumentation was based on Isa 59:2.

36 Allen, *Ezekiel 1–19*, 65; Block, *Ezekiel 1–24*, 173.

likely, 4:3 is an extension[37] to the two preceding verses that was written to under-line the harshness of the siege and God's hostile attitude.

The last sentence in 4:3 explicitly refers to the symbolic nature of the previ-ous action. Its keyword אות is a term covering both profane and theological as-pects. In the context of the account of the Israelites' exodus from Egypt[38] it often occurs combined with מופת. Both words refer to divine actions and phenomena that will and ought to be remembered by Yhwh's people. Roughly speaking it is a sign established by God. Thus, the divine hostility represented by the prophet's mimic and gesture directed at the miniature scene of the siege is to be kept in mind because it is a sign prefiguring the future that is to be remembered afterwards.

3.2 Ezek 4:4–8

The pronoun addressing Ezekiel serves as a signal that another subsection begins in 4:4. God commands the prophet to lie on his left[39] side. This action is not spectacular in itself. A bewildering aspect emerges in the following command: Ezekiel is to place Israel's עון on it or maybe on him,[40] as the next sentence says "you are to bear their עון for the number of days you are lying on it" (4:4). A first problem emerges here because the Hebrew word עון is ambiguous: it means either "iniquity, guilt", or 'punishment'.[41] In Hebrew, cause and effect merge in the same term – a translator, though, has to choose one of the meanings. That is to say, Ezekiel is a personification of the Israelites, and lying on his side repre-sents either the people's state of unrighteousness or their being subjected to a punishment God imposes on them. It is worthwhile to consider a prevailing con-cept in Hebrew thinking here, which dominates wisdom literature, namely the close ethical connection of cause and effect (*Tun-Ergehen-Zusammenhang*): ob-

---

37 See Zimmerli, *Ezechiel 1–24*, 113–114, following Gustav Hölscher, *Hesekiel. Der Dichter und das Buch*, BZAW 39 (Gießen: A. Töpelmann, 1924).

38 For this see Schöpflin, *Theologie*, 203–204.

39 The adjective may be an addition prompted by 'right' in 4:6, see Zimmerli, *Ezechiel 1–24*, 116.

40 There might be a textual problem here: Does the suffix refer to the side or rather to the house of Israel? As 4:4aβ is similar to 4:5b the verb form ושמת has been emended to ונשאת because of the analogy. Some critics emend the suffix to the second person singular, a *lectio facilior* reading "place the iniquity of the house of Israel upon you". BHS suggests deleting the preposi-tion altogether.

41 A prominent passage where the same problem occurs is Cain's lament in Gen 4:13. Allen, *Ezekiel 1–19*, 68; Block, *Ezekiel 1–24*, 176–179; and Joyce, *Ezekiel*, 85, recognize the double meaning of the word.

serving divine rules causes well-being, whereas misbehaviour results in misfortune and misery. The term עָוֹן comprises both cause (iniquity) and effect (punishment). Its ambiguity becomes evident in the immediate context here which was created by different hands. The prevailing sense of עָוֹן seems to be 'guilt', though. Critics discuss whether Ezekiel's bearing Israel's iniquity is rather just representative, or whether it is vicarious in a way reminiscent of the scapegoat's function in Lev 16:21, with the prophet atoning for the people's misdeeds.[42] Then a priestly touch would come in, and a connotation of punishment with it.

Resting on the same side for some time, thereby pressing a single side of the body exclusively, causes a physical imbalance. Possibly this is the point of comparison in the action, as the people's relationship with YHWH is disturbed. Considering the immediate context, the first choice is to translate עָוֹן as 'guilt' here. As a reference to Israel's former misbehaviour which caused God's punishing measures, it would be a flashback. As we shall see, the sequence of the original sign-acts follows the chronological order of events (beginning of the siege, during and after the siege). If עָוֹן was taken as 'punishment' it would refer to the exile (an opportunity taken by a redactor as we shall see in 4:6), implying that living in a foreign country means punishment and atonement for former misdeeds. This would form an anticipation in the wrong place within the series.

Anyway, the main problem is that lying on one's side is a concrete action whereas bearing someone's עָוֹן is an abstract occurrence which cannot normally be illustrated by just lying on the ground; a verbal explanation is required if spectators shall grasp this abstract meaning of the act. Readers, however, get the necessary information from God's words. Ezek 4:4 consists of imperatives referring to the action exclusively. YHWH does not tell the prophet to accompany the act by an explanation. Thus, it seems unrealistic that lying on his side and bearing Israel's עָוֹן metaphorically is a sign-act the prophet would actually perform. Rather, this strange activity imposed on Ezekiel originates with some scribe and was written to appeal to readers, not spectators. Obviously, the first redactor wanted to emphasize Israel's guilt and to offer an accusation and reason for the siege of Jerusalem which functions as a punishment for the people's misbehaviour.

Ezek 4:5 puts the aspect of time, namely the number of days, more precisely: In MT the days amount to 390, in the Septuagint to 190. One day represents one year of the people's misbehaviour.[43] Commentators have tried to find out to which

---

[42] For the vicarious, expiatory meaning see Yip, *Message*, 117–125. He examines at length the links between Ezek 4:4–8 and Lev 10 and 16. He even finds connotations of forgiveness and substitutionary suffering in Ezekiel.

[43] 4:5b comes very close to 4:4aβ.

period in Israel's history the number 390 (or 190 respectively) might refer. This problem gets even more complicated when you include the following verse (4:6) in the discussion. There Ezekiel is told to turn to his right side and to bear Judah's עָוֹן for another forty days.

Again, things are complicated here. As a rule, the term 'Israel' denotes YHWH's chosen people as a whole in the Book of Ezekiel.[44] It refers to the special relation between God and this particular community. The author of Ezek 4:6, however, took 'Israel' in 4:5 as a political notion designating the Northern kingdom. Hence, he added the lines referring to Judah so that both kingdoms are mentioned.[45] Ezek 4:6 is clearly a redactional extension. Besides, this redactor obviously interpreted Ezekiel lying on his side as referring to the exile in Babylonia. The number 40 he gives here, is intended to correspond to the duration of the Babylonian exile. That it lasted for fifty years (from 587/6 to 538 BCE) is a problem that concerns the seventy years in Jer 25:12 and 29:10 as well.[46] This implies that the redactor must have added his line in post-exilic times. In spite of this inaccuracy, interpreting the number 40 as a reference to the Babylonian exile, that lasted roughly speaking for one generation, is the easiest and most obvious way to explain it.

Concerning the numbers 390 or 190, 40 and the total amount of 390 + 40 = 430, or even alternatively 390 − 40 = 350, commentaries offer multiple suggestions to understand them with regard to Israel's history.[47] But none of these calculations is so convincing that it is unanimously accepted. All ideas about these details remain speculative; therefore, they will not be further discussed here.

Ezekiel 4:7 does not at all fit in with the immediate context. It is interrelated with Ezek 4:3[48] resuming the command to set the face against the besieged city represented by the brick. Ezekiel 4:7 adds another threatening gesture, namely the prophet's bared arm which he would probably stretch out confronting the

---

44 See Zimmerli, *Ezechiel 1–24*, 115.

45 Some commentators claim that this addition of Judah and the lying on the right side caused the insertion of the adjective "left" in 4:4. The adjective is missing in 4:9.

46 Cooke, *Ezekiel*, 53, though, interprets Jeremiah's seventy years as referring to Babylonia's supremacy in Syria (609–539).

47 The most plausible suggestion seems to interpret a period of 390 years as covering roundabout the period of the existence of Solomon's Temple, see Zimmerli, *Ezechiel 1–24*, 119; the number 190 in LXX would cover the time from 722/1 to 538, the exile for people from the Northern kingdom if they lived in the Southern kingdom. To Zimmerli, *Ezechiel 1–24*, 118, the numbers are a scribe's interpretation, the latest addition to the immediate context.

48 See Zimmerli, *Ezechiel 1–24*, 117.

city-brick.[49] It is an equivalent to rolling up one's sleeves in order to start some manual labour or fight. The gesture is set in between the stereotypical vocabulary introducing some of the oracles in the Book of Ezekiel, namely setting (here expressed by the otherwise uncommon verb כון in the phrase, as in 4:3) the face against an addressee and uttering prophetic words.[50] The verbal message is not presented in the text, though. Probably Ezek 4:3 and 4:7 were written by the same author who wanted to include a pantomimic prophetic threat that God is determined to impose judgement on Israel.

Ezekiel 4:8 then is interrelated to 3:25[51] where Ezekiel is confined to his house. In Ezek 4:8 Yhwh announces that he will bind Ezekiel by putting – metaphorical – cords on him so that he becomes unable to move and thus to turn from one side to the other until the number of days God imposes on him is completed. This intensifies the strain on Ezekiel[52] and makes him come closer to the concept of the suffering prophet as it was developed in the Book of Jeremiah. Ezekiel is constrained to absolute immobility. If you take the number of years in Ezek 4:5 (plus 4:6) seriously, the prophet will be kept lying in the same position for more than a year. No human being would survive a task like this.[53] This made some critics assume that Ezekiel would lie on his respective side only for a number of hours per day,[54] though the text does not say so. Anyway, the sign-act appears to be impracticable. Besides, would the prophet's co-exiles pay attention to his bizarre behaviour if it lasted that long? In addition, people witnessing Ezekiel's lying on his side will need an explanation as to what it means.

So, the sign-act in 4:4 is a literary fiction added by a redactor; the initial command to perform a rather simple, unspectacular action is followed by instructions that make Ezekiel do things that require explanations when he would actually carry them out. And with every further redactional extension the sign-act becomes more grotesque. Without a comment, spectators would not understand what is going on. Information in the text is reserved for readers only.

---

49 Allen, *Ezekiel 1–19*, 67, interprets it as God's readiness to act against the people. Block, *Ezekiel 1–24*, 180, takes it as a military gesture of a warrior preparing for battle.
50 All occurrences of the phrase (see note 33) used to be continued by an imperative to prophecy.
51 See Zimmerli, *Ezechiel 1–24*, 118.
52 Yip, *Message*, 126, says that God enables Ezekiel in this way to carry out his priestly role.
53 Hölscher, *Hesekiel*, 63, and Cooke, *Ezekiel*, 52, thought that the action was not performed. However, Joyce, *Ezekiel*, 86, is not sceptical as to an actual performance as he compares it to Isa 20 where the prophet is walking naked and barefoot for three years.
54 See Allen, *Ezekiel 1–19*, 67; Block, *Ezekiel 1–24*, 179.

3.3 Ezek 4:9–11

With Ezek 4:9 the focus switches over to the situation of the besieged. The subsection begins analogically to Ezek 4:1 with the second person singular pronoun and the imperative קַח־לְךָ. YHWH tells Ezekiel to make bread of the remains that would still be available in the besieged city (4:9a). Six ingredients are to be mixed, four cereals (wheat, barley, millet, and emmer) plus beans and lentils. It is uncommon to combine so many different elements in producing bread so that it clearly indicates a situation of need approaching even famine.

Ezek 4:9b looks back to the previous passage and resumes the feature of lying on his side for 390 days (4:5). This redactionally-added sentence intends to interrelate the two sign-acts.[55] It evokes the impression that rationing his provisions – an idea that only comes in with the next verse, though – is accompanying all the time Ezekiel's lying on the ground. Thus, the addition suggests a connection between the time of bearing Jerusalem's עָוֹן and the fairly long period of deficiency during the siege. But would the multi-grained bread last for about 200 days or more? This remark obviously causes an inconsistency.

At God's command Ezekiel is to divide the bread into fixed rations and to eat these at fixed hours during each day (4:10). This practice underlines the scarcity of food in the city because of the siege. According to Ezek 4:11 rationing also comprises drinking – Ezekiel has to measure a quantity of water for each day. So, God tells the prophet to live on a minimum of basic nourishment – bread and water. It literally goes without saying what this means: Ezekiel takes the role of the people, he is illustrating and foreshadowing what happens to the besieged citizens. After Ezek 4:1–2, this is the second sign-act that does not require an explanation when it is actually performed before an audience of exiled Israelites.

As compared to 4:1–2 the action Ezekiel performs is in itself neither metaphorical nor theatrically alienated: the prophet makes it real, through coarse bread he can really eat. In doing so, Ezekiel as an individual is representing a multitude of citizens. This reduction of multiple protagonists to just one person qualifies the action as symbolic, as a sign act.

3.4 Ezek 4:12–15

Ezekiel 4:12 adds the command to bake what is now called עֻגַת שְׂעֹרִים ("barley cake") – and thus contradicts the order to make bread from mixed ingredients

---

55 See Zimmerli, *Ezechiel 1–24*, 122.

in 4:9a – on human dung. This is a way to highlight the strain to which the besieged are subjected: it indicates that there are obviously no animals left in the city which could provide the Jerusalemites with fuel, e.g. bovine dung. As human dung is taken as unclean (cf. Deut 23:12–14) and as its uncleanness[56] would affect the substance baked in the fire nourished by it, the barley cake will be unclean as well. Taken at face value, it means that Jerusalemites cannot avoid uncleanness due to the restrictions caused by the siege. This would metaphorically increase their unsuitableness in God's eyes and further encourage his punishment on them.[57]

In the following verse, though, a redactor (employing the introductory formula ויאמר אלי[58]) deals with this problem in his own way. According to the words he puts into YHWH's mouth in Ezek 4:13, illustrating the people's uncleanness is exactly the intention of the order, but in the sense that it foreshadows the fact that the people will live outside the country of Israel in unclean conditions, i.e. exiled Israelites take on a cultically intolerable status. The remark is an extension of the section changing its meaning from siege to exile.[59]

Ezekiel 4:14–15 is dedicated to an alternative aspect of God's command in 4:12, namely the effect on the prophet when he is performing this action. YHWH's order provokes Ezekiel's objection (4:14). He protests because he does not want to defile himself: so far he has never violated the rules on clean and unclean food in his whole life. The prophet's words explicitly refer to Exod 22:30 and Lev 7:18; 19:7; so, he, viz. the scribal redactor is well-versed in the Torah. As Ezek 1:3 introduced Ezekiel to the readers as a priest or at least as a member of a priestly family, his request to preserve a state of cleanness is even more understandable. It is probable that adding Ezekiel's protest was prompted by the initial characterization as a priest. He is personally concerned since he wants to avoid a conflict between his flawless priestly state which corresponds to God's rules on the one hand, and his obedience to divine commands on the other.

It is exceptional that Ezekiel reacts to God's orders at all.[60] As a rule, he listens to YHWH, and it seems to go without saying that he always does as he is

---

56 Yip, *Message*, 128, finds a pun on 'idols' in the choice of the plural term גלל.

57 Note that 4:12 includes the only reference to an audience by the last word לעיניהם. It comes as a surprise, raising the problem of to whom the suffix is referring. Is it the audience of Ezekiel's fellow exiles? Or is it a logical slip because it refers to the not yet exiled people in Jerusalem?

58 This is an apparent formal indication of the secondary character here and in the following subsection 4:15.

59 See Zimmerli, *Ezechiel 1–24*, 127.

60 This occurs only in Ezek 9:8; 11:13, and 21:5 (MT). All of these appear to be additions in their respective context.

told. Here, God yields to Ezekiel's protest and grants him cow dung instead (4:15) so that the prophet will keep his immaculacy.

Again, the sub-segment was created by different hands. First, 4:12 introduced the aspect of the kind of fuel to be used in the process of baking. This inspired two different aspects: an interpretation in 4:13 connecting uncleanness with residing in non-Israelite countries and environment so that the exile in Babylonia is predicted; and the idea of uncleanness affecting the prophet when he performs the sign-act, in the short dialogue 4:14–15.

The entire passage offers contents that appeal to readers only: God's initial command (4:12) is in fact withdrawn when he grants the prophet cow dung[61] which is the normal thing to use for fuel – through this, the action becomes utterly unspectacular and in fact meaningless. Ezekiel would just bake his bread in a common way. Therefore, 4:12 is only a potential sign-act the prophet is commanded to perform. Ezekiel's fellow exiles would not witness the dialogue in 4:14–15; it is information reserved for the readers of the book. The same applies to 4:13 where the exile is anticipated in a context that primarily still deals with the situation of the besieged.

3.5 Ezek 4:16–17

YHWH's short speech resumes the motif of scarcity of provisions from 4:9a, 10–11. God says explicitly that he causes famine in the city, and he adds an outlook on the people's state of mind: they will experience anxiety and horror (4:16). In 4:17 he asserts that the lack of food will make them desolate and rotting away. YHWH's words are a piece of information addressed to Ezekiel. They form a redactional afterthought[62] related to 4:9a, 10–11, and they help to return to the train of thought after the interlude in 4:12–15. Formally, 4:16–17 is an oracle of doom, not an instruction to perform a sign-act. Commentators note its stereotypical language and interrelation with Lev 26:26, 39[63] – both indications that the verses are an extension.

---

61 Would spectators recognize that Ezekiel takes dried up dung of human origin, not bovine?
62 See Zimmerli, *Ezechiel 1–24*, 124, and even Greenberg. Again, the formula introducing God's words in 4:16 indicates this as well.
63 See Greenberg, *Ezekiel 1–20*, 108; Block, *Ezekiel 1–24*, 187, 189. Allen, *Ezekiel 1–19*, 92–96, offers a helpful excursus on the relation between Lev 26 and Ezek 4–6.

3.6 Ezek 5:1–4

The last part of the section begins analogically to 4:1 and 4:9 with the second person singular pronoun and the imperative קַח־לְךָ. YHWH commands a somewhat bewildering action: Ezekiel is to cut off his hair both on his head and on his cheeks, though not with a razor blade but with a sword (5:1a). The sword is most inconvenient as an instrument for shaving,[64] the more spectacular is it accordingly, if the prophet would perform this action. The main point about the sword, however, is its metaphorical quality because it represents the notion of war and hence of divine judgement. The following command (5:1b, starting with לְךָ לְקַחַת) focuses on the material produced by the act of shaving, namely the hair. Next, Ezekiel is to take balances for weighing in order to divide the hair into three portions. Metaphorically, scales are a symbol of judgement so that the process of weighing serves as an equivalent to God assigning different lots to distinct groups of the people. Then (5:2) YHWH instructs the prophet to give each portion its particular treatment: one third is burnt, the second third is destroyed by strokes of the sword, and the last third is scattered to the wind. These actions illustrate the threefold fate of Jerusalem's population after the siege, that is, when the Babylonian army has conquered the city. For anyone familiar with Israelite history, this is easily seen. As the Babylonians set Jerusalem on fire, burning one portion of hair represents those inhabitants that died in the conflagration. Others were killed by the invaders' weapons outside the gates of Jerusalem – as the Hebrew סְבִיבוֹתֶיהָ ("all around her", that is, the city) suggests. These Israelites tried to escape when the Babylonian army attacked and entered Jerusalem. Being scattered to the wind is a stereotypical metaphor often found in Ezekiel;[65] it denotes being dispersed all over the world, and refers especially to the Babylonian exile and Diaspora. The series of these sign-acts illustrates what is kept in store for the besieged in Jerusalem. The last phrase in 5:2[66] – probably an addition stressing the severity of punishment – says that YHWH is going to persecute the exiled even after they have left the city for good.

---

64 Zimmerli, *Ezechiel 1–24*, 128, thinks that it is a small sword, in fact a knife. Greenberg, *Ezekiel 1–20*, 108, identifies it as a "sharp tool".

65 Ezek 5:2 is the only occurrence of the verb זרה in the *qal* stem. Ezek 6:8 and 36:19 the *niphal* stem is combined with בָּאֲרָצוֹת. The latter appears as local object also with the *piel* stem in Ezek 12:15; 20:23; 22:15; 29:12; 30:23, 26. The *piel* stem also appears in Ezek 5:10, 12 and 12:14 where God will scatter persons "to every wind" (לְכָל־רוּחַ).

66 The phrase חֶרֶב אָרִיק אַחֲרֵיהֶם is found in 5:12; 12:14; 28:7; 30:11; see also Lev 26:33 (Greenberg, *Ezekiel 1–20*, 109; Allen, *Ezekiel 1–19*, 71; Block, *Ezekiel 1–24*, 194), a chapter that exerted much influence on Ezekiel.

The performance in 5:2 presupposes the sign-act in 4:1–2, as Ezekiel is obviously supposed to use the brick representing Jerusalem: he burns the first portion probably on the brick, strews the second portion around the brick and then hacks the hair with his sword. God does not offer a comment on the action he is commanding. Apparently they are self-explanatory, at any rate for readers.

Is the act of shaving in 5:1 supposed to carry further associations? We learn from other texts in the writing prophets that a man shaves himself when he performs rites of mourning and this custom is transferred to people suffering destruction.[67] At the same time prisoners were shaven, a practice that shames and dishonours them.[68] Does the bald prophet here represent God punishing his people and at the same time mourning their fate in spite of himself? Or is he representing the shame of his people at the same time?[69] Is he a representative of YHWH, to whom the Israelites are as close (and as dear) as a man's hair? Does Ezekiel personify God performing mourning rites for the loss of his beloved people?

By the way, according to Lev 21:5 priests are forbidden to shave off the hair on their heads and of their beards. But, unlike 4:14, Ezekiel does not object to the command.

As Ezek 5:2 has it, Jerusalemites suffer either death or exile. In fact, God did not destroy his people as radically as the threefold sign-act suggests. A number of Judahites survived the conquest of Jerusalem and remained residents in Judah. This made some redactor add Ezek 5:3. Ezekiel is told to take a small quantity of hair from the third portion, i.e. from those destined for exile. He gathers this portion of hair in the 'pocket' of his garment; this is to say that he saves and protects them, as at least some Jerusalemites will be delivered from the catastrophe. The redactor wanted to make this statement explicit, because God did not make an end of his people as radically as 5:2 suggests.

Ezekiel 5:4 forms another extension saying that an even smaller portion of the rescued hair,[70] i.e. some of the people, will be burnt; so they will be destroyed (5:4a). The text does neither tell us who these are nor for what reason this punishment is going to happen. The fire will affect all Israel (5:4b); again, we do not

---

67 See Isa 15:2; 22:12; Mic 1:16; the beard only in Jer 41:5. Zimmerli, *Ezechiel 1–24*, 129, and Joyce, *Ezekiel*, 88, refer to Isa 7:20 to explain the metaphor.

68 See Isa 3:24; 2 Sam 10:4–5. Zimmerli, *Ezechiel 1–24*, 129, rejects this interpretation without giving a reason for it, though.

69 Friebel, *Sign-Acts*, 236, argues that Ezekiel is presented in a double role here.

70 Yip, *Message*, 130, states that the hair is picked up from the ground, not taken from the remnant in the garment. Yip wants to find an element of hope and restoration here as well as in all redactional additions, save 4:16–17.

learn why. Maybe, it is a warning hint that the surviving ought not to feel sure that their safety is guaranteed?[71] It is not clear whether Ezek 5:4 alludes to some event in Israel's history either. Here, even the reader is missing an explanation.

However strange a performance of the commands in 5:1–2 would look, the actions might be performed[72] and their meaning would be self-evident. In contrast, the actions in 5:3–4 are very simple and unspectacular, but remain at least in part obscure.

Yнwн's following speech (5:5–17) does not help to explain the ambiguous or obscure elements in 4:1–5:4. From the first words – "This is Jerusalem" (5:5aα)[73] – one might expect to get an interpretation of the series of sign-acts, though. But instead, this is a passage in its own right which accuses Jerusalem of misbehaving and of disobedience. God announces different ways of punishing them most severely without mercy. Although the speech and the series of sign-acts share two elements these are not exactly corresponding: First, in his speech Yнwн emphasizes that the people will be punished by famine (5:10; 5:12; 5:17); the sign-act in 4:9a, 10–11 (and the oracle in 4:16–17) also deal with scarcity of food, but point to the necessity of rationing it. Second, in 5:12 God differentiates three parts of the people that will suffer different punishments, namely famine, sword and dispersion.[74] This triad is incongruous with the one in 5:2 – fire, sword, and dispersion –, though. Most critics agree that Ezek 5:5–17 is the result of a complicated development, a topic that cannot be dealt with in this context.

3.7 Summary

The investigation of Ezek 4:1–5:4 has shown that there is an original set of three sign-acts found in 4:1–2; 4:9a, 10–11; and 5:1–2. Each segment of the basic set starts with the imperative form קַח־לְךָ. These actions require quite simple equipment. Besides, the prophet gets personally involved as the maker of a city and the provider of the siege, as representative of the citizens afflicted by famine, and as both judged victim and divine judge. Ezekiel is told to enact three stages in their

---

71 See Zimmerli, *Ezechiel 1–24*, 131.

72 Pohlmann, *Hesekiel*, 95, says that Ezek 5:1–2 makes up a sign-act by reverting to older metaphorical material. Therefore it follows that the sign-acts are fictitious and only function in the book's composition.

73 Those critics who take the mentioning of Jerusalem in 4:1 as an addition claim that only 5:5 explicitly reveals that the series of sign-acts refers to Jerusalem and not to, say, Babylon. To Zimmerli, *Ezechiel 1–24*, 132, this is the interpretation of the three basic sign-acts.

74 5:17 talks about famine, wild animals, pestilence, bloodshed and the sword.

chronological order leading up to Jerusalem's annihilation: the Babylonian siege, the miserable existence inside the city, and the citizens' twofold destiny, as they suffer either death or exile. Historical events are reduced to miniature representations, and they are characterized by a theatrical alienation effect, either because the requisites Ezekiel employs have a symbolic function (brick, sword, hair), or because the prophet either plays God's part (causing the siege, judging the people) or functions as an individual representative of the people (rationing food, in part also by shaving). The sign-act most likely to have been performed is the one in the middle, when Ezekiel bakes bread and rations it for some time.

The basic tripartite series of performances does not necessarily require interpretation, as all three are self-explanatory – to readers anyway – given their position within the book's composition. Within the time frame provided by the book in its final form, the complex of sign-acts is situated between the first date in 1:1–3 (July 593) and the second one given in 8:1 (September 593), so that God commands Ezekiel to perform these acts in late summer 593 BCE – a rather short time before the events in 588–587 BCE they are anticipating. What the sign-acts prophesy will be fulfilled very soon.

The number of the original series was enlarged and extended by various elements. These additions originate with several redactors.[75]

- 4:3, 7 make Ezekiel enact God's hostile attitude towards Jerusalem and thus emphasize his anger and fierce determination to strike her.
- 4:4 introduces the aspect of the citizens' iniquity and thereby implies the reason for God's judgement. The verse prompted a number of further additions:
  - 4:5 provides precise information about the time the lying on the side should take; the aspect is resumed in 4:9b to interconnect the two actions (one accompanies the other).
  - 4:6 mentions Judah because "the house of Israel" (4:6) was understood as referring to the Northern kingdom. At the same time, 4:6 highlights the facet of punishment in עון. Now there is an allusion to exile.
  - 4:8 creates a link to Ezekiel's confinement to his house in 3:25.
- 4:12 brings in the notion of uncleanness, thereby adding a priestly touch. This provoked two further additions.
  - A reference to exile where the people are dwelling in unclean territory (4:13)
  - 4:14–15 deals with the priestly prophet's personal problem, as he wants to avoid uncleanness.

---

75 The order of the single points is not intended to reflect the sequence of their addition to the text.

- 4:16–17 comments on 4:9a, 10–11 and emphasizes that it is *God* who causes the famine.
- 5:3–4 considers the fact that some Israelites survived the disaster, thus taking clearly an exilic point of view.

On the whole the investigation has confirmed the nowadays widely agreed[76] exegetical view that originally Ezekiel was told to perform three sign-acts representing the siege and fall of Jerusalem. The final number of sign-acts in Ezek 4:1–5:4 amounts to seven.[77] The redactional expansions share an important feature: they would need explanations if they were performed because the text renders them here in a way that would not enable an audience to decode their meaning. The text presents God communicating with the prophet exclusively. Throughout Ezek 4:1–5:4 God does not tell Ezekiel to accompany the acts by commenting words; therefore, a pantomimic performance of the expansions in itself would not achieve any effect on an audience. It follows that the redactional parts of the unit were never performed by an historical Ezekiel, but are literary fictions from the very start.

4 Conclusion

Now what about the nature of the three sign-acts that were identified as the original series by a redaction-critical approach? Did Ezekiel perform them? And were they magic in quality? To answer both questions, a comparison with the two selected passages from Jeremiah that were investigated in the beginning, will be instructive.

Most exegetes take it for granted in general that prophetic sign-acts, including those in Ezek 4–5, were actually performed.[78] In his special approach Lang emphasized the effect a sign-act has on spectators as it evokes their attention and

---

76 In spite of his generally holistic approach even Greenberg, *Ezekiel 1–20*, 118, admits that with 4:6, 12–15 references to the exile interrupt the complex of siege symbols. He says that these verses form a self-contained little unit.

77 4:1–2; 4:3, 7; 4:4; 4:9; 4:12; 5:1; 5:3–4.

78 E.g., Fohrer, *Handlungen*; Zimmerli, *Ezechiel 1–24*, 103–104, calls the performance the essence of the genre; Bernhard Lang, *Kein Aufstand in Jerusalem. Die Politik des Propheten Ezechiel*, SBB 3 (Stuttgart: Verlag Katholisches Bibelwerk, 1978), identifies sign-acts in Ezekiel as "street theatre"; Allen, *Ezekiel 1–19*, 66, qualifies sign-acts as a "megaphone for prophetic words"; see Block, *Ezekiel 1–24*, 166, and especially Friebel, *Sign-Acts*, 99–112.

interest.[79] The assumed genre 'sign-act' was form-critically defined[80] by the sequence of a divine command as exposition, an account of the action, and an
interpretation that might already be included in the divine order.[81] If the action
is taken as a performance, especially the latter detail especially brings about a
complication, because God's command will not be part of the prophet's pantomime, but only accessible to the readers of the text. It is striking that Fohrer
himself, who established this pattern, found exceptions to his own rules[82] – a fact
which makes his attempts at a definition not that convincing, since a closer look
at the textual candidates for the genre reveals quite a number of exceptions to
the rule. Trying to systematize or categorize Old Testament sign-acts thus is a
tricky venture.[83]

Therefore, one is inclined to think that former exegetes bore in mind a clan-
destine standard sign-act that provided a pattern for interpreting similar passages. In fact, Jer 13:1–11 fits in best with Fohrer's form-critical pattern. But as we
have seen above, it is quite improbable that Jeremiah's handling of the girdle is
an authentic sign-act which the prophet really performed facing an audience. If
Jeremiah gave just an account of the sign-act to some of his contemporaries, the
effect would be the same as for readers.

Although an account of the actual performance is missing and Jer 19:1–2, 10–
11a is restricted to Yhwh's commands, the incident with the broken jug witnessed
by Jerusalemite authorities, whom its explanation and meaning would take by
surprise, is a most plausible realistic sign-act – one might call it a 'classic'.[84] For
the rather simple action Jeremiah employs an everyday utensil; but the jug evokes
associations of a ritual common at the time at least in Israel's environment. It is
God's comment – not the action in itself – that betrays the witnesses' expectations,
since it turns a ceremony usually hostile to non-Israelites into an outlook of divine
aggression concerning God's own people. To the observers as well as to readers
the sign-act conveys a powerful illustration of the future disaster – whether a

---

79 Considering Ezekiel's sign-acts Lang, *Aufstand*, contends that they were intended to impress
the observers so much that they felt a call to repentance so that there would be a chance of
avoiding judgement.
80 If you establish a definition this includes the possibility that the genre might deteriorate as
Zimmerli, *Ezechiel 1–24*, 132, has it (he finds in Ezek 5:3–4a a "späte Zersetzungsform" of a sign-
act).
81 See Fohrer, *Handlungen*, 17–18; Zimmerli, *Ezechiel 1–24*, 104.
82 Fohrer, *Handlungen*, 18.
83 One of the latest attempts at this is found in Ott, *Analogiehandlungen*.
84 Schreiner, *Jeremia*, 87, postulates that spectators and a moment of surprise are necessarily
ingredients of a sign-act.

magical aspect is still attached to it[85] is not easy to say,[86] but apparently this sign-act is performed with a ritual background in mind. Jeremiah's sign-act in Jer 19 functions as an impressive prophecy to the immediate audience and to the readers as well.

The form-critically paramount sign-act in Jer 13 also predicts future events, however, as information to the prophet exclusively. Jeremiah learns that God's plan to destroy Jerusalem is irreversible. It reassures Jeremiah and functions as a piece of legitimization of the prophet and his message. There is no magic quality or even touch to Jer 13:1–11 as far as we can tell. The girdle gets rotten because it is exposed to water for some time, which is a natural reason. But the observation that sign-acts appeal to the modern mind because of their metaphorical analogies, is not to deny that incantation and magic rituals were practiced and played an important part in people's lives in the ancient world. Modern readers cannot tell to what extent ancient readers would still associate magic aspects with prophetic sign-acts. And it is not at all impossible that sign-acts have their roots in magic procedures like the voodoo-like smashing of a vessel representing someone. But this idea remains hypothetical.

As the two examples taken from Jeremiah show, every passage presumably qualified as a sign-act has to be studied in its own right. Having identified a sign-act in a prophetic book does not automatically lead to the conclusion that the prophet actually performed it. One has to take into consideration that it may be a fictitious piece of literature.

Exegetes who take the basic text in Ezek 4:1–5:4 as reflecting factual performances need to gather information about the scene and the audience from the context of the unit, that is, from the book in its final form. Ezekiel was introduced as living among the exiles deported to Babylonia in 597 BCE (1:3; cf. 3:15). From 3:24b one learns that he has a house in Babylonia to which God confines him. Because he cannot leave his house the scene of the performance is inside the house.[87] Therefore, any spectator would have to enter Ezekiel's home. As Ezek 8:1; 14:1 and 20:1 (that is some time after we have read 4:1–5:4) tell us, at least some elders came to visit him occasionally. Commentators used to imagine that these men constitute Ezekiel's audience. To an assembly of exiled

---

85 Carroll, *Jeremiah*, 296, recognizes magical elements in the Jeremiah tradition, and warns "It would be unwise to allow anachronistic systems of explanation to obscure that fact or to rationalize the mantic world."

86 Do the priests and elders believe in magic? Or did at least part of the earliest readers still do so?

87 To Pohlmann, *Hesekiel*, 87, the prophet's seclusion prevents the performance from achieving an effect outside.

elders, the three basic sign-acts illustrate events that are imminent at home in Jerusalem. They experience tele-vision in the original sense of the word. To them, the performance would point out that there is no chance of God renouncing judgement, let alone of their own returning home. Those affected by the disaster are not addressees of Ezekiel's pantomime, then, in spite of the fact that in the call narrative God sends the prophet to the rebellious Israelites (2:3) and only in an expansion to the exiles (3:11). Anyway, most oracles of doom in Ezekiel concern Jerusalem and are addressed to the citizens still living there. The traditional approach to Ezekiel's series of sign-acts is interested in providing details and material that support the opinion that the prophet did perform them before an audience.

However, when the context of the sign-acts is taken into account, the sign-acts might be considered alternatively, namely within the book's composition: When God tells Ezekiel to perform these sign-acts he does so still within the introductory vision which comprises Ezekiel's call.[88] Since the vision was disrupted by the insertion of the watchman-passage (3:16b–21), the visionary nature of 3:24b*ff.* is explicitly re-established and confirmed by the addition of 3:22–24a. In his vision narrative Ezekiel first describes YHWH's overwhelming appearance on his heavenly throne (1:4–28a). In a second step God installs Ezekiel in the office of prophet (2:3–3:11) by describing his future task of prophesying to the rebellious Israelites who will not accept his message of doom – by the way, reflecting a Deuteronomic concept of prophecy. YHWH makes Ezekiel swallow the scroll (2:8–3:3) to seal the agreement. Swallowing the scroll is, in a way, a first sign-act, because it illustrates drastically that Ezekiel internalizes God's word in order to utter it, to proclaim it afterwards to the people. The call narrative continues in 3:24b where YHWH confines Ezekiel to his house,[89] and it goes on with God's orders to perform a set of certain sign-acts. The three original sign-acts illustrate the gist of Ezekiel's message of doom, namely the siege and fall of Jerusalem including the lot of her inhabitants. Ezekiel himself comes to know that this prophecy is fulfilled in 33:21. After this the nature of his prophesies changes from announcement of doom to proclamation of salvation. So, the sign-acts in Ezek 4:1–5:4 function as a programmatic summary of his message preparing the reader for what is to come. The tripartite series is fictitious; formally, it is embedded in the vision narrative;[90] thus, the question of whether it was really performed in this case is futile. And the problem of whether there is a magic aspect in them is pointless, as well. These sign-acts in Ezekiel are conveyed within a vision, that is,

---

88 For a detailed analysis and interpretation, see Schöpflin, *Theologie*, 127–254.
89 God also sets up Ezekiel's dumbness (3:26) here.
90 See e.g., Cooke, *Ezekiel*, 57: "all is taking place in vision".

on a special ontological level. They are an alternative literary way of transmitting prophecies to readers of a prophetic book. In the introductory chapters of the Book of Ezekiel the three sign-acts appeal to the reader's imagination exclusively. The preview they offer is enacted before the reader's mental eyes.

Kelvin Friebel

The Enigma of Ezekiel's Iron Wall (Ezek 4:3)

3a And you, take for yourself a griddle of iron;   וְאַתָּה קַח־לְךָ מַחֲבַת בַּרְזֶל

  b and you shall place it (as) an iron wall,   וְנָתַתָּה אוֹתָהּ קִיר בַּרְזֶל

      between yourself and the city.[1]   בֵּינְךָ וּבֵין הָעִיר

As part of the complex of sign-actions of 4:1–5:4, the sign-action of 4:3 – taking an iron griddle and positioning it – is a simple action. It is assumed that Ezekiel set the griddle on its edge, placing it strategically between the brick-city[2] and himself. A מחבת is a flat griddle or pan that is used for baking. The shape, whether rectangular or circular, or flat or convex, and the size of the griddle are unknown. Although it is only mentioned with respect to the *minḥa*-offering as one of the ways in which that offering might be presented (Lev 2:5; 6:14 [Eng 21]; 7:9; 1 Chron 23:29), it is not an exclusive priestly utensil confined to Tabernacle/Temple usage.[3] The instructions of Lev 2:5, related to the griddle-cooked offering, are for the people as to how they can bring their prepared offering. It thus must be assumed that a מחבת is a common household cookware item.

Along with the command to position the iron griddle, an interpretation of the iron griddle is given: it is "an iron wall". But the enigma concerns what precisely the "iron wall" references, as no further clarification is given as to what it signifies nor what its purpose or function is. Since no further interpretation is given, there is a broad diversity related to the understanding of the "iron wall."

---

1 The translations in the essay are those of the author.

2 The "city" in v. 3b is clearly the city incised on the brick of v. 1. It is called simply "the city" in 5:2 as well.

3 Contra R. Andrew Compton, "The Sign-Acts of Ezekiel 3:22–5:17: Formative Rituals of Priestly Identity", *Mid-America Journal of Theology* 29 (2018): 47–80, that it is "an item unique to the temple and thereby wielded exclusively or at least primarily by the priests as part of their professional duties" (66). Then, completely overlooking that the griddle signifies a "wall", he focuses on it being a priestly utensil that "draws attention to the placating and reconciling work of temple sacrifice" and interprets the "placing of the griddle" as Ezekiel functioning as a priest, "performing the role of an intermediary in an effort to mitigate YHWH's wrath". He then acknowledges that the rest of the actions in 4:3c-e contravene that proposed intermediary perspective (67).

https://doi.org/10.1515/9783111521015-006

1 Various interpretations of the "iron wall"

The interpretation of the "iron wall" revolves around what is being signified by the two components of the griddle being "a wall" and its "iron"-quality. At issue with the griddle as "wall" is whether it should be understood in a representational way, that the artifact resembles some type of real or actual wall, or understood as a figurative or metaphoric "wall". An associated issue is the signified function of the wall, whether it communicates defensive protection, such as a city fortification wall, or whether it is part of an offensive attack, such as a siege wall or metonymic for the siege as a whole, or whether it is a barrier wall that creates separation. With respect to its "iron"-quality, there is a high degree of unanimity that it, in some way, figuratively signifies the characteristic of hardness, with its various connotations of strength, severity, or impenetrability.

Other interpretation issues are whether its meaning is tied directly to the siege depictions of vv. 1–2, and what role Ezekiel takes on in the performance of the sign-action, whether he portrays YHWH, or the Babylonians, or himself as prophet.

The various ways that the "iron-griddle-wall" has been interpreted can be categorized as follows.

1.1 Representational of the fortification wall of Jerusalem

In representing the fortifications of the city of Jerusalem, when set in an upright position, the griddle would resemble and correspond to the already incised city wall on the brick (v. 1). The "iron"-quality of the griddle-wall is understood figuratively indicating that the city's fortifications would be impervious to being breached. In signifying the impenetrability of the city's literal defenses, its meaning would correspond to the popular theology of the Jerusalemites who were presupposing upon the inviolability of Jerusalem due to YHWH's protection.

Against that interpretation is that such a portrayal is totally contradictory to the point of the overall complex of the sign-actions in chs. 4–5, which rhetorically function to eliminate any notion of the inviolability of Jerusalem and to disavow the people of an expectation of divine deliverance of the city. There is no indication, either in the action or in the text, that the sign-act of the iron griddle is ironic, so as to understand it in the sense that the presumed "iron" defenses are going to be of no avail.

Also, against that interpretation, is the use of the term קִיר for "wall". In Ezek, in its twenty-four occurrences, that term always describes walls of buildings.[4] In contrast, whenever a city's defensive wall is referenced, the term is חוֹמָה (used ten times in Ezek).[5] So, קִיר is not the term expected in Ezek to refer to Jerusalem's fortification wall.

1.2 Representational of the siege wall of the Babylonians

If the griddle-wall represents the siege wall constructed around Jerusalem by the Babylonians, then it would be another additional specific item in the list of components of the siege warfare in v. 2 (siege wall – דָּיֵק; siege ramp – סֹלְלָה; besiegers' camps – מַחֲנוֹת; battering rams – כָּרִים). If a "siege wall", the "iron"-quality figuratively indicated the severity of the Babylonians' siege efforts.

But if it represents a "siege wall", it becomes redundant with the already mentioned דָּיֵק. So, either the two reference different kinds of siege walls, or, if identical, the latter command is then a resumptive reiteration that forms an inclusio that emphasizes the "iron"-quality of that previously mentioned siege wall.

Alternately, the "siege wall" has been understood as metonymic for the whole arsenal of the offensive siege weaponry or armaments, and thus possibly depicts the warriors' shields, their mail body armour, or the mobile battering ram machines. Thus the "iron"-quality would reflect the actual iron composition or plating of those items,[6] as well as figuratively communicating the strength of the Babylonian army and the severity of its attack.

Given the specificity of items listed in v. 2, if the "wall" signified, for example, a shield, it seems that such would have been stated in the command ("place it as

---

4 Of the twenty-four occurrences, eleven are in the Temple vision of chs. 41 & 43 (41:5, 6 [2×], 9, 12, 13, 17, 20, 22, 25; 43:8) and another three in the Temple vision of ch. 8 (vv. 7, 8, 10). Another four occur in the sign-action of ch. 12 (vv. 5, 7, 12), in which he digs and goes out through the wall, presumably of his own house. In 33:30, the people are speaking about him by the walls and doors of their houses. It is used in the metaphors in 23:14 and ch. 13 (vv. 12, 14, 15 [2×]).

5 The term occurs six times in chs. 26 (vv. 4, 9, 10, 12) and 27 (v. 11 [2×]) in talking about the siege against the "walls" of Tyre. In 38:11, it forms the contrast between unwalled and walled towns, and 38:20 speaks about the destruction of the latter. It is used two times in the Temple description in 40:5 and 42:20, referring to its outer wall.

6 Josephus describes the much later Roman siege tower used against Masada as being plated with iron (*Wars of the Jews*, Book VII, ch. 8, § 5). But it is extremely difficult to tell from the glyptic art of the Assyrians and Babylonians as to what material covered the battering rams and siege towers. It is usually assumed that they, as well as their shields, were covered with leather or wicker, rather than metal (Yigael Yadin, *The Art of Warfare in Biblical Lands* [New York: McGraw-Hill, 1963], 314–15, 391).

a shield"). To interpret the "wall" as representationally indicating not a "wall", but some other armament, seems to needlessly add an unnecessary layer of obfuscation.

Both interpretations ##1 and 2 take the "iron griddle" to be representational in nature, in that the griddle has some type of physical resemblance to that which it represents, whether Jerusalem's wall or the Babylonians' siege wall or apparatuses. But those two interpretations are antithetic opposites with respect to with whom the "wall" is associated – the besieged Jerusalemite defenders (#1) or the besieging Babylonian attackers (#2) – and with respect to its function--a defensive wall against the siege (#1) or an offensive siege wall (#2).

1.3 Figurative of the dispositions related to the siege

Unlike the representational interpretations of ##1 and 2, in this interpretation the "wall" is a metaphor for the dispositions behind the siege in toto, which has a dual aspect of being orchestrated by YHWH, but carried out by the human instruments, the Babylonians. As reflecting a dispositional attitude, this interpretation focuses more on the "iron"-quality of either the severity of siege as carried out by the Babylonian besiegers and/or YHWH, or the divine determination that the siege will be carried through to its ultimate conclusion of the capture and destruction of the city.[7]

1.4 Figurative of the barrier wall of separation

A frequent interpretation of the "iron griddle-wall" is that it is figurative of the barrier wall that has been erected between YHWH and the Jerusalemites and signifies the spiritual and relational disjuncture between the two. As such, it may give a causal explanation for the judgment with the separation "wall" symbolizing the people's sin and idolatry that have cut them off from YHWH. Or it may symbolize YHWH barricading himself off from the people, due to their rebelliousness. The latter thus corresponds to Ezekiel's assertions of the divine abandonment of the city, and YHWH "hiding his face" from the people as expressed, for example, in Ezek 39:23–24. The corresponding "iron"-quality then reflects the impenetrable nature of that separation such that access is barred between YHWH and the

---

7 This is the interpretation formerly held by this author in Kelvin Friebel, *Jeremiah's and Ezekiel's Sign-Acts: Rhetorical Nonverbal Communication*, JSOTSup 283 (Sheffield: Sheffield Academic Press, 1999), 206–209.

people, so any of the people's plea-laden communications and any intercessions on their behalf are fully prevented from reaching YHWH. Analogies to this kind of situation are Isa 59:2 and Lam 3:44, in which YHWH creates the barrier of separation in communicating with his people.

The "separation wall", may also function as an explanation of the siege's inevitable outcome. The "iron"-quality may be understood to reflect the hardened and even hostile determinedness and disposition of YHWH that prevents YHWH from acting favorably on the people's behalf. In his "iron"-like adversarial stance, YHWH will not intervene or rescue or relent from the punishment of the siege, thus assuring the fate of the city. Thus, what it signifies is analogous to the figurative expression that in his withdrawing, YHWH's "eye will not spare, nor will he have pity", as in Ezek 5:11; 7:4, 9; 8:18; 9:10; 24:14.

For interpretations ##1–4, the departure point for understanding the "iron griddle" is derived from directly linking it to the model siege enactment of vv. 1–2. Thus, the "iron griddle-wall" of v. 3 amplifies or illustrates some aspect of the siege, whether representationally as some type of defensive or offensive wall (##1–2), or figuratively, indicating the severe nature of the siege, or the posture or demeanor of YHWH or the human besiegers (#3), or the divine-human relationship that either caused the siege or determines its outcome (#4). Also, in these interpretations, since the griddle-wall is between himself and the brick-city, Ezekiel is positionally aligned with the besiegers, and, thereby, in his performance is portraying either the Babylonians or YHWH.

That there is a temporal and situational connection between the siege depiction in vv. 1–2 and the "iron griddle-wall" of v. 3 is without question. First, the location of the placement of the iron griddle is between the prophet and "the city" (העיר), that is, the city engraved on the brick of v. 1. Second, the *Leitwort* of "besiege" (צור) is used in v. 3d-e, which references back to the "siege" of v. 2. But even though there is an association, the issue is whether that means the artifact of the griddle-wall must be interpreted as a specific siege-element.

1.5 Wall of protection for the prophet

A less frequent way of interpreting v. 3 is that Ezekiel has shifted away from depicting the siege per se, but rather the "iron wall" coheres to Ezekiel's role as prophet. The "iron griddle" is figurative of the wall of protection that is erected between Ezekiel and the people, as he nonverbally enacts and verbally proclaims the impending fate of the city, and they react against those prophetic messages. There are several arguments that support this interpretation.

1.5.1 Ezek 4.3 in the literary structure of chs. 4:1–5:4

1.5.1.1 Literary division markers

With respect to the various differentiated groupings of sign-actions in chs. 4–5, a division marker is "and you" (וְאַתָּה) or "and you, son of man" (וְאַתָּה בֶן־אָדָם), which is followed by the specific command to "take" (קַח־לְךָ) an object (4:1, a brick; 4:3, an iron griddle; 4:9, various grains; 5:1, a sharp sword). The only exception to the occurrence of that verb is in 4:4, in which the commands do not involve an object external to himself, but rather his posture.

4:1–2	קַח־לְךָ	וְאַתָּה בֶן־אָדָם
4:3	קַח־לְךָ	וְאַתָּה
4:4–8	קַח־לְךָ	וְאַתָּה
4:9–17	קַח־לְךָ	וְאַתָּה
5:1–4	קַח־לְךָ	וְאַתָּה בֶן־אָדָם

By v. 3 beginning with "and you", it is structurally segmented off from the preceding commands in vv. 1–2, just as are the subsequent actions of lying on the sides in 4:4–8, eating of the foods in 4:9–17, and those with his hair in 5:1–4. With respect to those subsequent sign-actions, although associated with the initial siege depiction, all of them do not depict aspects of the "siege" itself. Some of the actions portray the resultant culmination of the siege and the exilic aftermath, such as the hair actions of 5:1–4, the exilic food of 4:12–13, and the lying on the right side of 4:6, which indicates the length of the exile. Thus, as a literarily segmented sign-act, it is not mandatory to interpret the "iron griddle-wall" as depicting a component of the siege, but, like the others, is part of the complex of sign-actions done in conjunction with the initial siege depictions.

1.5.1.2 "Thematic intrusions" re: prophesying & divine enabling[8]

In the structural groupings of the actions in ch. 4, the commands to perform the diverse sign-actions are interrupted by references either to the act of prophesying or to the enabling of the prophet so as to carry out the enjoined actions. Those two emphases of the "intrusions" directly echo the same themes highlighted in the commissioning narratives of chs. 2–3. The two actions of lying on the sides of 4:4–6 are followed by v. 7 by a reference to "prophesying" and in v. 8 to the divine enablement to carry out those actions by placing cords upon him, which echoes 3:25. The commands related to the culinary sign-actions of 4:9–17 are interrupted

---

8 By this is meant literary interruptions in the structural flow of the text and makes no conclusion about the diachronic development of the text as to whether these are editorial insertions.

by Ezekiel's objection in v. 14. And that is followed in v. 15 by an accommodation which makes the carrying out of the sign-action more palatable by giving to Ezekiel a greater sense of ritual comfortableness.

If 4:3 is understood as a reference to the divine protection of the prophet, such fits into the sequencing as a "thematic intrusion" focusing on prophesying and divine enabling:

A. 4:1–2 Sign-actions of the model siege
    B. 4:3 Sign-action of the iron griddle (symbol of divine enablement)
       & commands to prophesy (setting the face, laying siege)
A′. 4:4–6 Sign-actions of lying on the sides
    B′. 4:7 Command to take a prophetic posture and to prophesy
    C. 4:8 Divine enablement to perform the sign-actions
A″. 4:9–13 Sign-actions of eating & v. 14 Ezekiel's objection
    C′. 4:15 Divine enablement, through accommodation,
         to perform the sign-action

1.5.2 Topic of "Prophesying" in 4:3c–f and 4:7

The two "intrusions" of v. 3 and v. 7 share similar language and thematic motifs. The first part of v. 7 reiterates the wording of v. 3c–e, with the identical command to "set your face toward the city / Jerusalem", and also the "siege" motif.

3c	And set your face toward it[9]	7a	And towards the siege of Jerusalem, set your face;
3d	and it shall be under siege,	7b	and your arm is uncovered,
3e	and you shall lay siege against it.	7c	and you shall prophesy against it.

וַהֲכִינֹתָה אֶת־פָּנֶיךָ אֵלֶיהָ   וְאֶל־מְצוֹר יְרוּשָׁלַם
וְהָיְתָה בַמָּצוֹר   תָּכִין פָּנֶיךָ
וְצַרְתָּ עָלֶיהָ   וּזְרֹעֲךָ חֲשׂוּפָה
                            וְנִבֵּאתָ עָלֶיהָ

In vv. 3c and 7a, with respect to Ezekiel's "setting his face" (כון פנים אל), the verb כון is only used in these two places, where it indicates an actual movement and positioning of the face. That phraseology contrasts with the more frequent command that uses the verb שים (שים פנים אל/על): Ezek 6:2; 13:17; 21:7 [Eng 2]; 29:2; 35:2;

---

9 The referent of the third feminine suffix in v. 3c is not explicit, and could refer either to the feminine "griddle", "wall", or "city". The "city" is the most likely, as it is the immediate preceding feminine referent at the end of v. 3b. Likewise, the term "siege" in vv. 3d–e echoes the same term in vv. 2a & 7a, where it is the city of Jerusalem (represented by the incised brick) that is under siege. So the object of the siege in v. 3d–e is most probably the "brick-city", not the "griddle-wall".

38:2). The key difference in Ezek between the commands with כון and שׂים is that the latter does not involve an actual nonverbal facial movement, whereas the former does.[10] The command using שׂים is always conjoined with the command to "prophesy to/against" (הנבא אל/על), and thus, is an idiomatic expression meaning "prophesy" an impending judgment, while taking on an adversarial disposition.[11] Although employing different verbs, the signified meaning between the two expressions seems to be the same, as indicated in 4:7 where it is also conjoined with the command to prophesy (ונבאת עליה). Although the command to "prophesy" is not given in 4:3, the parallelism with v. 7 indicates that the gesture also signifies an adversarial posture of prophesying.

That adversarial stance is indicated in the following repeated commands to place the city under siege (vv. 3d-e), which references the nonverbal prophecy of the siege actions of vv. 1–2. Thus, the specific content of Ezekiel's prophesying that is cited is the impending judgment on Jerusalem.

Likewise, in 4:3f, Ezekiel's non-verbal enactment is declared to be a "sign" (אות), which relates to the function of prophesying:

3f   It[12] is a sign to the house of Israel.   אוֹת הִיא לְבֵית יִשְׂרָאֵל

More frequently in Ezek, the prophet himself is said to be the "sign",[13] in which case the term מופת is used (Ezek 12:6, 11; 24:24, 27). Although being synonymous in meaning, the distinction in Ezek between the two terms seems to be that when Ezekiel functions as a "sign" (מופת) it means that his behavior would or should be imitated by the people. Whereas in 4:3, the "sign" (אות) only communicates visualized information of what will happen to Jerusalem, and does not seek an imitative response.

In Ezek, "signs", which are always visually apprehended by the recipients, serve a rhetorical purpose of transmitting understanding so as to alter the observers' perceptions of the situation, which should, in turn, affect their beliefs and behaviors. Thus, at times in Ezek the two "sign" lexemes are connected with the recognition formula, "and you/they shall know that I am YHWH" (Ezek 14:8; 20:12, 20),[14] or the sign-actions themselves are to result in recognition of YHWH

---

10 On "setting the face" in Ezek, see Friebel, *Jeremiah's and Ezekiel's Sign-Acts*, 16, 209–10.
11 The adversarial connotation of the prophet "setting his face" is also reflective of YHWH's "setting his face against (נתן פנים ב ...)" those upon whom he is executing judgment, as in Ezek 14:8 and 15:7.
12 The third feminine pronoun is unspecified. But, consistent with the preceding, the likely referent is the brick-city under siege.
13 On "signs" in Ezek, see Friebel, *Jeremiah's and Ezekiel's Sign-Acts*, 27–31.
14 See similarly Jer 44:29.

(Ezek 12:15, 16, 20; 24:24, 27).[15] So the statement in 4:3f that Ezekiel's sign-action of the siege (vv. 1–2) functions as a "sign" must also be understood similarly as a statement about the rhetorical purpose of that nonverbal form of prophesying.

The setting of his face (v. 3c), his laying siege (v. 3d–e), and his sign-action (v. 3f) all deal with aspects of Ezekiel's carrying out the prophetic task and ministry to which he has been commissioned. The "setting his face" is an idiomatic expression meaning "prophesy" while taking on an adversarial posture. His "laying siege" is a summary of the content of the immediate prophetic message. His nonverbal message of the siege being a "sign" designates the intended rhetorical function of his prophetic activity.

As indicated by the parallels between vv. 3c–e and v. 7, the topic of v. 3c-f is that of "prophesying". Since structurally v. 3 is segmented off from vv. 1–2 and vv. 4–6, it suggests that the whole of v. 3 is concentrated on a single topic. It is thus reasonable to assume that the action of v. 3a-b of the iron griddle also deals with that same topic. As such, the "iron griddle-wall" should exemplify some facet of "prophesying", rather than being a siege-component. Such is further suggested by the connections between v. 3a-b and the commissioning narrative of chs. 2–3.

1.5.3 Connections to the "hardness" metaphor in the commissioning in chs. 2–3

The negative receptivity to Ezekiel's prophesying is highlighted in his commissioning in the corresponding passages of 2:3–7 and 3:4–9, 11. Commissioning commands to prophesy are directly juxtaposed with statements about the lack of reception due to the nature of the audience. The audience is characterized through the recurring description of being "rebellious" (2:3, 5, 6, 7, 8; 3:9, 26, 27), and through the motif of "hardness" (חזק). They are described in 2:4 as ones who are "stiff of face" and "hard of heart" (קשי פנים וחזקי־לב), and in 3:7 as "hard of forehead" and "stiff of heart" (חזקי־מצח וקשי־לב).

In response to the highlighted lack of responsiveness, YHWH stresses an internal strengthening that Ezekiel should not shrink back in his prophetic ministry due to fear (2:6 and 3:9b), and also reassures of a divine enabling so as to carry out the prophetic task. The latter is expressed through expanding on the previous imagery of "hardness". In 3:8–9a, the "stiff face" of 2:4 and the "hard forehead" of v. 7 morph into a metaphoric comparison of foreheads like that of šāmîr and ṣôr.

---

15 Similarly in Ezek 15:7, YHWH's "setting his face" is to result in the recognition of who YHWH is.

3:8	Behold I have made your face hard	3:8 הִנֵּה נָתַתִּי אֶת־פָּנֶיךָ חֲזָקִים
	against their faces,	לְעֻמַּת פְּנֵיהֶם
	and your forehead hard	וְאֶת־מִצְחֲךָ חָזָק
	against their forehead.	לְעֻמַּת מִצְחָם
9a	As *šāmîr* is harder than (flint-)stone,	9a כְּשָׁמִיר חָזָק מִצֹּר
	I have made your forehead.	נָתַתִּי מִצְחֶךָ

So the predominate imagery used in the commissioning to contrastively indicate both the reactance against the prophetic messages, as well as the divine enabling, is that of the quality of "hardness". The negative metaphoric quality of "hardness" related to the people in 3:7 is transformed into a positive quality in Ezek 3:8–9 when a greater hardness (*šāmîr*) is given to Ezekiel's forehead in fortifying him against the lesser hardness of the people's disposition.[16] It is that positive imagery of "hardness" that may be the interpretive key to the "iron-wall" metaphor in 4:3.

The concept of "hardness" is often expressed through the metaphoric signifier "iron", as a concrete exemplar of that quality. In Isa 48:4, the somatic signifier of "forehead" is also used to indicate the recalcitrant nature of the people, as in Ezek 3:8–9. In Isa 48:4 there is also a coalescing of "hardness" (using קשׁה as in Ezek 2:4 and 3:9) with the metal metaphors of "iron" and "bronze".

4	Because I know that you are stiff;	מִדַּעְתִּי כִּי קָשֶׁה אָתָּה
	and an iron sinew is your neck;	וְגִיד בַּרְזֶל עָרְפֶּךָ
	and your forehead is bronze	וּמִצְחֲךָ נְחוּשָׁה

Likewise, the two metaphoric qualities of "iron (ברזל)" of Ezek 4:3 and *šāmîr* (שמיר) of 3:9 may also not be that distant from each other. There is no certainty as to the specific mineralogical identity of שמיר. Based on the assumption that a stone (*šāmîr*)-to-stone (flint)[17] contrast is being made in 3:9, *šāmîr* is frequently translated as "adamant", or sometimes as "diamond". With respect to the translation "diamond", it is highly unlikely that diamonds were commonly known or used in that time period in the Levant. Thus, another suggested identification is corundum, varieties of which include sapphire and ruby.[18] But the use of *šāmîr* may be emphasizing it hard quality, rather than identifying it as a specific mineral.

---

16 Many have noted the play on Ezekiel's name, יחזקאלת, "YHWH will harden/strengthen".
17 In Exod 4:25 and Josh 5:2–3, צור seems to indicate "flint", specifically "flint knives" that were used for circumcision. But more often it is a general term for "rock", rather than specifying a specific mineral.
18 See Ruth V. Wright and Robert L. Chadbourne, *Gems and Minerals of the Bible* (New York: Harper & Row Publishers, 1970), 1–2 ("1. Adamant") and 54–57 ("25. Diamond").

Outside of Ezek 3:9, the only other uses of *šāmîr* (שמיר) as some type of mineral,[19] are Jer 17:1 and Zech 7:12, where it also bears the metaphoric connotation of an extremely "hard" material.[20]

The negative description of the people in Zech 7:12 is very similar to that of Ezek 2:4; 3:7–9, and Isa 48:4. The people's refusal to hear both the law and the prophetic messages is due to their stubborn shoulders, heavy ears (Zech 7:11: ויתנו כתף סררת ואזניהם הכבידו משמוע), and their *šāmîr*-hearts (v. 12: ולבם שמו שמיר). The *šāmîr*-quality of the people's heart corresponds specifically to Ezekiel's pejorative somatic description of the people's "heart-hardness" (Ezek 2:4: "hard of heart" – חזקי־לב; 3:7: "stiff of heart" – קשי־לב).[21] It seems clear that the metaphoric semantic field of describing the people's defiant oppositional disposition toward YHWH's messages includes both a variety of qualifying descriptors (stiff, hard, *šāmîr*-like, flint-like, iron-like, bronze-like), as well as somatic referents (face, forehead, heart, neck). Thus, the *"šāmîr*-heart" description of Zech 7:12 corresponds to the somatic metaphors of "(flint)-stone forehead" in Ezek 3:9 and "iron-neck" and "bronze forehead" in Isa 48:4.

The other use of *šāmîr* is in Jer 17:1 where the people's sins are written and engraved upon the tablet of their heart and on the horns of their altars with a "pen of iron" (בְּעֵט בַּרְזֶל) and with a stylus-point of *šāmîr* (בְּצִפֹּרֶן שָׁמִיר). The parallelism with "iron" (ברזל) may indicate that *šāmîr* (שמיר) is not a stone, but that the two are synonymous types of metals. Thus another suggestion as to the identity of *šāmîr* (שמיר) is that it is an iron compound, such as siderite, or magnetite and lodestone.[22] Given that *šāmîr* may be some kind of iron material, whether in its natural or refined form, it does raise the possibility that in Ezek 3:9, the metaphoric contrast between שמיר and צור is not that of stone versus stone, but rather a hard iron-metal versus stone. Even if *šāmîr* is some type of stone, Jer 17:1 illustrates that it can serve as an appropriate poetic word pair along with "iron". So the *šāmîr* imagery signifying a "protective hardness" in 3:9 may not be far removed from the metaphoric use of the "iron"-quality of the griddle-wall in 4:3.

---

19 The term only occurs elsewhere in Isaiah (5:6; 7:23, 24, 25; 9:17; 10:17; 27:4; 32:13) where it refers to "thorns".
20 The Versions are of no help in identifying שמיר. In the LXX, the Jer verse is lacking, and the translation removes the metaphor in Ezek and Zech. The Targum and Peshiṭta simply transliterate the term.
21 It is interesting that Ezek is the only one who uses the imagery of "heart of stone" (לב האבן: Ezek 11:19; 36:26).
22 Wright and Chadbourne, *Gems and Minerals*, 55.

1.5.4 Connection to the "bronze wall" in Jeremiah's commissioning narrative (ch. 1)

In the commissioning narrative of Jeremiah (ch. 1), similar descriptions of opposition and enabling are found as in Ezekiel's commissioning. In both 1:8 and vv. 17–19, Jeremiah is told to not "fear" (as in Ezek 2:6 & 3:9) and to strengthen himself for the task (17a), with such being predicated on the divine accompanying enablement and deliverance. Rather than the Ezek 3:8–9 imagery of YHWH giving (נתן) a hard forehead to the prophet, the divine enabling in Jer is spoken of as the prophet being made (נתן) into a "fortified city, an iron pillar,[23] and bronze wall". It is clear that the "wall" is protective in nature as its purpose is to counter the people's active opposition when the people "fight" against him (v. 19a). Yet, because of the divine protection, he will experience deliverance from those assaults.

18a	And I, behold, I have made you, this day,	וַאֲנִי הִנֵּה נְתַתִּיךָ הַיּוֹם 18a
	a fortified city,	לְעִיר מִבְצָר
	and an iron pillar,	וּלְעַמּוּד בַּרְזֶל
	and a bronze wall	וּלְחֹמוֹת נְחֹשֶׁת
	against all the land ...	עַל־כָּל־הָאָרֶץ ...
19	and they will fight against you.	וְנִלְחֲמוּ אֵלֶיךָ 19
	but they will not prevail against you;	וְלֹא־יוּכְלוּ לָךְ
	for with you, I am, ... to deliver you	לְהַצִּילֶךָ ... כִּי־אִתְּךָ אֲנִי

The same imagery is repeated in Jer 15:20, where the three distinct objects of Jer 1:18 (fortified city, pillar, wall) are reduced to a singular "bronze fortified wall".

15:20	And I have made you against this people,	וּנְתַתִּיךָ לָעָם הַזֶּה
	into a bronze fortified wall,	לְחוֹמַת נְחֹשֶׁת בְּצוּרָה
	and they will fight against you,	וְנִלְחֲמוּ אֵלֶיךָ
	but they will not prevail against you,	וְלֹא־יוּכְלוּ לָךְ
	for with you, I am, to save you and to deliver you	כִּי־אִתְּךָ אֲנִי לְהוֹשִׁיעֲךָ וּלְהַצִּילֶךָ

Although the imagery related to Jeremiah cannot be automatically transposed upon Ezekiel, their call narratives contain the same themes of divine fortifying of the prophet against the reactant opposition that they, as prophets, would as-

---

23 Although the specific identification and function of the "iron pillar" (עמוד ברזל), or possibly "iron (gate)-bolt", is debated, for the purposes of this discussion, such is secondary. What is significant is the pairing of an "iron object" with a "bronze object" in the context of referring to a protective wall.

suredly encounter. Although the specific metaphors in Ezek 3:9 and in Jer 1:18 and 15:20 are different, the material composition of both (respectively *šāmîr* and bronze) accentuate the quality of "hardness" of those objects of, respectively, "forehead" and "wall", and both serve as a defensive fortifying of the prophet.

It is the "metal (bronze) wall" imagery in Jer (1:8; 15:20) that corresponds more directly to the "iron wall" imagery of Ezek 4:3. Besides a different metal composition of the respective walls, the key difference is the use of different terms for "wall", (חומה) and (קיר). The term חומה normally refers to a "city fortification wall", while קיר is semantically broader and references various types of structural walls, whether of residential buildings (Ezek 12:5, 7, 12), the walls of the temple (1 Kgs 6:5, 6; Ezek 41:6, 17, 20, 25), or walls enclosing vineyards (Num 22:25 // גדר v. 24). But in Num 35:4 it does refer to a city wall. That reference along with Josh 2:15 in which the two terms refer to a house built conjoined to the city wall, suggest that a metaphoric parallel between the two types of walls cannot be categorically excluded.

With respect to the difference in metal composition, in numerous texts "iron (ברזל)" and "bronze (נחושה / נחשה / נהשת)" are a fixed word pair. In some cases, a single object is said to be composed of both "iron and bronze" (Jer 6:28; Dan 4:12a, 20b [Eng 15a, 23b]). In other cases, as in Jer 1:18 ("iron pillar, bronze wall"), the two terms occur as synonymously parallel, whether referring to the actual metals or being used in their metaphoric sense to emphasize the quality of "hardness" (Deut 8:9; Jer 15:12; Isa 45:2; 48:4; Mic 4:13; Job 20:24; 28:2; 40:18; 41:19 [Eng 27]; Dan 7:19). As a word pair the two seem to be interchangeable. Such is evident from the similar covenant curses in Lev 26:19b and Deut 28:23. In Lev 26:19b, YHWH will make

the skies like iron, and the land like bronze

וְנָתַתִּי אֶת־שְׁמֵיכֶם כַּבַּרְזֶל// וְאֶת־אַרְצְכֶם כַּנְּחֻשָׁה

Yet when the same curse is cited in Deut 28:23, the respective metals are paired with the opposites, the

skies will be bronze, and the land, iron

וְהָיוּ שָׁמֶיךָ אֲשֶׁר עַל־רֹאשְׁךָ נְחֹשֶׁת // וְהָאָרֶץ אֲשֶׁר־תַּחְתֶּיךָ בַּרְזֶל

So, from a purely poetic, metaphoric standpoint, what a "bronze wall" (as in Jer 1:18 & 15:20) signifies is not substantially different from what an "iron wall" (as in Ezek 4:3) signifies.

1.5.5 Other uses of the "wall" metaphor

The metaphor of "wall", whether קִיר, חוֹמָה, or גָּדֵר, signifies various meanings and connotations within biblical passages.[24] Among those meanings is that of "protection", which would be the chief function of a literal fortification wall of a city. In Exod 14:22, 29, the waters on both sides were a "wall" (חוֹמָה) to the Israelites as they passed through the Reed Sea. In 1 Sam 25:16, David and his men are viewed as being "a wall" (חוֹמָה) to Nabal's men who tended the sheep, preventing any harm from coming upon them. In Isa 25:4, YHWH is the protection, like a stronghold (מָעוֹז) and refuge (מַחְסֶה), to the poor and needy when distress assails them like "a storm against the wall" (כְּזֶרֶם קִיר). In Zech 2:9 [Eng 5], YHWH will be a "wall of fire" (חוֹמַת אֵשׁ) to the un-walled, resettled Jerusalem. In Ezek 13:5, the prophets are accused of not "building a wall (וַתִּגְדְּרוּ גָדֵר)" which would provide defensive protection in the day of battle (לַעֲמֹד בַּמִּלְחָמָה). So interpreting Ezekiel's "iron wall (קִיר)" as a wall of divine protection for Ezekiel as he carries out his prophetic ministry, is fully within the semantic field of the biblical metaphoric uses of "wall".

Within the broader Ancient Near Eastern context, the metaphor of "wall" as a signifier of "protection", is found in an Assyrian text. Ashurbanipal (second half of 7th century BCE) describes himself as "the (protecting) wall of the weak".[25]

The protective "wall" metaphor occurs numerous times within Egyptian texts ranging from the 19th through the 3rd centuries BCE, in reference to the pharaohs or rulers in their roles of protecting both the people they govern and the soldiers under their command when in combat.[26] Not only is the undetermined metaphor of "wall" used, but when specified as an "iron wall", a "bronze wall", or a "flint wall", the metaphoric quality is interchangeable.

– Senusret (Sesostris) III (mid-19th century BCE), is spoken of as "a walled rampart of copper of Sinai".[27]
– Thutmoses III (turn of the 15th century BCE), in the Gebel Barkal stela is called "an excellent fortress for his army, a rampart of iron".[28]

---

24 On the metaphoric use of "wall", see W. in der Smitten, "חוֹמָה chōmāh", *TDOT* IV (1980), 267–271 (270–71); Randall Bailey, "Jeremiah: Fortified City, Bronze Walls, and Iron Pillar against the Whole Land", *Hebrew Studies* 57 (2016): 117–138 (120–23).

25 "*dūru*", in *The Assyrian Dictionary of the Oriental Institute of the University of Chicago*, Volume 3, D, ed. A. Leo Oppenheim et al. (Chicago: Oriental Institute, 1959), 194b.

26 On the Egyptian use of the metaphor, see Albrecht Alt, "*Hic murus aheneus esto*", *Zeitschrift der Deutschen Morgenländischen Gesellschaft* 86 (1933), 33–48; Bailey, "Fortified City", 125–127; B. Couroyer, "L'Arc d'Airain", *Revue Biblique* 72 (1965): 508–14.

27 Hans Goedicke, "Remarks on the Hymns to Sesostris III", *Journal of the American Research Center in Egypt* 7 (1968): 23–26 (25).

28 Mark-Jan Nederhof, "Gebel Barkal Stela of Tuthmosis III" (2006, updated 2009), 6 (https://mjn. host.cs.st-andrews.ac.uk/egyptian/texts/corpus/pdf/GebelBarkalTuthmosisIII.pdf; accessed 4 June 2021).

- Amenhotep II (last quarter of the 15th century BCE), on the arch of his tomb, he is called a "great wall of Egypt".[29]
- In an Amarna letter (mid-14th century BCE), Abimiliki, king of Tyre, refers to pharaoh Akhenaten as "a bronze wall set up" for him" (EA 147, l. 53).[30]
- Seti 1 (first quarter of 13th century BCE), in the Karnak inscription of his attack of Kadesh and Amurru, is referred to as one "[who protects] his army, a rampart for myriads" (24:11).[31] In the second Beth-Shan stela, he is called "an iron rampart on the field on the day of battle".[32] And in the Abydos inscription, he is called "a wall of bronze" for Egypt.[33]
- His son, Rameses II (13th century BCE.), in the Beth Shean stela, is called "an effective wall for Egypt", and elsewhere, "the wall of his soldiers".[34] Similarly in the literary records that detail the battle of Kadesh, he is called "a strong wall about his army, their shield on the day of fighting" (P11), and "a wall for his soldiers on the day of fighting" (P304). He inquires from his troops, "Did you not know ... that I am your wall of iron?" (P262). And in the reliefs, he is referred to as "being behind them ... like a wall of iron for ever and ever" (R11).[35] In the first Hittite Marriage Stela, Ramesses II is called a "wall of flint" around Egypt.[36]
- Rameses III (first half of 12th century BCE), in the Medinet Habu temple inscriptions, is called several times "a great wall for Egypt", "a great wall shading Egypt", "a great wall to shelter Egypt", or "a wall for his country".[37]
- Nehtanebos (Nectanebo) II (mid 4th cent BCE) in the Naukratis Stela is called "a strong king, protecting Egypt, a wall of bronze on both sides of Egypt" (l. 3).[38]

---

29 Couroyer, "L'Arc d'Airain", 510–11.

30 W. F. Albright, "The Egyptian Correspondence of Abimilki, Prince of Tyre", *The Journal of Egyptian Archaeology* 23/2 (1937): 190–203 (199).

31 Kenneth A. Kitchen, *Ramesside Inscriptions Translated and Annotated: Translations*, vol.1 (Oxford and Cambridge, MA: Blackwell, 1993), 15.

32 Kitchen, *Ramesside Inscriptions*, 10 (line 4).

33 Couroyer, "L'Arc d'Airain", 511.

34 Couroyer, "L'Arc d'Airain", 511.

35 A. Gardiner, *The Ḳadesh Inscriptions of Ramesses II* (Oxford: Oxford University Press, 1960), the quotations come from pp. 7 (P= "Poem" 11 & 24), 12 (P262), 13 (P304), 37 (R = "Relief" 11).

36 Carolyn Graves-Brown, "The Ideological Significance of Flint in Dynastic Egypt" (PhD diss., Institute of Archaeology, University College London, 2010), 245.

37 Couroyer, "L'Arc d'Airain", 511.

38 Battiscombe Gunn, "Notes on the Naukratis Stela", *The Journal of Egyptian Archaeology* 29 (1943): 55–59 (58).

- It is also attested on a statue of the late Ptolemaic period (mid 4th cent BCE) of a territorial ruler: "a copper wall around his nome, (the one who) protects the citizens of his town" (l. 1).[39]
- Similarly on a statue of Ptolemy II Philadelphus (first half of the 3rd cent BCE), is the phrase "the living wall around his nome".[40]

Although from different social and cultural contexts, those Egyptian uses, along with the biblical uses, provide evidence that the use of the "wall" metaphor, and specifically that of an "iron/bronze wall" to signify "an impregnable defensive wall of protection", is part of the broader cultural semantic field of meaning for "iron wall".

2 Conclusion

Suggested by the accumulated weight of the arguments is the interpretation that Ezekiel's "iron griddle-wall" of 4:3 is a figurative protective wall shielding the prophet from the reactant opposition of the people that is evoked by his contrary prophetic messages of judgment. That interpretation fits well within the range of the metaphoric semantic fields of both the compositional materials used to indicate the quality of "hardness" and its indestructible nature, as well as the metaphoric wall that signifies fortification. Thus, through a metaphoric shift of images, the sign-action of the iron griddle-wall (4:3) enacts the promise of the *šāmîr* -forehead, given to the prophet in the call narrative (3:9) that YHWH would enable him by making the prophet harder than the hardness of the people in their reactance to him and his messages. Ezekiel's "iron wall" also functions like Jeremiah being made into an iron pillar and bronze wall (1:18; 15:20) to protect him from the oppositional attacks directed at him.

Thus, the visual image created through the placement of the iron griddle is that of a wall between himself and the people (v. 3b). As he then functions in his prophetic role of setting his face–taking on a posture of prophesying – and laying siege to the city through his nonverbal and verbal prophetic messages (v. 3c–f), the iron wall provides him protection against any opposition to his unreceptive messages.

---

39 Hassan Selim, "Three Unpublished Late Period Statues", *Studien zur Altägyptischen Kultur* 32 (2004): 363–378 (364).

40 Selim, "Three Unpublished Late Period Statues", 365.

Stephen L. Cook
Ezekiel's Dark Tunnel to Exile

Ezekiel's book presents his dramatic actions as densely symbolic, remarkably rich in meaning and nuance. Rarely straightforward, the sign-acts often entail improbable, abnormal, and/or disturbing behaviors, which both astound and confound the audience. They often probe behind or beyond observable things and events, using metaphors and allusions to reveal supernatural realities and underlying structures of existence. In what follows, I explore the rich symbolic act of nocturnal tunneling described in Ezekiel 12. I argue that Ezekiel's dramatic actions allude to coming deathly encounters associated with exile. They are suggestive of his penetrating into Sheol and contacting the unclean dead.

Biblical reports of symbolic dramatizations performed by prophets typically begin with God commanding a sign-act followed by a report of the prophet's enacting the instructions. Often there follows an interpretation of the symbolism. Isa 20:1–6 is a straightforward example. Verse 1 sets the context and v. 2 both relates God's command to walk about naked and reports the prophet's compliance. Then vv. 3–6 relay the meaning of the sign as a prophecy of the coming Assyrian conquest of Egypt and Ethiopia.

The symbolic action of Ezekiel 12 follows this outline but reveals complexities and theological subtleties far beyond the norm. The intricacy of this dramatization and others in the book suggests to many present-day scholars that Ezekiel 12 is most credible as an imaginative literary construct. It is a symbolic, hagiographic "legend." As such, its purpose is not historical recollection (*mimesis*). Ezekiel 12 is not recalling an observable, real-world event in which an audience was able to see in the dark (amid night's thick blackness, vv. 6, 7, 12). Rather, it is inviting us into an alternative, *intertextual* world.

1 A Simple Sign-Act Account that was Expanded over Time?

Missing the deep roots of a *non-mimetic*, allusive, inner-biblical style in Ezekiel, earlier scholars assumed that the book's literary and symbolic complexity arose over time as symbols were elaborated in writing and textual interpolations and errors crept in. Thus, G. A. Cooke reconstructed a relatively simple historical core

https://doi.org/10.1515/9783111521015-007

to Ezekiel 12.[1] He suggested the sign-act at first dramatized the exile of all of Jerusalem's inhabitants, not the unique flight of Zedekiah. The prophet packed a sack, dug a hole in the wall of his Babylonian house, and made an exit while enough light remained to be seen ("at evening" בערב, vv. 4, 7). Digging through the wall was a sign of ruined homes and frantic escape efforts.[2] The motif of nighttime darkness (עלטה, vv. 6, 7, 12) was not originally present. *"Thick darkness* [עלטה] would render [Ezekiel's] action invisible," defeating the drama's whole purpose (see v. 4).[3] Neither was his covering his eyes part of the original sign-act.[4]

By the time he recorded the symbolic action in writing six years later, Ezekiel had discovered an uncanny fuller sense to his prophecy. At the city's fall, King Zedekiah had fled Jerusalem under cover of darkness (2 Kgs 25:4; Jer 39:4). The enemy was everywhere (Jer 52:7), so he likely covered up with a mask or disguise (see Job 24:15). Ezekiel adapted his narrative to fit his enlarged understanding. He introduced the idea of a mask, a face covering, into the sign-act (Ezek 12:6, 12, 13). It symbolized Zedekiah's concealing his visage, avoiding recognition by the enemy. The LXX preserves this sense of covert measures: "You shall go out concealed. You shall veil your face" (v. 6, see also vv. 7, 12). Verse 12 (LXX) prophesies that Zedekiah "shall not be seen by eye." Cooke argues that the scribes behind the MT misread the vocalization of ראה ("see") in v. 12, which the LXX shows was

---

1 G. A. Cooke, *A Critical and Exegetical Commentary on the Book of Ezekiel*, ICC (Edinburgh: T&T Clark, 1936), 128–33, following F. Giesebrecht, *Die Berufsbegabung der alttestamentlichen Propheten* (Göttingen: Vandenhoeck & Ruprecht, 1897), 166–71.

2 Cooke, *Ezekiel*, 130. Cooke compares the generalized prophetic imagery of Amos 4:3.

3 Cooke, *Ezekiel*, 130. Ezek 12:3–7 repeats "in their sight" seven times. Thus, the term עלטה must, in Cooke's view, be a later elaboration relating to Zedekiah's flight under cover of darkness. Also see Jörg Garscha, *Studien zum Ezechielbuch: eine redaktionskritische Untersuchung von 1–39* (Europäische Hochschulschriften: Reihe 23, Theologie, Bd. 23; Bern: Lang, 1974), 104, 111; Walther Zimmerli, *Ezekiel 1*, trans. R. E. Clements and James D. Martin, Hermeneia (Philadelphia: Fortress, 1979), 272–73. Friebel asserts that עלטה means "dusk," when one can still see, but he misses the paralleling of "deep darkness" (v. 14) and עלטה (v. 17) in Gen 15. See Kelvin G. Friebel, *Jeremiah's and Ezekiel's Sign-Acts: Rhetorical Nonverbal Communication*, JSOTSup 283 (Sheffield: Sheffield Academic Press, 1999), 265, n. 420.

4 Cooke's assumption that the original sign-act would not have anticipated Zedekiah's blinding has been challenged by F. E. Deist, "The Punishment of the Disobedient Zedekiah," *JNWSL* 1 (1971): 71–72. Deist (72) notes that the curses in the Aramaic Sefire treaty (ca. 750 BCE) include the blinding of the king (I Sefire A 39). He concludes that "the penalty which befell Zedekiah was ... an inescapable consequence of breaching the oath of loyalty." The Vassal Treaty of Esarhaddon (672 BCE), treated below, also contains a curse of blindness. Section 40 reads: "May Shamash ... remove your eyesight. Walk about in darkness!" See Christopher B. Hays, *Hidden Riches: A Sourcebook for the Comparative Study of the Hebrew Bible and Ancient Near East* (Louisville, KY: Westminster John Knox, 2014), 174; Friebel, *Sign-Acts*, 270, n. 432.

originally יֵרָאֶה ("be seen").[5] Taking ראה as transitive (יִרְאֶה, Qal, not יֵרָאֶה, Niphal) they added an object, "the land," and a subject, "he himself."[6] Key elements of v. 12 were then taken up and used to expand vv. 6–7.

A covert escape now became the primary signification of the sign-act's original timing after sunset. "After sunset" now meant "under cover of darkness." The shrouding was a further attempt at cover. It was a type of mask, veil, or disguise. In v. 13, however, Ezekiel allowed the symbolic face covering to take on an additional, fuller sense. After being captured, Zedekiah's eyes had been gouged out (2 Kgs 25:7; Jer 39:7; 52:11). He had been taken to Babylon blind. Pointing to this fact, Ezek 12:13 plainly states that Zedekiah "shall not see" Babylonia, the "land of the Chaldeans," where he will die. Greenberg, after much wrestling, comes to accept this view, finding that "the glossator" of v. 13, "perhaps the prophet himself," added the clause "but he [Zedekiah] shall not see it [Babylonia]" to embed a new deeper understanding of the sign-act in the text's wording.[7]

Whether or not Cooke is correct to reconstruct a relatively simple historical core to Ezekiel 12, his astute observations of the passage's complexities and inner tensions should not be ignored. His exegesis both uncovers real textual seams and leaves puzzling unanswered questions. A furtive evening departure to avoid capture makes sense (v. 4). Performing a drama for public viewing "in the dark" (vv. 6, 7, 12) does not. Enacting a masked escape is intelligible, but normally one disguises one's face without blindfolding oneself (v. 6). Besieging armies do breach city walls, but a city's terrified inhabitants do not scramble out through the breaches. They run the other way! (see 2 Kgs 25:4).[8] If Ezekiel's tunneling is not about Jerusalem's breached walls in 586 BCE, what does it signify?

---

5 Cooke, *Ezekiel*, 132. See BHS v. 12 note f. Verse 12 does not yet refer to Zedekiah's being blinded; this comes in v. 13. Moshe Greenberg (*Ezekiel 1–20*, AB 22 [Garden City, NY: Doubleday, 1983], 213–14) agrees with Cooke in avoiding a premature importing of blindness into "the context of escape." He finds Cooke's interpretation of the LXX data "plausible but not inevitable."

6 See BHS v. 12 note g-g. The reference to not seeing the "land" is absent in the Chester Beatty papyrus B967. Cooke (*Ezekiel*, 132) suggests the MT scribes noticed the reference to "land" in v. 13 and copied it here.

7 Greenberg, *Ezekiel 1–20*, 215. His acquiescence comes as a somewhat surprising turn. Friebel (*Sign-Acts*, 270) insists that v. 13 is still talking about Zedekiah not seeing Judah ever again, as in vv. 6, 12, but this stretches the Hebrew syntax beyond the breaking point.

8 In this case, Zedekiah fled through a southern gate at the opposite end of the city from the breached wall. For the details, consult Marvin A. Sweeney, *I & II Kings: A Commentary*, OTL (Louisville: Westminster John Knox, 2007), 466–67. Cooke (*Ezekiel*, 131) dismisses this problem as a "trifling inconsistency." Greenberg (*Ezekiel*, 210) calls him on this and concludes that, at the end of the day, the tunneling in the sign-act does not interrelate with Jerusalem's breached wall in 586 BCE. Friebel (*Sign-Acts*, 271–73, 278, 424) thinks Ezekiel is digging *into* his house, acting the part of the Babylonians, the besiegers.

Perhaps Cooke is correct that the passage underwent refinement over time to bring out the surprising conformity with Zedekiah's blinding. As the account of the sign-act developed, Ezekiel or an early scribe realized its original form veered only slightly off the details of an unknowable future by a margin as small as the vocalization of a verbal form. Cooke's reconstruction is clever, and Greenberg ends up accepting it. "After Zedekiah's blinding" Greenberg surmises, the "primary text (written only consonantally) [was] subtly altered by reading the verbs [of seeing] as actives."[9]

One wonders, however, whether noting the text's remarkable capacity to match an originally unforeseen future, to fit a historical contingency, fully illuminates its highly suggestive nuances. By focusing on the text's future fulfillment, does this perspective overlook its placement in Ezekiel and its echoes of earlier scripture? Does it miss the symbolic nuances of key idioms? I believe that a better appreciation of the passage arises by shifting the focus away from redaction and historical reconstruction and toward inner-biblical allusion and preternatural vision. Ezekiel's texts are known for such allusive, dialogic rhetoric and transcendent perspectives. Ezekiel is known, as well, for his extensive use of detailed imagery about the underworld, the world of the dead.

2 Inner-biblical Echoes of Genesis 15:7–21

In my view, considering Ezekiel 12's intertextual links to an earlier priestly Pentateuchal passage more fully clarifies its complexities and oddities. The passage at issue is a priestly text of Genesis that, like Ezekiel 12, foretells a coming exile of Israel. As in Ezekiel 12, references to nighttime, to darkness, and to eerie terrors pepper the text. The two passages resonate powerfully. The passage I have in mind is Gen 15:7–21.

As I have noted, a key puzzling feature of Ezekiel 12 is the emphasis on night and lack of visibility. An especially rare Hebrew word for "darkness," עלטה, occurs three times as part of the sign-act report (in Ezek 12:6, 7, 12). As Ibn Ezra notes, the only other biblical use of the term is in Gen 15:17. Just as Ezekiel tunnels into darkness, so Abram before him penetrated a deep and terrifying blackness. A priestly layer within Gen 15:7–21 connects this with a coming foreign captivity of Abram's descendants. The text, Gen 15:13–17, parallels Ezekiel 12 in warning of a

---

9 Greenberg, *Ezekiel*, 215. Greenberg connects the evolution behind the MT's present form with a homiletic technique known in Talmudic times.

future exile of darkness. Some evidence suggests the text is Holiness School (HS) material authored by Zadokite priests like Ezekiel.

Scholars have long debated how Gen 15:13–17 fits within the literary development of Genesis. Identifying it as "E" material was never convincing. Rather, it appears to represent a late editorial stratum of the chapter, since v. 17 functions as a resumptive repetition of v. 12 (*Wiederaufnahme*).[10] Both verses display a double temporal clause referring to nighttime followed by a report of a preternatural experience. Editors must have carefully crafted v. 17 to function in this resumptive fashion and thus to help fit vv. 13–16 smoothly into the present context. The second half of v. 17 may take up and redeploy some of the wording already present in an earlier J formulation of Genesis 15.

Konrad Schmid notes that recent investigations have uncovered an editorial hand here that was familiar with and postdates P. He concludes that at least Gen 15:13–17 dates from after P.[11] Diction in vv. 13–17 (in particular) is known especially from priestly texts. Language of death at a "good old age" (שׂיבה טובה, Gen 15:15) is reused from PT ("Priestly Torah" material, see Gen 25:8). Diction about identifying with life as aliens in a foreign land (Gen 15:13) occurs in HS at Lev 19:33–34. The term רכשׁ ("possessions") in v. 14 occurs in HS texts at Num 16:32 and 35:3. In my view, a hypothesis that Gen 15:13–17 represents HS redaction is far likelier than the older identification of it as "E."[12] The focus on a holy land set aside for Israel and belonging to God, which is vulnerable to its occupants' iniquity (v. 16), fits a core theological dynamic of Zadokite texts (Lev 18:25 HS; Ezek 36:28).

If v. 17 doubles back to repeat the structure and sense of v. 12 (*epanalepsis*), then v. 17's rare term עלטה ("dark") should be understood as resuming the conno-

---

10 Isaac Kalimi describes the phenomenon as follows: "Resumptive repetition (*Wiederaufnahme*) is the repetition of a word or phrase after an interval ... in order to renew the connection with the central descriptive theme of the text ... [T]he resumptive repetition served as a literary technique that a later writer used to signal the fact that he had introduced his words into an earlier, already formulated text" (*The Reshaping of Ancient Israelite History in Chronicles* [Winona Lake, ID: Eisenbrauns, 2012], 275).

11 Konrad Schmid, "Genesis in the Pentateuch," in Craig A. Evans et al., *The Book of Genesis: Composition, Reception, and Interpretation* (VTSup 152; Leiden: Brill, 2012), 27–50 (41). See Thomas Römer, "Gen 15 und Gen 17: Beobachtungen und Anfragen zu einem Dogma der 'neueren' und 'neuesten' Pentateuchkritik," *DBAT* 26 (1989/90): 32–47; and John Ha, *Genesis 15: A Theological Compendium of Pentateuchal History*, BZAW 181 (Berlin: De Gruyter, 1989).

12 On the Genesis text as a JE document, see John Skinner, *A Critical and Exegetical Commentary on Genesis* (ICC; Edinburgh: T&T Clark, 1910), 282; Hermann Gunkel, *Genesis: Übersetzt und Erklärt* (Göttingen: Vandenhoeck & Ruprecht, 1922), 177–78; Cooke, *Ezekiel*, 130; Otto Eissfeldt, *The Old Testament: An Introduction* (Oxford: Blackwell, 1965), 199–200; Antony F. Campbell and Mark A. O'Brien, *Sources of the Pentateuch: Texts, Introductions, Annotations* (Minneapolis: Fortress, 1993), 166–67.

tations of תרדמה ("deep sleep") and אימה חשכה גדלה ("deep and terrifying darkness") of v. 12. The NJPS understands עֲלָטָה to mean "very dark" (v. 17, also see NASB). Everett Fox has Abram experience "night blackness" (v. 17, Schocken Bible). Kimhi understood this blackness to be "so intense that, when the sun sets, there is no light whatsoever. Not even the stars can be seen." For him, "This hints at the redoubled difficulties of the exiles."

Ezekiel 12 has more in common with Genesis 15 than simply the diction of 15:17. The emphasis on knowing God's power in Ezek 12:15–16 resonates with Abram's question "how am I to know?" in v. 8. The likening of Israel to animal prey in Ezek 12:13 connects back to the attacks of birds of prey on carcasses in v. 11. Both hunting nets and raptorial birds are symbols of death and tools of Sheol. The two symbols are parallel in Mesopotamian exorcism rituals. Two Netherworld demons most troublesome to the living are *Alluḫappu*, "net," and the bird-headed *Upholder-of-Evil*. As I will argue momentarily, the covering of Ezekiel's face also symbolizes death, at least in part.

Ezekiel 12 and Genesis 15 both anticipate exile and portray it with symbols of darkness and death. Trappers' nets (Ezekiel 12) and birds of prey (Genesis 15) are paired as wielders of death in the victory monument known as the Stele of the Vultures (ca. 2450 BCE).[13] Ezekiel 32 pairs the symbols as well. After being caught in a net (32:3), Pharaoh's carcass is flung out for consumption by birds and animals (32:4). So too, in Ezek 13:20–21, spirits are hunted as prey and netted. Victims of raptorial necromancers, they are מצודה, "netted prey," the term in our text, Ezek 12:13. The parallel term "שחת" in 19:8 means both "trap/net" (NJPS: "snare") and "pit/netherworld/Sheol."[14] Ezekiel is aware that שחת can mean "Sheol" (see 28:8) and could be punning on that sense in 19:8.

Ezekielian allusion to a broad swath of Genesis 15 is intelligible since Gen 15:13–17 had no independent prior existence outside its present literary lodgement. Anyone alluding to these verses could as easily draw on their wider context, which is bound up with them in the text's present form. In fact, Genesis 15 already reflects the supplement's air of foreboding as early as v. 11, when raptorial birds swoop down on the carcasses that Abram has prepared. The gloom intensifies in

13 In one image, the god Ningirsu holds a net full of enemy captives fastened by anzu, a large bird of prey, emblem of Ningirsu. Another image depicts flying vultures carrying the body parts of the same enemies of Lagash in their beaks. For discussion, see Daniel Bodi, *The Book of Ezekiel and the Poem of Erra*, OBO 104 (Freiburg: Universitätsverlag, 1991), 176–78. Images are available online on Wikipedia: https://bit.ly/SteleVultures.

14 On the term שחת, see Daniel I. Block, *The Book of Ezekiel, Chapters 1–24*, NICOT (Grand Rapids: Eerdmans, 1997), 98 n. 42. In Psalm 9:15 and Ezek 19:8 שחת is parallel to רשת ("net"). M. Held distinguishes between שחת I, "netherworld" and שחת II, "net." See his "Pits and Pitfalls in Akkadian and Biblical Hebrew," *JANES* 5 (1973): 173–90.

v. 12 as a deathly darkness accosts Abram. So too, v. 7's formulaic style shows that Egyptian slavery, explicit in vv. 13–17, is on the agenda. The divine self-introduction of v. 7 parallels the formulation of Exod 20:2. The God now present to Abram is the God who will later help his descendants in captivity.

3 Intimations of An Infernal Encroachment

At first, vv. 7–10 give the impression that the animals – heifer, goat, ram, and birds – are simply part of a ritual that assures Abram of God's commitments. Verses 17–18 confirm a covenant ritual is in fact in play, one in which God obligates himself to Abram through a self-curse. In this regard, as Jer 34:17–22 shows, the animals represent the curse of dismemberment applicable (shockingly!) to God. As covenantal grantee, God subjects himself to this grizzly threat. Yet amid the theme of oath taking, vv. 11–16 interject a chilling note of "terrifying darkness" (v. 12). Birds of prey representing horrors to befall Israel (see vv. 13–16) swoop down on the carcasses (v. 11). The dead animals are not just elements of a ritual. They also symbolize Abram's vulnerable descendants.

Have the carrion birds come to bring Abram's family to Sheol? Bound up as they are with dead creatures, such birds may symbolize death. Eating corpses makes them unclean agents of the underworld. Ravens and owls are denizens of ruins, and their croaks and hoots bespeak infernal chaos (Zeph 2:14–15). The gathering of raptorial birds in the sky signifies death's approach (Hos 8:1; Job 39:30). When Pharaoh's baker dreams of birds eating from baskets (Gen 40:16–19), it is an omen of death.[15] Ezek 39:17 evokes the image of carrion birds and unclean beasts partaking in a drunken funerary feast (an ancient *marzēaḥ*). The archetypally evil Gog and his underworld army supply the main course.[16]

The mutterings of ghosts appear to sound like birds chirping (Isa 8:19). A spirit "speaking from the underworld" often sounds like a bird: "from the dust you will chirp" (Isa 29:4 NET). The Nergal and Ereshkigal text from Mesopotamia describes the dead dwelling in darkness, unable to see, moaning like doves" (iii 7).[17] A sev-

---

[15] Among the Juruna of the Xingu Indigenous Park to dream about vultures near someone means they will die; "vultures only eat carrion." See Sidarta Ribeiro, *The Oracle of Night: The History and Science of Dreams*, trans. D. Hahn (New York: Pantheon, 2021), 319.

[16] See the discussion in Stephen L. Cook, *Ezekiel 38–48*, AB 22B (New Haven: Yale University Press, 2018), 101–102. Ezekiel's animalized ritual feasting appears primarily to be a mock sacred drinking banquet, a satirical *marzēaḥ*.

[17] Quoted in Esther J. Hamori, *Women's Divination in Biblical Literature: Prophecy, Necromancy, and Other Arts of Knowledge*, AB Reference Library (New Haven: Yale University Press, 2015), 174.

enth-century BCE Babylonian necromancy ritual counteracts the evil brought by strange birds (winged dead?) that hover over a person or enter a house. A flying demon of the Mesopotamian Netherworld *Upholder-of-Evil* (noted above) had a bird's head and outstretched wings.[18]

The association of birds with interment and escort to the Netherworld is very ancient, with the avian spirits sometimes viewed neutrally or even positively. In Mesopotamia, the underworld's ferryman *Humuṭ-tabal* had an *anzû*-eagle head (the *anzû* bird also seen in the Stele of the Vultures noted above). An Assyrian tablet from Nineveh's library describes the gate of the underworld as staffed by bird spirits such as *Ua-ua*, an owl, and *Qua-qua*, a crow between the walls. According to Irving Finkel, "birdseed is the going currency" there.[19] Much more archaic, vulture images on the walls of Neolithic shrines at Çatal Hüyük interconnect with burial rites and the veneration of ancestors.[20] One painting shows a funerary rite with humans dressed as vultures. A striking vulture panel depicts seven or more birds pecking at six headless human corpses.

In biblical symbolism, a chief horror of death and key torment of Sheol is isolation/exile from communal fellowship and family ties (see Ezek 37:11). Thus, Jer 7:33 prophesies poetic justice for parents sending their children's spirits to the underworld (7:31). They will make their graves in vultures' guts, cut off from the lands and burials of kin. To prevent such a horror, Rizpah, at an earlier time, set a vigil by the bodies of her sons and their half-brothers, guarding them from carrion birds of prey (2 Sam 21:10).

We cannot insist that the birds in Gen 15:11 must be underworld spirits, but the "deep sleep" (תרדמה, v. 12) that follows them presses us to ponder the prospect.[21] Such sleep is part of Jonah's gradual descent into Sheol (Jonah 1:5). So too, an induced sleep of God entails terrors in Job 33:16 and paranormal apparitions in Job 4:13–15. Isaiah 29:9–10 describes this kind of sleep (תרדמה) as preter-

---

18 Irving Finkel, *The First Ghosts: Most Ancient of Legacies* (London: Hodder and Stoughton, 2021), 192, 232; Stefan Maul, "Totengeist und Vögel: Eine Vogelliste aus dem neubabylonischen Grab 433 in Uruk," in R. M. Boehmer, F. Pedde, and B. Salje, eds, *Uruk: Die Gräber* (Mainz: von Zabern, 1995), 218–20 (220).

19 Finkel, *First Ghosts*, 213–14.

20 For the warrants behind an interpretation of an excarnation rite, see Rose L. Solecki and Thomas H. McGovern, "Predatory Birds and Prehistoric Man," in Stanley Diamond, ed., *Theory and Practice: Essays Presented to Gene Weltfish* (New York: Mouton, 1980), 79–96 (87–89).

21 Ribeiro (*Oracle of Night*, 319) provides ethnographic notes on common notions of oneiric access to ancestors. For example, he quotes an indigenous Pirahä man: "When we dream, we are close to the dead, we are with them." Franz Boas found that 25 percent of dreams among the indigenous Kwakiutl people referred to dead relatives or funeral scenes.

natural, a "spirit [רוח] of deep stupor" (REB). As in Ezekiel 12, the Isaian text (in 29:10) speaks of heads covered and eyes blinded. Isaiah 29 is thus remarkable in linking Ezekiel 12's symbols (here, face covering and blindness) with a second rare term in Genesis 15 (*viz.* "deep sleep," תרדמה).

The curses of the Vassal Treaty of Esarhaddon (672 BCE) specifically threaten direct contact with the underworld and its denizens, including demon, devil, and evil spirit. They depict the vassal's living-dead spirit cut off in the netherworld (section 56).[22] This is the likely allusion and symbolism of carrion birds, deep sleep, and dark terrors in Genesis 15 and netted prey, black darkness, tunneling, and face masking in Ezekiel 12.

4 Incubating an Encounter with Sheol

To be covered with תרדמה, to undergo sensory deprivation, has at least two possible effects, which may interconnect. It may effect isolation (Isa 29:10) and it may open up access to ethereal spirits (Job 4:15).[23] How these two effects may interconnect is illuminated by Wiebke Friese's work on Greco-Roman oracle-caves, where rites and spatial design catalyzed contact with dead spirits. Cultic staff at these entrances to Hades made their visitors receptive to transcendence through seclu-

---

22 Hays, *Hidden Riches*, 175.

23 The term's etymology may indicate being shut off from the empirical world and thus open to the world of spirits. The LXX of Gen 15:12 speaks of a "trance" (ἔκστασις) falling upon Abram. Hartley understands תרדמה to often signify "a stupor blocking out all other perceptions," training the focus on the preternatural. See John E. Hartley, *The Book of Job*, NICOT (Grand Rapids: Eerdmans, 1988), 112. Gordis suggests that Jonah 1:5–6 makes ironic use of the תרדמה theme, portraying Jonah sleeping deeply "not in order to establish contact with God, but to escape it." See Robert Gordis, *The Book of Job: Commentary, New Translation, and Special Studies*, Moreshet Series 2 (New York: Jewish Theological Seminary of America, 1978), 48–49. Indeed, in my view Jonah's תרדמה fits in with his tunneling progressively away from God into netherworld depths (cf. Isa 14:13–15; see n. 41 below). For its part, Job 4:13–16 links תרדמה with a veiled apparition and with what Habel calls "a faint sound uttered by a fleeting specter," "something unknown." See Norman C. Habel, *The Book of Job: A Commentary*, OTL (Philadelphia: Westminster, 1985), 121–22. As noted below, ecstatic contact with the dead in Greco-Roman culture could take place in a netherworld antechamber known as a *nekuomanteion*, often a natural cave. Contact was facilitated through sleep incubation, through inhalation of subterranean psychoactive vapors, or through mind alteration through sensory deprivation. On the latter, see Wiebke Friese, "Facing the Dead. Landscape and Ritual of Ancient Greek Death Oracles," *Time and Mind: The Journal of Archaeology, Consciousness and Culture* 3 (2010), 29–40, esp. pp. 34–39.

sion, complete darkness, and spatial disorientation. Their clients often found themselves "in the infinity of the Hades."[24]

In part, the face covering of Ezek 12:6, 12, 13 may signify a process of incubating an encounter with Sheol or having one's living soul snagged like a bird in a trap (Ezek 13:21). The veil may catalyze the soul's *alienation* from life (Job 7:9–10; Ps 88:5; Lam 3:54), an affiliation with the *anonymity* of the dead (see Job 4:16; 7:21b), and a descent into *decay* (see Job 21:26; Ps 49:14; Isa 14:11).[25] Menippus experienced much of this in his journey to Hades, a visit facilitated by a specialist in Babylon. The adventure is recorded by Lucian of Samosata in the *Necyomantia*, a second-century CE work.[26]

Menippus's preparations for travel to Hades do not involve a blindfold, but he does avoid eye-contact with the living and even starts walking home backwards. To avoid standing out among the dead, he disguises his appearance, allowing him to pass as a habitue of Hades (preferably as Heracles, Odysseus, or Orpheus).[27] As Menippus's tour of Hades progresses, he observes the dead losing their identifying features (as in Job 21:26). Many dead souls have become "as like as could be, eyes glaring ghastly and vacant, teeth gleaming bare." You cannot tell beggar from king, beauty from beast, line cook from hero.

Various features of Mesopotamian funerary rituals aim to counteract the horrors of being an *eṭemmu*, of becoming anonymous, indistinct, and abstract. The dead one is given a chair or is represented by a figurine to focus and prolong individuality.[28] The grasp of the underworld grows tighter as one removes distinctive jewelry and strips off favorite clothing, as Inanna did in descending to the netherworld. Ties with kith and kin dissolve when one is no longer recognized,

---

24 Wiebke Friese, "'Through the Double Gates of Sleep' (Verg. Aen. 6.236): Cave-Oracles in Graeco-Roman Antiquity," in Fanis Mavridis and Jesper Tae Jensen, eds. *Stable Places and Changing Perceptions: Cave Archaeology in Greece*, British Archaeological Reports International Series 2558 (Oxford: Archaeopress, 2013), 228–38 (232–34).

25 Halperin speaks of Ezekiel symbolically being "carried enwrapped" to the "womb of death." See David J. Halperin, *Seeking Ezekiel: Text and Psychology* (University Park, PA: Pennsylvania State University Press, 1993), 228. Dead spirits notoriously appear veiled. Thus, Eliphaz describes an apparition of a trance state as follows: "Someone stood there – I did not know his face, but the form stayed there before my eyes" (Job 4:16 NJB).

26 See Finkel, *First Ghosts*, 122. The text is found in H. W. Fowler and F. G. Fowler, *The Works of Lucian of Samosata* (Oxford: Clarendon, 1905). It is available online at the Lucian of Samosata Project, https://bit.ly/Necyomantia.

27 In *Gilgamesh, Enkidu, and the Netherworld*, Gilgamesh similarly warns Enkidu not to draw unwanted attention to himself in the underworld if he wishes not to be held prisoner there. There appear to have been generic rules for always keeping a low profile in Sheol.

28 See Laura Quick, *Dress, Adornment, and the Body in the Hebrew Bible* (Oxford: Oxford University Press, 2021), 29.

is no more visible to the eye (Job 20:9).[29] Surely, this loss of individuality is one aspect of the symbolism of Ezekiel's face covering.

Menippus's observations about "eyes glaring ghastly" resonate with the cross-cultural practice of covering the faces of condemned or dead persons.[30] Why do these faces demand covering? Lykke finds that the condemned, the fresh corpse, the zombie – each radiates, simultaneously, both sentient vitality and putrefying carnality. The head shroud mends the uncanny contrast between the two conflicting presences. It counters the dissonance generated by every imminently dead or newly dead corpse. It relieves the living from the weight of the dead soul's sunken, abject, and threatening character.[31]

The necromancers of Ezekiel 13:17–19, specialists at netting human spirits, appear to employ head-veils to help pry open infernal portals to Sheol, tunnels to the chambers of death.[32] These specialists were able both to escort the living ("souls who should not die") into contact with dead spirits and to call back into our world living-dead spirts of the departed ("souls who should not live") (Ezek 13:19 ESV). In Mesopotamia Shamash had the same role, as a *namburbû* ritual aimed at ghosts declares: "O Shamash ... You carry those from Above down to Below, those from Below up to Above."[33]

For present purposes we concentrate on the former power, that is, taking living souls – "persons who should not die" – and leading them along "paths to the shades," cut off from life (Prov 2:18). Ezekiel understands this as usurping God's

---

29 Important here are Quick's observations (*Dress, Adornment, and the Body*, 23) about the role of one's visible appearance in indexing one's status as a vital, living soul. One's jewelry, clothing, skin, hair, and countenance are the "very stuff of self." They encode one's personhood and they create a boundary holding back Sheol's threat to individuation.

30 The practice stretches back in time to the covering of the face of the condemned Haman in Est 7:8 and references to covering a deceased corpse's head in Assyrian elegies. It is older than the metaphor of Isa 25:7, where doom's pall, death's shroud, already cloaks all earth's peoples and nations. All the world's inhabitants are veritable veiled prisoners, waiting on death row. The New American Bible Revised Edition (NABRE) translation of Isa 25:7 captures well the symbolism of a veil of death: "The veil that veils all peoples, The web that is woven over all nations."

31 For discussion, see Nina Lykke, *Vibrant Death: A Posthuman Phenomenology of Mourning* (New York: Bloomsbury, 2021), 76–77; Christine Quigley, *The Corpse: A History* (Jefferson, NC: McFarland, 1996), 116.

32 Helpful treatments of Ezekiel 13 illuminating its necromancy include Marjo Korpel, "Avian Spirit in Ugarit and in Ezekiel 13," in Nicholas Wyatt et al., eds., *Ugarit, Religion, and Culture: Proceedings of the International Colloquium on Ugarit, Religion and Culture, Edinburgh, July 1994* (Münster: Ugarit-Verlag, 1996), 99–113; Jonathan Stökl, "The מתנבאות in Ezekiel 13 Reconsidered," *JBL* 132 (2013): 61–76; and Hamori, *Women's Divination*, ch. 11, pp. 167–83.

33 Finkel, *First Ghosts*, 229 (see also pp. 57–58, 99, 102, 179, 235, 243); JoAnn Scurlock, *Magico-Medical Means of Treating Ghost-induced Illnesses in Ancient Mesopotamia*, Ancient Magic and Divination III (Leiden: Brill, 2006), 178–79.

prerogative. God alone has rights to say, "I kill and I make alive" (Deut 32:39). God thus intends to tear off the powerful head veils, prying free the necromancers' human "prey" (Ezek 13:21).

The idea of necromancy as a threat from which one needs protection is known outside of Ezekiel 13. A Mesopotamian *Ušburruda* incantation for reversing necromantic arts turns "face veiling" back on the medium who wields it, sending *her* to the dead. The spell finds the enchantress and delivers karma. It informs her it aims to "cover your face with cobwebs," as would a spider, and "direct your face to a hole toward sunset."[34] The necromancers of Isa 8:20, 22; and 9:1 are likewise viewed as a threat, and Isaiah subjects them to a similar poetic justice: groping in darkness. Isaiah mocks those who would seek preternatural illumination through assuming the guise of the blind, un-cared-for dead. They look to the underworld only to peer into darkness.[35] Did not the symbolism of Ezekiel's blindfolding partly entail this sort of assuming the guise of the Sheol-bound?

5 Tunneling to the Dead

Yet another element of Ezekiel's sign-act equates the Jerusalemites' coming exile with a severing of connections with life and a descent into netherworld privations and desecrations. In both Job 24:15–16 and Amos 9:2 the rare verb חתר ("dig") used in Ezek 12:5, 7, 12 specifically entails entering Sheol. In each text, the wicked hide in deathly gloom. They think, "No eye will see me" (Job 24:15). Job 24 describes rebels waiting for twilight, covering their faces (v. 15), digging through houses (v. 16), and befriending deep darkness (v. 17). This sounds like a poetic recasting of Ezekiel 12!

Not only Job 24:15–16 and Amos 9:2 but also Babylonian burial practices foster the suggestion that Ezekiel is digging into Sheol. Penetrating the walls of a Babylonian house risked encountering a baby's or young child's burial site.[36] It also

---

34 Tzvi Abusch and Daniel Schwemer, *Corpus of Mesopotamian Anti-Witchcraft Rituals, Volume One*, Ancient Magic and Divination, 8/1 (Leiden: Brill, 2011), 186; Tzvi Abusch, *Essays on Babylonian and Biblical Literature and Religion* (HSS; Leiden: Brill, 2020), 30. The image of wrapping a victim in spider silk parallels the weaving of a veil of death in Isa 25:7 (NABRE): "The veil that veils all peoples, The web that is woven over all nations."
35 See Christopher B. Hays, *Death in the Iron Age II and in First Isaiah*, FAT 79 (Tübingen: Mohr Siebeck, 2011), 276, and the bibliography he cites.
36 Finkel, *First Ghosts*, 17, 44; Philip J. King and Lawrence E. Stager, *Life in Biblical Israel*, Library of Ancient Israel (Louisville: Westminster John Knox, 2001), 368; Bastian Still, *The Social World of the Babylonian Priest*, Culture and History of the Ancient Near East (Leiden: Brill, 2019), 207;

evokes a comparison with Mesopotamian magical procedures for dispelling ghosts through walls. Akkadian texts for ridding homes of annoying spirits prescribe passing magical figurines with sacks of provisions through walls. One could, for example, mate a male ghost with a figurine and then, at sunset, place the latter with a travel pack in a hole in one's wall.[37]

Ghosts may be fascinating as well as bothersome. Far from dispelling ghosts, some Greco-Roman pilgrims sought them out at the cave shrines noted earlier. At the coast of Daunia, seekers squeezed through a breach in the rock, clambered up a slope to a recessed chamber, and met the dead through sleep incubation. At another cave portal, pagan pilgrims pressed through a breach in the rock to a small chamber with a narrow gap in the back wall. Strabon (13.4.13) describes it as flooded with a blinding, mind-altering vapor coming up from a dark chasm behind the wall. Plinius (*HN* 2.207) reports that the vapor induced ecstatic trances, enabling the cave's priestly staff to contact dead spirits.

A visionary contact with Sheol of a parallel nature takes place in chapter 8 of Ezekiel. Translated from Babylonian exile back to Jerusalem before its capture, the prophet sees scenes of detestable ritual within the sacred precincts that are outrageously incongruous with everything Ezekiel ever understood the temple to represent. As part of the visionary tour, God orders Ezekiel to dig (חתר, 8:7) through a wall at the temple complex. Complying immediately, the prophet digs into a hidden infernal sacrarium in the temple (Ezek 8:7–13, scene 2 of the temple tour). There, Judah's elders, making the shadow of death their companion, secretly offer incense to "loathsome animals." As Job would say, they make "friends with the terrors of deep darkness" (Job 24:16–17).

Karel van der Toorn, *Family Religion in Babylonia, Syria and Israel: Continuity and Change in the Forms of Religious Life*, Studies in the History and Culture of the Ancient Near East 7 (Leiden: Brill, 1996), 60–61.

37 As early as 1450 BCE an Akkadian exorcism text (the Boghazköy tablet) describes creating such a female figurine to attract a ghost. A hole in the house's wall must be enlarged to enable the figurine's exit with the smitten ghost in tow. The figurine is placed in the hole with travel rations, facing the setting sun, ready for departure. From his sickbed, the victim of possession shouts to the ghost, "Take your wife and go away!" See Finkel, *First Ghosts*, 108–112. Finkel notes that a sixth-century BCE Babylonian tablet overlaps with this material, as does a fourth-century tablet from Uruk, also in southern Iraq. The former tablet (BM 40183+), like the one from 1450 BCE, instructs the exorcist to place a magical female figurine in a drain-hole in the victim's wall facing the setting sun provisioned with a travel sack (Finkel, *First Ghosts*, 118).

Blenkinsopp is likely correct to connect the images of loathsome creatures on the walls of the anti-sanctum (Ezek 8:10) with the paintings of divinities on the walls of Egyptian burial chambers.[38] Prominent among such tomb images was the jackal-headed Anubis, who could either warm the hearts of the dead or weigh and judge them harshly. Were the elders in this liturgical netherworld offering incense to Egyptian deities to enlist their support (see Ezek 17:15; Jer 37:5, 7, 11)? Were they warding off terrible demonic powers, identified with an imminent enemy assault? The latter suggestion is provocative, given that there is an ironic reversal of Num 16:41–50 (MT: 17:6–15) here in Ezekiel. The episode of liturgical censing in Numbers 16 aimed to drive away a terrible plague. I suggest below a possible parallel to the censers in the flaming torch of Gen 15:17.

6 Conclusions

To sum up, Ezek 12:1–15 resists the efforts of redaction critics such as Cooke to attribute its complex form to *ex eventu* fine tuning (adjusting the text in accordance with the unfolding of history). As Block, Friebel and others show, the sign-act does not correlate well with biblical accounts of Zedekiah's attempted escape.[39] At the same time, positivist interpretive efforts to construe the text as an historical, univocal sign-act also fall short. Friebel's attempt in this regard is heroic but would require us to violate the syntax of v. 13, miss the connotations (numbing darkness and dream incubation) of the thrice-used term עלטה, and see Ezekiel playing the part of the Babylonian army in his digging.

Though valuable at points, these interpretations miss our sign-act's layered and intertextual character. Directly before the sign-act, the prophet had performed a parallel act of digging in which he tunneled into an unclean "netherworld" beneath the temple. So too, in the immediately succeeding chapter, Ezekiel associates ritual head-covering with penetration into Sheol and contact with the dead. Lodged amid these parallels, surely the sign-act's elements of digging and head covering reveal expansive symbolic meanings.

The sign-act's reuse of Gen 15:7–21 reinforces its symbolism of exile as a terrifying brush with Sheol. In Genesis 15, Israel is likened to exposed corpses, threat-

---

38 Joseph Blenkinsopp, *Ezekiel*, Interpretation (Louisville, KY: Westminster John Knox, 2012), 55. For sample images, see Charles K. Wilkinson and Marsha Hill, *Egyptian Wall Paintings: The Metropolitan Museum of Art's Collection of Facsimiles* (New York: The Metropolitan Museum of Art, 1983), 21, fig 16; 136, figs. 23.2.84–86; 137, fig 23.2.82; 138, fig 30.4.1; 139, fig 15.5.18; 153, fig 15.5.10 (to access online, visit: https://bit.ly/3vLRJ6w).
39 Block, *Book of Ezekiel*, 366; Friebel, *Sign-Acts*, 270–71.

ened with lack of safe burial (v. 11). The sun twice enters the netherworld (vv. 12, 17), opening the way for descending spirits.[40] A תרדמה falls (v. 12), recalling Jonah's descent to Sheol and Eliphaz's encounter with a veiled phantom (Job 4:12–17).[41] Finally, a flaming torch appears, passing around the carcasses. Most directly, this symbolizes God as covenant oath taker. Some early readers, however, may also have thought of the setting sun accompanying Israel into underworld exile. After all, the Canaanite goddess Shapshu, "the gods' torch," accompanied souls down there.[42] Or, if in Mesopotamian exile, readers might have envisioned an exorcist's protective fumigation. Anti-ghost magic from Nineveh's library instructs exorcists to pass a flaming torch by victims of ghost harassment, along with a censer of burning fumigant (see Ezek 8:10–11).[43] That this was a longstanding necromantic protective measure is shown by its mention much earlier in the Boghazköy tablet and in the much later account of Menippus, both noted above.[44]

---

40 In the Ugaritic royal funerary text, CAT 1.161, Shapshu, the sun goddess, appears to use her illumination to guide the living king Ammurapi down to the underworld to visit with his dead ancestors. So too, in the Ugaritic Baal Cycle, CAT 1.6, Shapshu likewise accompanies a mourning family member to the realm of the dead. Sixth-century BCE necromancy manuals from Babylon designate the sun god Shamash as ghost-master, "who can open the darkness!" See Finkel, *First Ghosts*, 235, and the references in n. 33 above.

41 Gunn puts it this way: "Jonah ... goes down to the port of Joppa, onto a ship, and, as a storm breaks, into the 'innermost part' of the ship, where he falls into a 'dead sleep.' Thrown into the sea by the sailors, he sinks to the roots of the mountains, the belly of Sheol, the Pit of Death." See David Gunn, "Jonah," in James D. G. Dunn and John W. Rogerson, eds., *Eerdmans Commentary on the Bible* (Grand Rapids, MI: Eerdmans, 2003), 699–702 (699).

42 See n. 40 above and Mark S. Smith, *The Origins of Biblical Monotheism: Israel's Polytheistic Background and the Ugaritic Texts* (New York: Oxford University Press, 2001), 127, 267 n. 190. On one hand, Zadokites like Ezekiel strongly dissociate God from death and Sheol. On the other hand, the Zadokites were clear that God's presence accompanied Israel into their impure and deathful exile (Ezek 11:16; 37:11–13). Further, the torch's movement through the carcasses recalls the promise of Lev 26:12 (HS).

43 British Museum tablet K 2175+; see Finkel, *First Ghosts*, 94–98; Scurlock, *Magico-Medical Means*, no. 232.

44 Irving, *First Ghosts*, 112, 122. To protect him from the ghosts he would encounter, Menippus's necromancer sanctified him with torches, applied bulbous herbs, and poured a magic circle of flour.

John T. Strong
Where is Ezekiel's Wife? An Examination of Ezek 24:15–27 through the Lens of Performance Art

"¿Donde está Ana Mendieta?" (Where is Ana Mendieta?) raged the 500 protestors outside the entrance to the Guggenheim Museum in New York.

The day (*that very day*) was June 25, 1992. The Guggenheim was opening an exhibit that featured the work of six artists, only one of whom was a woman, and only one being a person of color. Mendieta, in contrast, was both – a renowned female artist of Cuban descent. Her oeuvre included influential works of performance art. But Mendieta and her work were absent that day. So, the protesters screamed: "Where is Ana Mendieta?"

The protesters' cry did not just highlight the absence of Mendieta's work, but it screamed out her absence altogether, the fact that *Mendieta was dead*. In 1985, Mendieta had fallen from the bedroom window of her 34th floor apartment in New York City, where she lived with her husband, artist Carl Andre, who was home at the time, and who had been arguing with her when she fell. Andre was in fact indicted for her murder, though acquitted of the charge in a court of law.

"Where is Ana Mendieta?" therefore publicized the fact that at the Guggenheim's opening, on that day in 1992, not only that Mendieta was absent, but that Carl Andre and his artwork were present. Indeed, he was one of the six artists being featured. Hence the crowd's rage.

In this essay, I will read Ezekiel's sign-act in which he does not mourn the death of his wife (Ezek 24:15–27) through the lens of performance art, specifically drawing from several parallels with the life and art of Ana Mendieta. I will not place Ezekiel in the role of Carl Andre, charging him with murder. Instead, I want to explore several important features that prophetic sign-acts share with performance art, and how this form of art – even if, for me at least, it is something of an academic forced migration – can help us conceptualize Ezekiel's ancient performances.[1] A note of warning, Mendieta's work includes perfor-

---

1 I want to thank Donna Bowman of the University of Central Arkansas for introducing me to the possibilities that performance art offers to the study of prophetic sign-acts, when she delivered her lecture, "The Needle and the Bullhorn: Cloth-Making as Religious and Political Expression," at Missouri State University, October 23, 2012. In her lecture, she discussed "yarn bombing," citing the work of yarn artist Olek (Agata Oleksiak), who on Christmas Eve, 2010, covered the *Charging Bull* (the statue in front of the New York Stock Exchange on Wall Street) with yarn. See Olek's video on YouTube: https://youtu.be/zT0HhNvDFRQ.

https://doi.org/10.1515/9783111521015-008

mance art in response to a rape and murder, which will be discussed later in this chapter.

I will argue here that, like Ana Mendieta, Ezekiel's wife died in exile, equating the idea of exile with absence. Unlike Carl Andre, however, Ezekiel transferred his wife's "breath of life" to a future generation of exiles, whom he promised would one day serve in the presence of God.

1 Ana Mendieta is in Exile

1.1 Locating Performance Art[2]

In the latter half of the twentieth century, especially in the 1960s and 1970s, a segment of avant-garde artists began to shift the presence of art "from art's object to art's audience, from the textual or plastic to the experiential."[3] Art, this new avant-garde argued, was in its essence not an object, but rather an experience. Jane Blocker has suggested that to some extent the aesthetic of the seventies "can be defined by lack – lack of authorial privilege, lack of commodity, lack of object-hood, lack of permanence, and lack of celebrity."[4] Even a visitor to a traditional gallery of Renaissance masterpieces fundamentally experienced the art. The paintings themselves were mere catalysts for an experience, but it was this experience that was central, not the painting hanging on the wall. A new set of artists, such as Marina Abramović, Vito Acconci, Bruce Nauman, Eleanor Antin, Carolee Schneemann, Lorraine O'Grady, and Ana Mendieta, began to engage in performances that were aimed at eliciting a reaction, an emotion. What the artist wanted to create was not an object, but rather an experience between the artist and the audience. The art object, e.g., the painting or sculpture, was deemed unnecessary, perhaps even a distraction to the art experience, which took over the entire focus of the artist.

---

2 For discussions of scholarship relating performance art to prophetic sign-acts, see Jeanette Mathews, *Prophets as Performers: Biblical Performance Criticism and Israel's Prophets* (Eugene, Ore.: Cascade, 2020), 32–59; and Johanna Erzberger, "Prophetic Sign-Acts as Performances," in *Jeremiah Invented: Constructions and Deconstructions of Jeremiah*, ed. Else K. Holt, Carolyn J. Sharp, LHBOTS 595 (New York: Bloomsbury, 2015), 104–6.
3 Henry M. Sayre, *The Object of Performance: The American Avant-Garde since 1970* (Chicago: University of Chicago Press, 1989), 1–7, with the quote being taken from p. 5. Not surprising, this shift in art coincides with the rise of reader-response criticism in biblical studies.
4 Jane Blocker, *Where Is Ana Mendieta? Identity, Performativity, and Exile* (Durham: Duke University Press, 1999), 6.

Performance artists have gone to outlandish, shocking lengths to generate the audience's experience.[5] In this essay, I will feature the performance art of Ana Mendieta, though I want to open with an illustration, using a 1975 piece titled "The Lips of Thomas," performed by Marina Abramović. The script for her performance is as follows:

> I slowly eat 1 kilo of honey with a silver spoon.
> I slowly drink 1 liter of wine out of a crystal glass.
> I break the glass with my right hand.
> I cut a five-pointed star on my stomach with a razor blade.
> I violently whip myself until I no longer feel any pain.
> I lay down on a cross made of ice blocks.
> The heat of a suspended heater pointed at my stomach causes the cut star to bleed.
> The rest of my body begins to freeze.
> I remain on the ice cross for 30 minutes until the public interrupts the piece by removing the ice blocks from underneath me.[6]

Not all performance art is masochistic, though examples like this abound. Abramović herself denies being masochistic, or that her works are masochistic:

> "All the aggressive actions I do to myself I would never dream of doing in my own life – I am not this kind of person. I cry if I cut myself peeling potatoes. I am taking the plane, there is turbulence, I am shaking. In performance, I become, somehow, like not a mortal. All my insecurities – having a fat body, skinny body, big ass, long nose, a gut, being abandoned, whatever – aren't important." What makes it art? Context and intention, she said: "The sense of purpose I feel to do something heroic, legendary, and transformative; to elevate viewers' spirits and give them courage. If I can go through the door of pain to embrace life on the other side, they can, too."[7]

The extreme nature of Abramović's performance and other performance art pieces virtually guarantee a strong reaction by an audience. Abramović's piece "The Lips of Thomas" illustrates that audiences are intended to experience something,

---

5 Kelvin Friebel's work, *Jeremiah's and Ezekiel's Sign-Acts: Rhetorical Nonverbal Communication*, JSOTSup 283 (Sheffield: Sheffield Academic Press, 1999), should be brought in early into this discussion. Friebel does not explore performance art in his examination of the sign-acts of Jeremiah and Ezekiel. He nevertheless recognizes that the power of the prophetic sign-acts lay in their sensational quality and the emotional investment they evoke. See especially his discussion on pp. 411–18.
6 The text is reproduced here from an article by Judith Thurman, "Walking through Walls," *New Yorker* 86/3 (March 8, 2010): 25. "Thomas' Lips" was reperformed in 2005 in the rotunda of the Guggenheim Museum in New York. See the online curation of the piece at https://www.guggenheim.org/artwork/5176.
7 Ibid., 26.

often a mixture of fascination and revulsion, as the artist takes what is normal and turns it into something grotesque, in many instances by some means of violence.[8] At this juncture, we might recall several of Ezekiel's actions – lying on his side bound for 390 days, shaving his head, eating food prepared over dung. While not all are made grotesque by violence, were they not profoundly shocking to both Ezekiel and his audience (4:14–15)?[9]

Still, what separates the performance out as art and not just masochism is, as Abramović stated, intent and purpose. Sayre observes that "performance was initially intensely political in orientation,"[10] and he traces its origins to the political protests of the late 1960s. By its very nature, then, performance art is intended to disturb the audience, with the purpose of exposing unstated assumptions and biases and challenging the status quo. So, for example, Carolee Schneemann performed a work titled "Interior Scroll," first in 1975, and again in 1977, when she performed it at the Telluride Film Festival.[11] At the Telluride festival, Schneemann's portion of the program had been designated "The Erotic Woman." This assignment, she believed, allowed for the passive viewing of women and therefore the safe categorization of women artists. Schneemann challenged this comfortable, recognizable categorization with a performance, in which she confronted a man she referred to as a "happy man." In her performance, Schneemann stripped off her clothing, painted the contours of her body to emphasize her shape, and then proceeded to read the script of a scroll that she pulled from her vagina that concluded with the "happy man" dismissing her as a serious filmmaker, writing her off as simply a dancer. Schneemann's purpose with this performance was to step out of the safety of film and disturb the audience with her live nude body. Then, out from the interior of her vagina, which permitted the "happy man" to dismiss her in the first place as a serious artist, Schneemann condemns him with her sarcastic scroll.

Returning to Ezekiel, the prophet clearly, like Schneemann, acted with purpose, for having seen his performance, his audience felt driven to ask: "Will you not explain to us what these actions mean for us?" (24:19; 37:18; and see also 12:9; 21:7 [Heb 21:12]).[12]

---

8 See the discussion of Kelly Baum, "Shapely Shapelessness: Ana Mendieta's 'Untitled (Glass on Body Imprints: Face)'" *Record of the Art Museum, Princeton University* 67 (2008): 87.

9 See Mathews, *Prophets as Performers*, 155–92.

10 Sayre, *Object of Performance*, 13–17, the quote being found on p. 13.

11 Schneemann's performance is discussed in Sayre, *Object of Performance*, 90–2.

12 Performance artists do not typically leave interpretation of their own work, a statement of what they intended. Friebel, however, argues that this was a requirement of prophetic sign-acts (*Sign-Acts*, 415), a point that distinguishes performance art from performed prophecy.

In the literature, performance art is also called "time-based art" because it is ephemeral by its very nature.[13] Since the art is the audience's experience, how, simply put, does one curate performance art?[14]

> By nature, [performance art] is an ephemeral activity, which, in a culture obsessed with materiality and posterity, prove problematic. It raises questions about how the library or archivist records art and can preserve an impression of it for future generations. Must performance art as part of its nature disappear? How can the immaterial, the fleeting, be captured and preserved, and does that in some way change it? Does performance art perhaps exist after the fact solely in its documentation to the extent that the documentation and the performance merge and become one in the same?[15]

Certainly, photography has played a significant role in documenting performances, and as we will see with Mendieta, she planned much of her work from the beginning with an idea of how to capture it on film.[16] The two examples of Abramović's and Schneemann's work, noted above, were reperformed, a practice some purists view with disdain.[17] The mediation and curation of performance art involves preserving artifacts, such as scripts, props, drawings, interviews, in addition to photographs and films and other such objects, that are the residuals of the objectless art. Mendieta herself left a warehouse of films and other items as documentation of her performed art.[18] But the issue – and for curators, it is one of professional ethics – is that these artifacts are secondary to the art; they are not the art.

---

13 See Linda Burnham, "'High Performance,' Performance Art, and Me," *The Drama Review* 30/1 (Spring, 1986): 15–16.

14 I want to thank Martha Scott Burton (Manager of Presidential Special Projects and Research, Office of the President, The Andrew W. Mellon Foundation), who in conversation about this paper introduced me to both Ana Mendieta and, even more importantly for this study, the problems and issues of curating performance art. As will be elaborated upon below, it is the challenge of preserving and curating time-bound works of art that provides interesting insights to Ezekiel's sign-acts and what he thought he was doing.

15 Christina Manzella and Alex Watkins, "Performance Anxiety: Performance Art in Twenty-First Century Catalogs and Archives," *Art Documentation: Journal of the Art Libraries Society of North America* 30 (Spring, 2011): 28.

16 See the discussion of Mark Alice Durant, "Photography and Performance," *Aperture* 199 (Summer 2010): 30–37.

17 Reperformance has been criticized by some performance artists. Vito Acconci has questioned the principle of reperformance, holding that the integrity of time-based art is inseparable from its transience, and that no performance can or should be resurrected. Abramović, who once held to this position, has rethought her position. "In the seventies, we believe in no repetition. ... O.K., but now is a new century, and without reperformance all you will leave the next generation is dead documents and recordings. ... I think it is selfish of the artist not to let her work have its own life" (Thurman, "Walking through Walls," 29).

18 See the lecture by Mendieta's niece, Raquel Cecilia Mendieta, "The Films of Ana Mendieta," Annual Stanley and Pearl Goodman Lecture on Latin American Art; NSU Art Museum, Fort Lau-

The documentation and archiving of performance art for posterity is the crux for our discussion of Ezekiel's sign-acts here.[19] For though performed roughly 2600 years ago, we are still discussing them with a full volume of essays. What exactly are the implications of the documentation and archiving of Ezekiel's sign-act for our understanding of those actions? Did Ezekiel have any idea what he was doing?

1.2 Locating Ana Mendieta

My art comes out of rage and displacement.[20]

Mendieta was born into a privileged and politically elite family in Cuba in 1946. The Cuban revolution in 1959 changed everything for her family and for her. In September 1961, Ana and her sister, Raquelín, were sent by their parents to Iowa, as a part of "Operation Peter Pan," a program sponsored by the Catholic Church and the U. S. State Department. She was thirteen years old at the time; Raquelín was fifteen. While in Cuba, Mendieta and her sister had lived in a warm, stable, upper-middle-class home. In Iowa, they were placed with foster families and grew up in an orphanage. She and her sister were the only Latinas in their new home city, where no one spoke Spanish. Mendieta's move was in every way a forced migration, an exile.[21]

Her art was a product of her sense of being "othered" as a woman, as a Latina, and as an exile. As an "Other," she was in a sense absent from the easily seen and recognizable male-dominated, Caucasian society of Iowa. Her performances forced her audience to see her, to recognize her presence in their midst. Mendieta's art transported her from being absent to present. Suddenly, her audiences felt her as Other, and in doing so, they experienced the disturbing fact that within their communities, some were Us and some were Other, some were Present and some were Absent, some were Marked and some were Unmarked. Mendieta's performances forced the issue; that in their everyday gaze, they sub-

---

derdale, FL (February 27, 2016), available on the internet: https://nsuartmuseum.org/exhibition/covered-in-time-and-history-the-films-of-ana-mendieta/.

19 See Erzberger, "Prophetic Sign-Acts as Performances," 112–16, especially her comments on p. 115. Erzberger correctly states that prophetic sign-acts, whatever their historical reality, are "accessible only as mediated by the text …." (p. 112).

20 Eva Mendieta, quoted in Eva Cockcroft, "Culture and Survival," *Art & Artists* (February 1983): 16.

21 Laura Roulet, "Ana Mendieta and Carl Andre: Duet of Leaf and Stone," *Art Journal* 63/3 (Autumn 2004), 89–91.

consciously "Othered" her and women in general, as well as people of different ethnicities and origins.

While completing her MFA at the University of Iowa, in 1972–1973, Mendieta engaged in several performances titled *Untitled (Rape Scene)*, which was a response to the rape and murder of a female student at the University of Iowa. In one performance, Mendieta invited colleagues to view a performance in a wooded area close to campus. When they arrived at the specified location, they found Mendieta lying face down in the woods, half naked, her clothes torn, and her legs covered with blood. Her intent was to expose the violence and control by men that women experienced.

In another series of performances, *Untitled (Glass on Body)*, Mendieta took a pane of glass and pressed it up against her face, breasts, pubis, and other regions of her body, disfiguring each. In this series, Mendieta sought to make explicit the violence inflicted on women by the gaze of men and society writ large. Mendieta openly displayed her face and breasts for the viewer to gaze at, but with the pane of glass she distorted her lips, her cheeks, and breasts by smearing them across the pane in a grotesque manner. The effect is that the viewer is forced to recognize not just their gaze at a female body, but also experience the violent, distorting effect that gaze has on women. Along these same lines is her visually disturbing, satirical pieces, *Untitled (Facial Cosmetic Variations, Wig and Make-up)* and *Untitled (Facial Cosmetic Variations, Stocking)*, both dating to 1972. With these, Mendieta's focus was not just on the gaze of men and society, but of the violence done to women by the cosmetic and fashion industry.

In yet one final example from 1975, *Untitled (Ape Piece)*, Mendieta dressed up in a gorilla costume and black tights, and then caged herself within a wooden pen at the All Iowa Fair. In this piece, Mendieta's purpose was to bring her sense of being "othered" as a Cuban who supported Castro[22] and was exiled to Iowa as a teenager to the consciousness of the Iowans visiting the fair. Had it ever dawned on them that they somehow "othered" Mendieta with their gaze? Her performance brought the invisibility of their gaze to their consciousness, confronting them with their own biases. Ostensibly, Mendieta made a spectacle of herself and subjected herself to public humiliation, but the performance effectively exposed the reactions of her onlookers, some of which were predictably antagonistic. As one critic commented: "In the end, though, who is being shamed? Precisely whose

---

[22] Mendieta's relationship with the Castro regime was complicated. Ideologically, she was a Marxist (and Carl Andre was as well). She also expressed her support of the Castro regime several times, and she traveled to Cuba to perform several of her pieces. However, in the end she refused to return to Cuba on account of conflicts with the Cuban government. See Roulet, "Duet of Leaf and Stone," 91.

belief system is being objectified? If anyone or anything was being scrutinized and mocked during the performance, I would argue, it was the very spectators who were scrutinizing and mocking the artist."[23]

To reiterate, the documentation and curation of performance art for later audiences is crucial for this discussion of Ezekiel's sign-acts. In this regard, Mendieta intentionally documented many of her performances, initiating the curatorial process herself. Of her performance *Untitled (Body on Glass)*, she recorded the work on 36 slides.[24] Five black and white photographs document *Untitled (Ape Piece)*.[25] She left 104 Super 8 films of performances, such as *Blood and Feathers* and *Sweating Blood*, some of which have been remastered.[26] While the art itself – the performance and the immediate reaction of the audience – was time bound, Mendieta thought about and planned for the afterlife of, if not her art, the intent and purpose of her art. If future audiences would not have experienced viscerally her demonstrations of Otherness, Mendieta understood well that they could nevertheless study her art through photographs, films, and other documentation, and that her message could still effectively travel forward in time, beyond the moment of her performance.

In her retrospective of Ana Mendieta, Jane Blocker set out to locate Mendieta and her work within the field of art history. She concludes:

> Exile is itself the perfect answer to the question with which I began. Where is Ana Mendieta? To say that she is in exile is both to answer the question and to render it unanswerable.[27]

By exile, Blocker refers to Mendieta's absence, which is how I am using exile in this essay. Certainly, at the surface level, she means Mendieta's death, but Blocker's examination of Mendieta focuses more on her work as an artist. The objectless nature of her art, as time-bound art, is one aspect of Mendieta's absence/exile. But with her work itself Mendieta pointed to her own absence, for her performances made her audiences feel her removal, her distance from them, that normalcy hid. Her art demanded that onlookers feel how she is "Other." With *Untitled (Body on Glass)* and *Rape Scene*, for example, Mendieta discomfited her audiences, so that they experienced the exile a woman feels when the target of male gaze or the victim of sexual violence. *Ape Piece* caused Iowa fair goers, in their very act of looking away, to confront her identity as Cuban and Latina.

---

23 Baum, "Shapely Shapelessness," 87–88.
24 Ibid., 81; and see 92 n 4.
25 Ibid., 88.
26 Raquel Cecilia Mendieta, "The Films of Ana Mendieta."
27 Blocker, *Where Is Ana Mendieta?* 26–27, in her larger discussion in the section, "Performativity, Identity, and Exile" (23–7).

Blocker defined nationality as the effect of narrative repetitions, which once enacted, bring a national identity into existence. Mendieta's art, Blocker states, created not a national identity, but an exile, or as she puts it, "a set of meanings that both engage and undermine the narrative of the nation."[28]

Ana Mendieta is in exile. The same with Ezekiel's wife.

2 Ezekiel's Wife is in Exile

As Blocker intended absence and removal by her use of the notion of exile, so too do I mean in this section the absence and removal of Ezekiel's wife, who, of course, in his performance stood for Jerusalem. The examination of the sign-act in 24:15–27 below will underscore two ways in which Jerusalem's exile/absence was theologically significant for the prophet and his audience. First, Jerusalem as Yahweh's consort was dead to Yahweh, forever absent, never to be revived. In this instance, Ezekiel's performance shares a message with Mendieta's *Rape Scene*. Second, Jerusalem as host of the temple was forcibly removed in space, away from the sacred compound, and so, from God's presence. In this sense, Ezekiel shares a message with Mendieta, in her *Ape Piece*.

Ezekiel, however, had a larger agenda than Mendieta, and his performance in chapter 24 has another side to it. Mendieta's work, like all good art, was singular in focus, demanding that her audiences be shocked by sexual violence, or feel revulsion in the presence of a grotesque female body created by the male gaze. While exiling Jerusalem, however, Ezekiel had in mind as well a replacement. It was his concern for Jerusalem's replacement that explains why anyone ever bothered to curate his otherwise time-bound performances.

2.1 Locating Ezekiel and the Exiles

You! Lie on your left side ... I give to you for the number of days: 390. ...
(Then) you shall lie upon your right side ... 40 days.
(Ezek 4:4–6, my translation)

In ancient Israel and Judah, history was arranged according to periods or epochs. There does not seem to have been an agreed upon standard concerning the length of eras or which events were definitive, for different intellectual traditions demarcated history according to their own theological agendas. As David Miano

---

28 Ibid., 27.

explains,[29] the Deuteronomistic traditions defined the period between the exodus and the building of the temple as lasting 480 years (1 Kgs 6:1), that is to say, an epoch of twelve generations, each one 40 years in length. Miano points out that P, on the other hand, assigned the period of the Israelites enslavement in Egypt as being 430 years (Exod 12:40–41). Its exact meaning is obscure, however, when Miano adds to this figure another 130 years, the time from Jacob's birth to his entry into the Egypt (Gen 47:7–9[30]), and also forty years, the span of time from the exodus to the entry into the land (Num 14:33–34), the figure amounts to 600 years, which is a multiple of twelve times fifty (Lev 23:15, the Festival of Weeks; Lev 25:10, the year of jubilee). Importantly, Miano states the obvious; these periods were imposed on the history and represent theological understandings, not nice, neat coincidences, produced by careful record keeping. Even though the sources that Miano cites date to the post-exilic period, it seems most reasonable to postulate that the periodization of history was practiced already in pre-exilic times and inherited by later Deuteronomistic and Priestly tradents.

The periodization of history necessitates, therefore, beginnings and endings, though it is the latter – given that I am discussing the death of Ezekiel's wife – that I am initially concerned with here. Because of its widespread scholarly use, I will use the term *eschaton* in this context, despite its Greek derivation. The Hebrews used the term קץ (Ezek 7:2, 3; 21:25 [30], 29 [34]; Amos 8:2).[31] In introducing his discussion of eschatology in the Hebrew Bible, Stephen Cook states:

> Broadly understood, [eschatology] may encompass any biblical or cognate expectation that present experience, in all its complexity, will find a definitive resolution or culmination in God's time. In many biblical texts, such a denouement ushers in a revolutionary new reality, where God has seized the initiative and redefined the parameters of existence. Eschatology provides the faithful with a sense of an ending to current experience and a firm confidence in the ultimate fruition of God's work. It offers assurance that that God's activity on behalf of God's people, humanity, and creation has a definite direction and goal (telos). God's purposes for God's people and their world are both good and definitive, and God will bring them to consummation.[32]

---

29 David Miano, *Shadow on the Steps: Time Measurement in Ancient Israel*, SBL-BS 64 (Atlanta: Society of Biblical Literature, 2010), 56–8.

30 Although Gen 47:7–12 is attributed to the E source, Miano's argument still holds, as this date would have been known to the priestly source.

31 Shemaryahu Talmon defines קץ primarily as denoting a temporal end. See "קץ," vol. XIII of *TDOT*, ed. G. Johannes Botterweck, Helmer Ringgren, and Heinz-Josef Fabry, trans. David E. Green (Grand Rapids: Eerdmans, 2004), XIII: 79–81.

32 Stephen L. Cook, "Eschatology of the OT," *The New Interpreters Dictionary of the Bible*, volume 2, D-H, ed. Katharine Doob Sakenfeld (Nashville: Abingdon, 2007), 299–306, here, 299.

I want to draw attention to an important part of Cook's statement. True enough, while eschatology involves a "definitive resolution or culmination," it also encompasses the expectation of "a revolutionary new reality." *Endzeit wird Urzeit*. The ancient Israelites' periodization of history and its associated form of eschatology also encompassed a period of transition. Think, for example, of the year when land should enjoy a sabbath (Lev 25:1–7), or the seventy years of exile expected by Jeremiah, after which the people will return to the land (Jer 29:10–14). Ezekiel, likewise, anticipated the exile to be limited, lasting 50 years (see 40:1 as the halfway point of the exile), in keeping with his priestly roots, and so a period of transition. In a past essay, I have argued that the idiosyncratic language of Ezekiel reflects his understanding of a period of de-creation, to be followed by a period of re-creation.[33]

Before moving on to Ezek 24, something should be said about the meaning of "Day of Yahweh." Specifically, at the end of the seventh century, so, the time of Ezekiel, *it did not connote an eschaton*. The earliest text to use the expression "Day of Yahweh" is Amos 5:18–20, an eighth century text. Here, Amos cites the people's longing for the Day of Yahweh, but then turns it back around on them, so that it becomes a day of "darkness, not light." Though with this oracle, Amos predicts judgment upon Samaria and the northern kingdom, Amos' use of the Day of Yahweh in chapter 5 is not connected with his discussion of the northern kingdom's קץ, its eschaton, in chapter 8:1–3 and 9:1–4. Yair Hoffmann has brought much clarity to the meaning of the Day of Yahweh in Amos, and thus, in the pre-exilic period.[34] He argues that although Amos may have coined the term, the prophet was nevertheless referring to a commonly held and well understood concept that expressed 1) the notion of a theophany; 2) Yahweh's saving acts (plural); 3) destructive and frightening phenomena; and 4) judgment.[35] He is emphatic that the concept, as used by Amos, lacked any eschatological content; that it was, as he puts it, entirely *"noneschatological."*[36] The use of Day of Yahweh in the mid-seventh century by Zephaniah (1:7–13; 2:2–3) reflects this same non-eschatological under-

---

[33] John T. Strong, "Cosmic Re-Creation and Ezekiel's Vocabulary," in *Ezekiel: Current Debates and Future Directions*, ed. William A. Tooman and Penelope Barter, FAT 112 (Tübingen: Mohr Siebeck, 2017), 245–84.

[34] Yair Hoffmann, "The Day of the Lord as a Concept and a Term in the Prophetic Literature," *ZAW* 93 (1981): 37–50.

[35] Ibid., 41–5.

[36] Joseph Everson reached a similar conclusion. See A. Joseph Everson, "The Days of Yahweh," *JBL* 93 (1974): 331. Everson states: "The texts demonstrate that the Day of Yahweh was not viewed in the pre-exilic eras of Israel's history as a singular, universal, or exclusively future event of world judgment. Rather, the Day of Yahweh was a powerful concept available to the prophets for their use in interpreting various momentous events – past, present, or imminent" (335).

standing of the Day of Yahweh and may be a later application of a phrase that Amos made prominent a century earlier. Actually, Ezekiel seems to provide the pivot at which the Day of Yahweh acquires an eschatological meaning.

"Write the name of today, this very day. The King of Babylon has besieged Jerusalem on this very day." (Ezek 24:2). "Day of Yahweh" does not appear in Ezekiel, but the day of the Jerusalem temple's eschaton does; it is the tenth day of the tenth month of the ninth year of the exile (January 15, 588 BCE).[37] The expression עצם היום הזה ("this very day") is very specific in Ezekiel, found only here and in 40:1, when Ezekiel announces the coming of the next epoch centered around a rebuilt temple.[38] (A similar expression is found in 2:3, which is conceptually related to 24:2.) "This very day" defined turning points in Israel's ancestral past (Gen 17:23, 26; Exod 12:17; Deut 32:50), and in this capacity, it served in the pre-exilic traditions to mark epochal shifts (Exod 12:41). Ezekiel, therefore, found this phrase convenient to define that particular January 15th as the eschaton of the first temple era. It was useful to him, not only because of the meaning it carried, but also because he apparently needed it to follow up his refutation of the popular proverb "the days are prolonged, and every vision comes to nothing" (12:22; and see also 12:26–28). This proverb seems to reflect the delay in the end predicted earlier, perhaps in Ezek 7:1–4 (see the use of קץ in 7:2, 3). In Ezekiel, then, יום and קץ in the sense of "eschaton," were joined perhaps for the first time, at least according to the data that has been left to us. This permitted later readers of the texts to apply the significance of קץ to the Day of Yahweh, essentially repurposing this phrase. If this tracing of breadcrumbs is correct, Ezekiel forms a pivot in the evolution of ancient Israel's language of eschatology.

---

[37] I am using the date given by Walther Zimmerli, *Ezekiel 1*, Hermenia (Philadelphia: Fortress, 1979), 498, who is citing Parker-Dubberstein.

[38] Within Ezekiel studies, scholars debate the nature of the temple envisioned in Ezek 40–43. I argue that Ezekiel envisioned in chapters 40–43 a physical second temple, located in physical space. See my article "Grounding Ezekiel's Heavenly Ascent: A Defense of Ezek 40–48 as a Program of Restoration," *Scandinavian Journal of the Old Testament* 26:2 (2012): 192–211; and more famously, Jon D. Levenson, *Theology of the Program of Restoration of Ezekiel 40–48*, HSM 10 (Missoula, MT: Scholars Press, 1976). In contrast, Steven Tuell and Paul Joyce have argued that the second temple of chapters 40–43 was envisioned as a heavenly temple, never to be physically built, and that Ezekiel's future program amounted to a total rejection of the Jerusalem temple cut. See Steven S. Tuell, *The Law of the Temple in Ezekiel 40–48*, HSM 49 (Atlanta: Scholars Press, 1992); idem, "Ezekiel 40–42 as Verbal Icon," *CBQ* 58 (1996): 649–64; Paul M. Joyce, "Ezekiel 40–42: The Earliest 'Heavenly Ascent' Narrative?" in *The Book of Ezekiel and Its Influence*, ed. H. J. de Jong and J. Tromp (Aldershot: Ashgate, 2007), 17–41; and Paul M. Joyce, "Dislocation and Adaptation in the Exilic Age and After," in *After the Exile: Essays in Honour of Rex Mason*, ed. John Barton and David J. Reimer (Atlanta: Mercer Press, 1996), 45–58; and Paul M. Joyce, *Ezekiel: A Commentary*, LHBOTS 482 (New York: T&T Clark, 2007), 220–1.

Ezekiel and his exilic audience were not just located in a visible spatial exile, but according to Ezekiel, they existed in a temporal exile as well. Their temporal exile was more difficult to recognize, because in a sense they were absent in time. From their location, they would observe from afar the eschaton (קץ) of the first temple epoch, but this end only presaged the coming of the epoch of the next temple (Ezek 40–43). They themselves would span the in-between time, that sabbatical period that bridged the two epochs. Although their spatial and temporal exile provided them with "a firm confidence in the ultimate fruition of God's work,"[39] Ezekiel and his immediate friends had no hope of living to see it.

2.2 Locating Ezekiel's Wife/Jerusalem

The boundaries of the city you will establish: five thousand cubits in breadth, twenty-five thousand cubits in length, to be adjacent to the holy district. ... The name of the city will be "Yahweh is over yonder."
(Ezek 45:6; 48:35, my translation – with an assist from my Arkansas grandfather)

Let's begin with a discussion of two sides. There are two sides to a coin. Two sides to every story. With Ana Mendieta and Carl Andre, there are also two sides: absent and present, or as they have also been labeled: "unmarked" and "marked," respectively.[40] Even with an eschaton, quoting Stephen Cook yet again: "it provides ... a sense of an ending to current experience and a firm confidence in the ultimate fruition of God's work." In Ezek 24:15–27, we will see that there were two sides to Ezekiel's sign-act: one who died, and one who did not die. Sadly, Ezekiel's wife ended up on the wrong side of that coin.

In keeping with our approach to Ezekiel's sign-act in 24:15–27, we find the "script" for his performance in vv. 16–18:

[16] I am taking from you the delight of your eyes in one blow.

You shall not wail. You shall not weep. Your tears shall not well up. Crying must cease. [17] Sigh, but keep silent (about it). You shall not perform any funerary rituals. Instead, bind up your turban upon your head, strap your sandals on your feet. Do not wrap your moustache. Do not eat the bread of mourners (לחם אנשים).[41]

---

39 Cook, "Eschatology of the OT," 299.

40 Unmarked and marked were applied to Mendieta and Andre by Elizabeth Hess, "Born Again," *Village Voice* 7 (July 1992): 38, cited by Blocker, *Where is Ana Mendieta?* 2.

41 For this paper, I am willing to accept the NRSV's translation of this phrase. Many commentators repoint the MT אֲנָשִׁים to אוֹנִים, "food of sorrow." See Zimmerli, *Ezekiel 1*, 503 n 17c; Daniel I. Block, *The Book of Ezekiel 1–24*, NICOT (Grand Rapids, MI: Eerdmans, 1997), 784 n 4; Leslie C. Allen, *Ezekiel 20–48*, WBC 29 (Dallas: Word Books, 1990), 56 n 17c. Greenberg (*Ezekiel 20–37*,

The script of Ezekiel's performance is two-sided. Negatively, all normal outward signs of mourning, e.g., crying, formal rituals, must be noticeably absent.[42] Positively, actions such as putting on a turban, sandals, and maintaining proper grooming – quite unremarkable, just a part of the normal, everyday routine before heading out the door for another day's work – must be noticeably present. And, in order that these subtleties not be lost, Ezekiel announced his performance prior to his wife's death (v. 19). His actual performance is only briefly stated (24:18b), not described, the point being merely to emphasize Ezekiel's obedience and adherence to the script.

As with Mendieta and other modern performance artists, Ezekiel intended his performance to evoke a reaction from his audience, for it was his audience's emotional experience of the moment that constituted the art/prophetic communication. And indeed, the performance hit its target: "Will you not explain to us what these things that you are doing mean for us?" (v. 19).[43] The challenge for the modern reader is to experience the absurdity and offensiveness of Ezekiel maintaining mundane habits in the intimate presence of death, for a silent reading of Ezekiel's art is in danger of missing the emotional impact of his performance.

In Ezekiel's sign-act, his wife is found on the negative side of his performance, her death being equated with that of Yahweh's wife, Jerusalem (24:21). This sign-act in chapter 24 fulfills what was promised in the pornographic allegories found in chapters 16 and 23, that Yahweh would execute Jerusalem, as Julie Galambush has put the matter so forcefully in her seminal work on this subject.[44] Galambush

---

AB 22A [New York: Doubleday, 1997], 509) maintains the reading of the Massoretes, translating it as "food of [other] men," and referring to the meal that friends would bring to mourners.

42 Ezekiel's refraining from performing any mourning rituals should be read in the broader context of mourning national calamities in ancient Judah. See Kerry M. Sonia's discussion of depiction of Ahijah's sign-act in 1 Kgs 11:30 ("Torn Garments and Calamity Mourning in 1 Kings 11:30," *JBL* 139/4 [2020]: 691–700), which would have been "hot off the press" in Ezekiel's day.

43 Thomas Renz notes that this is the only time we hear directly from the prophet's audience (*The Rhetorical Function of the Book of Ezekiel*, VTSup 76 [Boston: Brill, 1999], 138; we do hear indirectly from Ezekiel's audience in 12:8). In this verse, they voice the experience of the implied audience on behalf of the intended readers/recipients of the book, the exilic audience who outlived Ezekiel and survived the exile. Otherwise, all dialogue is between Yahweh and Ezekiel.

44 Galambush stated: "... just as Yahweh destroys the temple, so also must he preside over the death of his metaphorical wife (16:40), not only to vindicate his dishonored name, but to remove the potential for *future* defilement that the city's feminine persona represents" (*Jerusalem in the Book of Ezekiel: The City as Yahweh's Wife*, SBLDS 130 [Atlanta: Scholars Press, 1992], 88; author's italics); and see also, "... rather than being a prediction of judgment ..., 23:46–49 is a *call* to judgment. Yahweh summons the throng, commanding that they begin the long threatened destruction" (p. 124, author's italics). Galambush notes that while the prophet and Yahweh are typically conflated in sign-acts, Ezekiel is distinguished in his treatment of his wife (pp. 140–1).

points out further that Yahweh never revitalized his wife, Jerusalem, but instead turned her to stone.[45] Galambush is, of course, correct in her observation, however, attention needs to be drawn to the fact that Ezekiel separated the city from the temple. Certainly, while Jerusalem with the temple as her vagina was not revitalized as Yahweh's wife,[46] Ezekiel nevertheless envisioned both a rebuilt city (40:2; 45:6; 48:15–20, 30–35) and a new temple in which God would dwell (40:1–43:12; see 43:7). To put the matter more precisely, the two have been divided. While the temple and its environs shall be holy (40:48–43:12; 45:1–5), the city has been demoted, having become "ordinary" (48:15), whose purpose is to house workers supporting the flow of pilgrims (48:18–19).[47] On account of its displacement and demotion, the name of this future city will not be Jerusalem, but rather – contrary to what is found in many translations –"Yahweh is over yonder" (48:35; יהוה שׁמה).[48] Yahweh executed his wife, Jerusalem, by surgically removing her from the temple and Yahweh's presence.[49]

Like Ana Mendieta, the city, which before the eschaton of the first temple period lived with Yahweh in his presence, would become noticeably absent in the epoch of next temple. In Ezekiel's theological schema, and so in his sign-act, Jerusalem has been forcibly removed into exile.

Surprisingly, the prophet and his fellow exiles are found on the positive side of his performance, being commanded to don turbans and, *for God's sake, put on your shoes!* Much speculation has gone into understanding Ezekiel's actions and

---

45 Galambush, *Jerusalem in the Book of Ezekiel*, 129, 145, 147–8.

46 "If the city is a woman, then the temple is her vagina, and the offense of Jerusalem's granting illicit 'access' to foreign men and competing gods becomes plain, both as a legal transgression and as a personal injury to the husband" (*Jerusalem in the Book of Ezekiel*, 87).

47 See the comments of Stephen Cook, *Ezekiel 38–39*, AB 22B (New Haven: Yale University Press, 2018), 291–2.

48 Read "The Lord is There" in KJV, NRSV, NJPS, NIV, NASB. See also Robert Alter, *The Hebrew Bible: Volume 2: Prophets* (New York: W. W. Norton and Co., 2019), 1197. The final ה, however, is locative; see Paul Joüon, *A Grammar of Biblical Hebrew*, revised ed., trans. and rev. T. Muraoka; Subsidia Biblica 27 (Rome: Pontificio Istituto Biblio, 2006), § 93c, p. 256. Much more sophisticated than my Arkansas-influenced translation, Stephen Cook renders the name as "The Lord is Just Over There," *Ezekiel 38–48*, 293. For a discussion of the phrase, see Soo J. Kim, "*YHWH Shammah*: The City as Gateway to the Presence of YHWH," *JSOT* 39 (2014): 199–206.

49 Jerusalem's removal from the presence of God is consistent with Ezekiel 8:6: "See what they are doing to remove themselves from my presence?" Note that this verb is passive in the G stem, so that the infinitive identifies the people as the subject being acted upon. See Ka Leung Wong, "A Note on Ezekiel VIII 6," *VT* 51 (2001): 396–400; Margaret S. Odell, *Ezekiel*, Smyth and Helwys Bible Commentary (Macon, GA: Smyth and Helwys, 2005), 107; and my essay, "The God that Ezekiel Inherited," in *The God that Ezekiel Created*, ed. Paul M. Joyce and Dalit Rom-Shiloni, LHBOTS 607 (New York: Bloomsbury, 2015), 41, and the bibliography in note 62.

his instructions to his audience. Many scholarly readings of the prohibition to mourn and the concomitant command to continue to wear turbans and sandals and all the rest understand this as compounding the "bad news," as Joyce puts it.[50] Daniel Block, however, sees something quite different in Ezekiel's refusal to mourn when read, as he argues it should be, with the opening of Ezekiel's mouth (24:25–27):

> [Together they] signified a turning point in Israel's history: the old era of sin and judgment had come to an end; the new era of hope and salvation could begin. The exiles would refrain from mourning not because they would be paralyzed by grief or calloused by sin, but because they would recognize the dawn of a new age.[51]

In my view, Margaret Odell has made a significant contribution to the understanding of the positive, active elements of Ezekiel's performance, highlighting important parallels with Lev 10:1–7.[52] In this narrative, Nadab and Abihu, two sons of Aaron, brought an offering of ordinary/unholy fire before Yahweh, of the kind that Yahweh had not commanded (v. 1). Fire came out from the presence of Yahweh and consumed them (v. 2). After their bodies had been disposed of outside of the camp by their cousins, replacement priests were elected by Yahweh, Eleazar and Ithamar (v. 6), who were told to remain in the Tent of Meeting, retain their priestly vestments and not to mourn. Note that on a small scale, Lev 10:1–7

---

50 See Joyce, *Ezekiel*, 168. See also Zimmerli, (*Ezekiel 1*, 506), "the grim harshness of suffering, which symbolically shows the immense suffering of Israel that is coming"; and Franz Sedlmeier (*Das Buch Ezechiel: Kapitel 1–24*, NSKAT 21/1 [Stuttgart: Katholisches Bibelwerk, 2002], 326): „Er hat statt dessen in inneren und äußerer Erstarrung zu verharren, Zeichen der Schreckensstarre, die das commende göttliche Gericht über das Gottsvold bringen wird." ("[Ezekiel] had, instead [of mourning], to persevere in internal and external stoicism, signs of the terror-induced-numbness, which the coming divine judgment of the people of God would bring.") Stephen Cook argues that Ezekiel's eschewing of mourning is the proper response to theophany, according to the Holiness School. His sign-act, then, calls for his audience to turn away from their own "egocentric interests," a release of their own interest in power, and toward a "theocentric" interest in the will of God ("The Speechless Suppression of Grief in Ezekiel 24:15–27: The Death of Ezekiel's Wife and the Prophet's Abnormal Response" in *Thus Says the Lord: Essays on the Former and Latter Prophets in Honor of Robert R. Wilson*, ed. John J. Ahn, and Stephen L. Cook [New York: T & T Clark, 2009], 222–33).
51 Block, *Ezekiel 1–24*, 794. See also G. A. te Stroete, "Ezekiel 24:15–27: The Meaning of a Symbolic Act." *Bijdragen: Tijdschrift voor Filosofie en Theologie* 38 (1973): 163–75.
52 Margaret S. Odell, "Genre and Persona in Ezekiel 24:15–24" in *The Book of Ezekiel: Theological and Anthropological Perspectives*, ed. Margaret S. Odell, John T. Strong, SBLSymS 9 (Atlanta: Society of Biblical Literature, 2000), 200–2; and idem, *Ezekiel*, 317. Stephen Cook ("Speechless Suppression," 224) has similarly argued that Ezek 24:15–27 is an "inner-biblical reactualization" of Lev 10. In contrast, however, Cook draws from these parallels a message of judgment, not election.

fundamentally represents an eschaton concerning priestly lines. The first scene brings about an end to one line of Yahweh's elected priests by means of fire. However, that end only cleared the way for the election of another. As Block stated above, read within the context of Lev 10:1–7, Ezek 24:15–24 implies that the command not to mourn, alongside the command to put on headdresses (to be discussed momentarily), signaled Yahweh's election of the exiles as an initial promise of a new future era.

Odell argues further that putting on turbans symbolizes new status for the exiles, that of election.[53] In the Hebrew Bible generally, putting on clothing marks Aaron's status and sanctification for cultic service (Exod 28:3, 41). In the Priestly instructions concerning the priestly vestments in Exod 28:1–43, vv. 37–39 instruct Moses to create a single turban for Aaron, on which a special emblem will be placed that reads "Holy unto Yahweh" (see also Exod 29:5–6; and 39:27–31). These instructions are carried out when Aaron is ordained, in Lev 8:9.

Ezekiel's prophecies share this priestly practice, but even more he provides an amazing look at the role that turbans play, either in their removal or their binding on, in signaling an eschaton. On the losing side, Ezek 21:30, a notoriously difficult passage, announces to the Prince of Israel" "You vile, wicked Prince of Israel, whose day has come with an eschaton (קֵץ) brought about by punishment ..." (my translation).[54] The prophecy continues in v. 31, with a pair of H infinitives stating the fact of his removal of the turban and lifting off the diadem. Following this description of the prince's end is a statement of reversal: "This will not be that. The low will be raised; the high will be leveled" (21:32). Here, Ezekiel expresses succinctly and perfectly a pre-exilic eschatology.[55] Then, when this day arrives, Ezek 24:2, Ezekiel

---

53 See Odell, "Genre and Persona," 203–4; *Ezekiel*, 319. See also the comments regarding clothing and social status by Victor H. Matthews, "Cloth, Clothes," in *The New Interpreter's Dictionary of the Bible*, ed. Katharine Doob Sakenfeld et al. (Nashville: Abingdon Press, 2006), 1:692–5; and idem, "The Anthropology of Clothing in the Joseph Narrative," *JSOT* 65 (1995): 25–8; and Ora Horn Prouser, "Suited to the Throne: The Symbolic Use of Clothing in the David and Saul Narratives," *JSOT* 71 (1996): 30.
54 The Hebrew reads as: בְּעֵת עֲוֹן קֵץ. The בְּ introduces a temporal phrase, modifying the coming day. Regarding the construct phrase, עֵת and קֵץ are related adjectivally, falling into Waltke and O'Connor's classification *attributive genitive*, meaning "time of an end" (Waltke and O'Connor, § 9.5.3b). The construction עֲוֹן קֵץ is adverbial, what Waltke and O'Connor identify as *genitive of effect*, meaning that the nomen regens *causes* the nomen rectum (§ 9.2.c).
55 Of Ezek 21:30, Zimmerli separates the concept of end found here from a "philosophical doctrine of the end of time" (*Ezekiel 1*, 446). He argues this conclusion on the basis of his interpretation of Ezek 7 as not referring to an eschaton. Of course, I agree with Zimmerli that Ezek 21:30 should be read in context with Ezek 7, but I differ with him in that I do understand Ezek 7 to prophesy an eschaton, as long as the eschaton in Ezek 7 is understood within the larger theological framework of pre-exilic eschatology.

announces with the positive side of his sign-act (24:17, 23) that it will be the exiles who are to take up what the prince has taken off; they are the low who will be raised.

Then Ezekiel confuses everything by saying of his newly elected exiles: "You will rot to the bone in your iniquities and be reconciled[56] to one another" (24:23). The root מקק appears only 10 times in the Hebrew Bible, spread over just seven verses, three of those being found in Ezekiel. It connotes the putrefaction of the flesh on the bones, as in Zech 14:12, "their flesh shall rot while they are still on their feet; their eyes shall rot in their sockets, and their tongues shall rot in their mouths" (NRSV), as well as in the lexicons (*HALOT*, "to rot, to decay"; and *BDB*, "decay, rot, fester"). Te Stroete recognized in 1973 that Ezekiel seems to have drawn this gruesome image from the covenantal curses in the Holiness Code, Lev 26:39.[57] How in the world does the purification of flesh indicate election?

By applying the curse in Lev 26:39 to the exiles, whom he signals will be the new elect, Ezekiel seems to have painted himself into a theological corner. The prophet solves this problem, however, with his vision of the dry bones in 37:1–14. In Ezek 37, the dry bones that Ezekiel sees are not all of Israel, but rather they are specifically the exiles who become all of Israel (37:11).[58] This narrow identification is demanded by the location of the bones; to find them, Ezekiel has to be brought to *the valley –with the definite article* (הבקעה; 37:1). All other mentions of בקעה in Ezekiel refer to the specific valley that was near the river Chebar, where he met the exiles (3:22–23; 8:4). Hence, while declaring the exiles to be the next elected priests of Yahweh, Ezekiel does not protect them from the shame and punishment of exile. They are corpses whose flesh has decomposed; they are desiccated skeletons. Ezekiel's pre-exilic eschatology, however, permits him to declare that their existence as disintegrating corpses is merely a process of transformation, and that it is exile itself that will transform these Judahite captives in Babylon into a nation capable of obeying Yahweh's eternal covenant

---

56 I follow the LXX and emend the text to וְנִחַמְתֶּם, the D perfect of נחם. I understand נחם as connoting a person's recognition and acceptance of their new status or situation, often times in regard to punishment. See Ezek 14:22–23. In Ezek 24:23, even while being declared elect, Ezekiel still calls upon the exiles to recognize the shame of their punishment, of being in exile (Ezek 16:63).

57 Te Stroete, "Ezekiel 24:15–27," 174–5. I am convinced by Michael Lyons' argument Ezekiel borrowed from the Holiness Code, and not the other way around (*From Law to Prophecy: Ezekiel's Use of the Holiness Code*, LHBOTS 508 [New York: T & T Clark, 2009], 59–75; and see his comments on Lev 26:39 // Ezek 24:23, p. 184).

58 I interpret העצמות האלה ("these bones"; 37:11) to identify specifically the bones in the valley, so the exiles. The next verbless clause, with המה referring reiteratively back to the bones, states that these bones are all of Israel.

(16:59–63).[59] While Ezekiel's wife/Jerusalem may have breathed her last, with 37:10, Ezekiel commanded the breath of life to come into and revitalize the exiles.

Ezekiel's wife died in exile, and he was not allowed to be sorry about it at all. God would not allow it because God was not sorry about the absence of Jerusalem. Ezekiel's wife and Jerusalem were both left "unmarked," as was Ana Mendieta. In contrast, Ezekiel "marked" the exiles, as has been said of Carl Andre, for the prophet identified them as the elect who would ascend to positions of honor in the next epoch. And like Andre, the descendants of these exiles would appear at the grand opening of the next temple, at the beginning of the next epoch.

Ezekiel's audience did not just hear this message – they certainly did not read it in silence, as we do today – but rather, they felt it; they experienced the shock of it all. Still, the question remains: Why do we know about the exiles' time-bound experience of what Ezekiel did not do?

2.3 Curating Ezekiel's Performance

According to Thomas Renz, "… the book [of Ezekiel] received its final shape to function in a specific way for the second generation of exiles."[60] Renz's focus is on the rhetorical argument achieved by the final form of the text, not, as are the interests of this essay, on the individual oracles of the prophet, or as the case of Ezek 24:15–27, with a particular performance.[61] That is not to say, however, that Renz understands there to have been a wide temporal separation between the prophet and the redactors responsible for arranging the final shape of the book. The creation of the book of Ezekiel, Renz points out, would not have any function in a post-exilic setting,[62] which means that the redactors' shaping of the book must be squeezed into a fairly narrow window of time, and that the message of the redactor(s) of the material and Ezekiel shared a common goal.[63] The rhetoric

---

59 See Jacqueline E. Lapsley, *Can These Bones Live? The Problem of the Moral Self in the Book of Ezekiel*, BZAW 301 (New York: Walter de Gruyter, 2000), 129–57; and Jacqueline E. Lapsley, "Shame and Self-Knowledge: The Positive Role of Shame in Ezekiel's View of the Moral Self," in *The Book of Ezekiel: Theological and Anthropological Perspectives*, ed. Margaret S. Odell and John T. Strong, SBLSymS 9 (Atlanta: Society of Biblical Literature, 2000), 143–73.

60 Renz, *The Rhetorical Function*, 1.

61 Ibid., 137–8.

62 Ibid., 37–8. In support, Renz quotes Kuenen (see p. 37). See also the comments of Paul Joyce (*Ezekiel*, 219; citing Ronald E. Clements).

63 Here, Renz enlists the assistance of Brevard Childs (*Introduction to the Old Testament as Scripture* [Philadelphia: Fortress, 1979], 361): "the strongest continuity between the original oracles and the final canonical shape. The prophetic material in this case did not undergo a major

of the book, Renz argues further, is 'epideictic' in its genre, meaning that it functions to arouse within the audience a sense of connection between the rhetor and the audience, to intensify an adherence to a common set of shared values.[64] Notice the overlap in what Renz identifies as the rhetoric of the book and what Ezekiel achieved with his performance – the arousal and intensification of emotions. This overlap was achieved because the redactors of Ezekiel's performance art effectively curated his art/prophecy. The curation of Ezekiel's performance in 24:15–27 and elsewhere was necessary so that this second generation of exiles, the revivified dry bones of the valley, felt the impact of their election, in order to prepare them for their service in the temple of the next epoch.

To put the matter differently, Renz's description of the rhetorical function of the book for the second generation, when viewed through the lens of performance art, is not at all dissimilar from a museum catalogue archiving, documenting, and curating a past time-bound work of art.[65] The scroll of Ezekiel used the technology available to the prophet and his disciples to curate his performances for the inheritors of the exiles' election. Even more, the tight timeframe of this curatorial work closely parallels Mendieta's own curation of her performances through film, photography, and the warehousing of props and other artifacts.

Ezekiel's oracles are unique in that they are introduced by dates, not historical circumstances.[66] Previously, prophetic oracles were tied to specific events, not too distant from a known historical setting (e.g., Isa 7–8). The fact that Ezekiel's oracles were abstractly located by a date and not concretely tied to a particular historical circumstance indicates that something else was going on. In her important work, *Swallowing the Scroll*, Ellen Davis explored the nature and qualities of

---

literary or historical transformation in order to serve its new canonical role." Renz adds: "This 'unusual relationship between the original function of the oracles and its subsequent canonical shaping' (quoting Childs again) is best explained by assuming that someone who shared the outlook of the prophet edited the book so that it would address the second generation in exile in the same way that the prophet addressed the first generation" (*The Rhetorical Function*, 10).

64 Ibid., 58–9.

65 Concerning the characterization of the book of Ezekiel as an archive, Renz states: "The thesis advanced here is that the book of Ezekiel was to function not only as an archive, but also as an argument, interpreting Ezekiel's prophetic ministry for the following generation" (*The Rhetorical Function*, 15). Semantics aside, Renz's statement highlights what a good curator attempts to do when compiling a catalogue of performance art – recapture for a later audience the rhetorical power of the initial performance.

66 See the comments of Block, *Ezekiel 1–24*, 26–7, and see note 35. Outside of Ezekiel, only Jeremiah, Haggai, and Zechariah have oracles identified with a date formula precise to the day. The form of the date formulae in Jeremiah is to be distinguished from those in Ezekiel, Haggai, and Zechariah. See the discussion of Miano, *Shadow on the Steps*, 99–100.

Ezekiel's prophecies as written texts.[67] Within this context, Davis argued that the dates in Ezekiel served an archival function.[68] This archival function points not to Ezekiel's day and circumstances – he lived in spatial and temporal exile – but instead, as Lapsley has argued, to the circumstances of a later audience.[69] Such an archival function is precisely the motivation behind the command in Ezek 24:2: "Write the name of today, this very day. The King of Babylon has besieged Jerusalem on this very day."

Tyler Mayfield has proposed an interesting thesis regarding the date formulae in Ezekiel, which may have some relevance to my discussion here.[70] Mayfield has argued that the 13 formulae in the book provide a literary structuring device at the macro level, intended to create the context in which to read the prophecies of Ezekiel as they are currently arranged in the final form of the text.[71] According to Mayfield, the date formulae open each segment with a narrative, which is then followed by prophetic oracles introduced by a secondary formula, "The word of the LORD came to me."[72]

Although Mayfield, as with Renz, is interested in the function of the date formulae at the literary level, I wonder if his basic observations do not reflect something about the historical development of the texts. First, I am not comfortable with Mayfield's thesis in all of its particulars. For example, his approach leads him to group the oracles of the priestly meal (24:3–14) and Ezekiel's refusal to mourn (24:15–27) with the four foreign nation oracles (25:1–17), one of Mayfield's

---

67 Davis, *Swallowing the Scroll: Textuality and the Dynamics of Discourse in Ezekiel's Prophecy*, JSOTSup 78 (Sheffield: Almond Press, 1989). Davis states her research agenda as follows: "The question to be pursued is a functional one: what factors operative in Ezekiel's environment constitute a new kind of challenge to the prophet in communicating his message, and how does writing afford him the linguistic means to answer that challenge? My goal is to find a way of accounting for the elements in this book which violate our preconceptions about prophetic speech (as, perhaps, they violated those of Ezekiel's contemporaries), while yet taking seriously his own claim to stand in the line of Israel's prophets" (p. 25).

68 Ibid., 58–64; and see also Block, *Ezekiel 1–24*, 27. While I use the term "archives," what I envision would fit Niditch's description of an ancient library (*Oral World and Written Word: Ancient Israelite Literature* [Louisville: Westminster John Knox, 1996], 60–9; and especially 66–7).

69 Lapsley states: "Thus the purpose of the prophet's activity is not to bring about a change in the people's behavior in the present, but to instill a particular kind of knowledge in them in the future" (*Can These Bones Live?*, 120). To be precise (and fair to Lapsley), the knowledge she is referring to is moral knowledge, while I am pointing here to the exiles' knowledge of their election.

70 Tyler D. Mayfield, *Literary Structure and Setting in Ezekiel*, FAT 2/43 (Tübingen: Mohr Siebeck, 2010).

71 Ibid., 11; and see also the essay by Mayfield's mentor, Marvin A. Sweeney, *The Prophetic Literature*, Interpreting Biblical Texts (Nashville: Abingdon Press, 2005), 131–2.

72 Mayfield, *Literary Structure*, 11, and 80–121, especially 94 and 117–21.

case-studies.[73] Still, it seems clear that at some point prior to the intrusion of the oracles against the nations (Ezek 25–32), the statement about Ezekiel's mouth being opened when the refugee from Jerusalem came to the exiles (Ezek 24:25–27) was purposefully placed close to the fulfillment of that promise, in 33:21–22. Moreover, even at an early stage of the development of the text, Mayfield's observation that the dry bones vision was intended to be read within the context of the appearance of the refugee 33:21–22 may reflect the intention and arrangement of the early redactors. Admittedly, we are trying to look into the night through a tinted window. Nevertheless, given the short timeframe for the early arrangement of the text, as argued by Renz, and the archival function of the date formulae, per Davis and Lapsley, we get the sense from Mayfield for how the earliest curators of Ezekiel's prophecies and performances may have attempted to preserve their impact for the second generation of exiles, those who would be present in the next epoch.

3 Marking the Absence of Ezekiel's and Yahweh's Wives

The 1992 rally before the opening of the Guggenheim exhibit was not the last group of protesters to pose the question "Where is Ana Mendieta?" There have been many others, one of which was held at the opening of a 2013 exhibit of Carl Andre's work at the Contemporary Visual Arts Centre, Firstsite, in Colchester, England.[74] At that opening, a number of performance artists laid down on the gallery floor and covered themselves with sheets, as if they were Ana Mendieta's fallen corpse. A member of the troupe sat nearby to interpret for baffled patrons what exactly the shrouded corpses were marking. Their performance was intended to evoke discomfort among the gallery visitors, and in this way, they sought to mark the absence of Ana Mendieta, and by implication, unmark the presence of Carl Andre.

Returning to the prophet's performance in 24:15–27, Ezekiel marked the exiles for election, and by implication he unmarked Jerusalem and those remaining in the land. If we leave the historical-critical method behind for a moment and switch to a reader-response approach to the text, might we be able to play with

---

73 Ibid., 157–68.
74 This performance was filmed and has been curated on YouTube. See https://www.youtube.com/watch?v=E4_jCx5AT34.

the text a bit and read some of the post-fall actions of those remaining in the land as performances protesting the absence of Jerusalem?

In the case of Gedeliah, he set up his administration in Mizpah, outside of Jerusalem (Jer 40:7–12). Gedeliah in essence performed what Ezekiel already stated in 8:6: "Do you see what they are doing, the great abominations they are performing there to remove themselves from my sanctuary?" Viewed as performance art, Gedeliah and his court made visible God's execution of Jerusalem, that is to say, of his wife. The power and emotion of the absence of Jerusalem generated by this "performance" was clearly felt by his audience, seen in those who passed through Mizpah on their way to worship in Jerusalem (41:4–8). Yet another performance might be found in the actions of the community that left the land for Egypt, taking Jeremiah and Baruch with them (Jer 43:1–7). Similar to Gedeliah, they absented the land, forcibly removing Jeremiah and Baruch as well, fleeing to Egypt where they would all die (44:12–14).

Of course, neither of these two actions, as catalogued in this brief biographical novella, were reported as prophetic performances or protests. Nevertheless, they reflect the emotion-filled experiences of those remaining in the land, and these episodes were curated for the purpose of generating within later readers an emotional experience of losing the land and Jerusalem.

For later generations, and for us too, those left in the land raged: Where is Yahweh's Wife?

Stefano Salemi

Ezekiel's Wife's Death: Femicide, 'Divine Election,' Metaphor, or Mimic?

1 Introduction

Ezekiel 24 contains a message about the condition of Israel. The message is crucial as it refers to the city of Jerusalem and the "long section of the book constituted by chs. 4–24 here reaches its climax."[1] The prophet is informed about the loss of his wife who would represent the destruction of the beloved temple. The drama of the prophet becomes the drama of the people. The narrative highlights the tender love of the prophet for his wife, emphasizing the painful event of her death. This lends itself well to visualizing the loss of the city and the temple of Jerusalem, so loved by the people. The unusual behaviour of the prophet at his wife's death plays a role in the comparative framework of YHWH's relationship with his people and the people with the city and the temple.

How can the death of a woman constitute a pivotal element in the experience of the exilic community within the theology of the book of Ezekiel? Is it an act of 'divine election'? A metaphorical element of a traumatic narrative? An essential characteristic of a bizarre sign-act of Ezekiel? Moreover, as Ezekiel 24:24, 27 use the lexeme מופת to identify the prophet in relation to the house of Israel (לָכֶם לְמוֹפֵת), why does YHWH want the prophet to be a מופת for the house of Israel when his wife dies? What is a מופת? What is the purpose of Ezekiel's מופת-identity for the story of Ezekiel's loss and for the theology of the book that bears his name?[2]

Ezekiel uses the term מופת in only two chapters of the book, with two occurrences per chapter (12:6, 11; 24:24, 27). The term is used to designate or describe the function of the prophet before the people. Ezekiel is 'appointed' to be a מופת (12:6) for the house of Israel. The lexeme has often been rendered with 'sign'. However, its semantic meaning may go beyond the strict lexical understanding of the term.[3] This is reflected in the numerous translations, though less frequent,

---

1 Paul M. Joyce, *Ezekiel: A Commentary*, LHBOTS 482 (New York, NY and London: T&T Clark, 2009), 165.
2 For a broader discussion on the use of מופת in Ezekiel, his מופת-identity, and the narratives of ch. 12 and 24, see Stefano Salemi, *A Linguistic-Theological Exegesis of Ezekiel as* Môphēt – *"I have made you a sign"* (Ezekiel 12:6) (Studia Semitica Neerlandica; Leiden: Brill, 2024). This chapter substantially draws upon the insights and analysis presented in Salemi's monograph published by Brill.
3 For a semantic and linguistic analysis of מופת in the Hebrew Bible, see Salemi, "Semantic Analysis of מופת" in idem, *A Linguistic-Theological Exegesis of Ezekiel as* Môphēt.

https://doi.org/10.1515/9783111521015-009

of the lexeme as 'portent,' 'show,' 'warning,' 'type,' and many more.[4] This is done to render the broad semantic field expressed by מוֹפֵת, often used to describe divine portents such as the plagues of Egypt, to confirm an oracle or the work of a prophet, to remember a divine action, to show divine authority, to anticipate a judgment, or even to identify the function of a human being in relation to YHWH's intentions and activities.[5] The meaning expressed by the terms used to render מוֹפֵת is somehow implied in both contexts of ch. 12 and ch. 24 where Ezekiel is involved with a symbolic action related to the Exile. Ezekiel should be a מוֹפֵת for the house of Israel, in a way signalling to Israel what YHWH intends to do. This happens at the level of actions and behaviours, as the prophet is often confined and unable to express words if not intermittently when divinely allowed. Therefore, his personal life and being become the means of YHWH's revelation, and his drama represents the drama of the Judahites. Ezekiel is made a מוֹפֵת for them through the experience he lives, especially the death of his wife. However, how should this tragedy be interpreted? How does this relate to the prophet's role of being a מוֹפֵת to the house of Israel? What has this experience to do with the presence of YHWH? Why does his wife die? Who is the agent of her death?

---

4 The JPS Bible, "for I make you a portent to the House of Israel"; New International Reader's Version, "All of that will show the people of Israel what is going to happen to them"; The Good News Translation, "What you do will be a warning to the Israelites"; Young's Literal Translation, "for a type I have given thee to the house of Israel."
5 Here, a few examples of the use of the lexeme: Plagues – Exodus 4:21, 7:3, 9, 11:9; Confirmation of an oracle or the work of a prophet – Deuteronomy 13:2–3, 34:11, 1 Kings 13:3, 5; Memorial of divine actions – 1 Chronicles 16:12, Psalm 78:43; Anticipation of judgments – Joel 3:3 [v. 2:30 in Eng.]; Identification of the function of a human being – Psalm 71:7; Isaiah 8:18; Ezekiel 12:6, 11; 24:24, 27.

In biblical texts, מוֹפֵת is more frequent in prose contexts (29 prose to 7 poetic verses), more generally in the narrative context of the Pentateuch (in reference to Israel's deliverance from Egypt), in Psalms (in songs, praises, and prayers), and in Ezekiel (referring to the prophet).

The lexeme is used 36 times in 12 books of the Hebrew Bible (Exodus 4:21; 7:3; 9; 11:9; 10; Deuteronomy 4:34; 6:22; 7:19; 13:2 [v. 1 in Eng.]; 3 [v. 2 in Eng.]; 26:8; 28:46; 29:2 [v. 3 in Eng.]; 34:11; 1 Kings 13:3[x2]; 5; Isaiah 8:18; 20:3; Jeremiah 32:20, 21; Ezekiel 12:6, 11; 24:24, 27; Joel 3:3 [v. 2:30 in Eng.]; Zechariah 3:8; Psalms 71:7; 78:43; 105:5, 27; 135:9; Nehemiah 9:10; 1 Chronicles 16:12; 2 Chronicles 32:24, 31).

It is used also twice in Ben Sira (36.6, 48.12). The context of 36 is that of a prayer to God to perform signs and wonders, while in 48 it serves to present Elijah as a performer of signs and wonders with the utterances of his mouth.

It is used also 21 times in the Dead Sea Scrolls with a meaning that does not differ significantly from its use in the Hebrew Bible (1QHa 5.33, 7.33, 8.9, 15.24; 4Q185 f1_2i.15; 4Q377 f2ii.1; 4Q378 f26.5; 4Q392 f1.8; 4Q392 f2.2; 4Q416 f1.8; 4Q422 3.5, 3.11; 4Q422 f0.1; 4Q435 f5.2; 4Q437 f2i.12; 4Q451 f1.3; 4Q511 f26.4; 4Q511 f48_49+51.5; 4Q546 f10.2; 11Q11 3.3; 11Q19 54.9).

This discussion will include, especially, an analysis of the pericope of 24:15–27,[6] where the narrative of the symbolic behaviour of Ezekiel in reference to his wife's death sheds light on how מוֹפֵת points to the life of Ezekiel as a divine agent embodying YHWH's relationship with Israel. The persona of Ezekiel, as Launderville writes, "manifests how new life can arise from death"[7] and his embodied witness of commitment to YHWH "speaks clearly of the abiding presence of Yhwh in the lives of the faithful."[8]

2 Ezekiel's Experience and Symbolic Role

The harrowing experience of Ezekiel serves the purpose of anticipating the loss of the temple and the destruction of the city and many lives. Cook confirms this concept by saying that "Ezekiel's experience is to be a sign of a coming tragic loss for the exiles, which will entail a forfeiture of the very inspiration of their lives. They are about to lose both the Jerusalem temple and their children, their most treasured possessions."[9] The emotional bond represented by the relationship of Ezekiel with his wife presents that of Israel with the temple and the beloved city of Jerusalem. Consequently, Ezekiel's wife's death serves well to visualize Israel's coming tragedy.

This emotional bond is marked by three descriptors: the pride of your power (גְּאוֹן עֻזְּכֶם), the delight of your eyes (מַחְמַד עֵינֵיכֶם), and the desire of your soul (מַחְמַל נַפְשְׁכֶם). These descriptive expressions tell of the supreme importance of Jerusalem for the house of Israel as well as the importance of Ezekiel's wife for the prophet. Joyce argues for the absence of a love-terminology in reference to YHWH in

---

6 For questions of redaction, see Walther Zimmerli, *Ezekiel 1*, Hermeneia (Philadelphia: Fortress, 1979), 504–505; see also Daniel I. Block, *The Book of Ezekiel Chapters 1–24*, NICOT (Grand Rapids: Eerdmans, 1997), 785–786.

7 Dale F. Launderville, *Spirit and Reason: The Embodied Character of Ezekiel's Symbolic Thinking* (Waco, TX: Baylor University Press, 2007), ix.

8 Launderville, *Spirit and Reason*, ix.

9 See Stephen L. Cook, "The Speechless Suppression of Grief in Ezekiel 24:15–27: The Death of Ezekiel's Wife and the Prophet's Abnormal Response," in *Thus Says the LORD: Essays on the Former and Latter Prophets in Honor of Robert R. Wilson*, ed. S. L. Cook, and J. J. Ahn (New York, NY and London: T&T Clark, 2009), 222–233; see Andrew Mein, *Ezekiel and the Ethics of Exile*, Oxford Theological Monographs (Oxford: Oxford University Press, 2001), 155, "YHWH's turning away from his people represents his rejection of them which indirectly profanes the temple by allowing in outsiders to pillage it. The image is furthermore shocking in 24:21, where it is YHWH himself who profanes his sanctuary 'Behold I will profane my sanctuary, the pride of your power, the delight of your eyes, and the desire of your soul.'"

Ezekiel.[10] However, the above-mentioned epithets may well be considered expressions of the love-relationship between Ezekiel and his wife, the people and their temple/city, but also YHWH and Israel.[11] Ezekiel's symbolic behaviour represents these three levels of relationship. Therefore, the tragic experience of the destruction of the temple, like that of the death of the prophet's wife, and the emotional implications of this drama, point to Israel as the object of YHWH's love. There is reason to argue that the temple may be perceived as a sign of the relationship between YHWH and Israel. Its destruction would mean both YHWH's real 'loss' of his people, as many Judahites would be killed, and the end of a form of collective religious relationship represented by the temple as the place of worship, sacrifice, and national identity.[12] Therefore, in a sense, the death of Ezekiel's wife constitutes the termination of such relationships, a shared or corporate drama including YHWH. Consequently, the lexeme מופת here plays a role in pointing to the prophet as an embodiment of YHWH's relationship with Israel.

The prophet seems to mimic the experience of Israel.[13] This non-verbal theatrical display has the purpose of visualizing the outcome of the 'prophecy.'[14] In this

10 Paul M. Joyce, *Divine Initiative and Human Response in Ezekiel*, JSOTSup 51 (Sheffield: Sheffield Academic Press, 1989) 100.

11 Nissinen argues that "the metaphor involving marital/sexual relationship between Yahweh and Israel in Ezekiel and elsewhere (Ezek 16; 23; cf. Jer 2–3; 13; Hos 2) reveals further fractures in God's masculinity. As God has no real body, there is no real marriage between God and the people, and God is no real husband but the sovereign divine autocrat [...]," Martti Nissinen, "Biblical Masculinities: Musings on Theory and Agenda," in *Biblical Masculinities Foregrounded*, ed. O. Creangă, and P.-B. Smit, Hebrew Bible Monographs 62 (Sheffield: Sheffield Phoenix Press, 2014), 271–285 (esp. 278). I argue that the 'glory' of YHWH that leaves the temple and then returns is precisely the equivalent of the 'bodily' presence of YHWH among His people even in marriage. In chapter 1, YHWH does appear in a sort of bodily form. Moreover, Ezekiel's presence in his מופת-embodiment of YHWH is further proof of YHWH's 'bodily' presence. Ezekiel's marital status is equivalent to YHWH's marital status with Israel.

12 However, a different form of YHWH's presence with the exiles could be understood in the expression of Ezek 11, the מִקְדָּשׁ מְעַט. See further for more discussion on this topic.

13 The term is used here with the sense of 'reproducing' and not of 'making a parody of,' nor in the full sense of mimetic prophecy. See Joseph Blenkinsopp, *Ezekiel*, Interpretation (Louisville, KY: John Knox Press, 1990); Carolyn J. Sharp, *Irony and Meaning in the Hebrew Bible* (Bloomington, IN: Indiana University Press, 2009), 125; see also David Stacey, *Prophetic Drama in the Old Testament* (London: Epworth, 1990).

14 The expression "Street Theatre" as used of Ezekiel goes back to the research of Bernhard Lang, *Ezechiel: Der Prophet und das Buch*, ErFor 153 (Darmstadt: Wissenschaftliche Buchgesellschaft, 1981); Bernhard Lang, "Street Theater: Raising the Dead and the Zoroastrian Connection in Ezekiel's Prophecy," in *Ezekiel and his Book. Textual and Literary Criticism and their Interrelation*, ed. J. Lust, BETL 74 (Leuven: Leuven University Press, 1986), 297–316; see also Victor H. Matthews, *Social World of the Hebrew Prophets* (Peabody, MA: Hendrickson, 2001), 135.

line, Olley states that the "Lord does not leave the sign for Ezekiel to work out; as with previous sign-acts (4:1–17; 5:1–4, 11–17) its meaning is given to him. [...] What Ezekiel is doing is Lord's sign of what is going to happen to the house of Israel."[15] The narrative of Ezekiel's sign-acts sees their purpose in anticipating, with visual performances, the coming experiences of the house of Israel.

3 Ezekiel 24: The Prophet's Loss

The pericope of ch. 24 is divided into two large sections describing the dramatic event of the loss (vv. 15–19), and the uncommon behaviour of the prophet (vv. 20–24).[16] It opens with an announcement of YHWH's intention to take (לקח) the life of Ezekiel's wife (לֹקֵחַ מִמְּךָ אֶת־מַחְמַד עֵינֶיךָ בְּמַגֵּפָה). The statement is very drastic, and the lexical choice makes the scene even more effective. The narrative uses מגפה, often glossed as 'plague,' 'epidemic,' 'torment,' 'pestilence,' 'stroke,' and even 'blow', to indicate the cause of Ezekiel's wife's death. Zimmerli notes that the term is used in the Hebrew Bible to refer to divine anger or judgment, and battles, often of a sudden character.[17] Block argues that the narrative suggests a sudden death that leaves the prophet unprepared before an act that sees "Yahweh as the agent of death."[18]

The LXX uses παρατάξει to render מגפה, thus indicating a sort of 'battle array' and suggesting a violent act or an unexpected blow of a sudden character and devastating effect. The rendering of some translations with 'pestilence' follows the general understanding of the term as to indicate a 'plague' or 'epidemic' or a sort of deadly sickness.[19] I argue that it is difficult, if not impossible, to infer the

---

15 John W. Olley, *Ezekiel, A Commentary based on Iezekiēl in Codex Vaticanus* (Leiden and Boston, MA: Brill, 2009), 301–308.
16 Block divides this into four sections: 1. The command to perform a sign-act (vv. 16, 17); 2. The report about it (v. 18); 3. The request for explanation (v. 19); 4. The interpretation of the sign-act (vv. 20–24). See Block, *Ezekiel 1–24*, 787.
17 Zimmerli, *Ezekiel 1*, 505, "a disastrous battle (1 Sam 4:17; 2 Sam 18:7) [...] divine anger in a long lasting plague (2 Sam 24:21, 25) but also, especially in the priestly language, the fatal blow of divine judgment (Nu 14:37, cf. 17:13–15; 25:8f, 18f; 31:16, also Ps 106:29f). Thus Yahweh removes Ezekiel's wife by her sudden death, which completely overwhelms the prophet."
18 Block, *Ezekiel 1–24*, 788.
19 Block, *Ezekiel 1–24*, 788, "[...] that he was not alone in 597, but was deported with his wife. His wife died suddenly and unexpectedly, not 'old and full of years' (Gen 25:8), roughly ten years after the deportation and shortly before the fall of Jerusalem at the time of the renewed siege"; Zimmerli, *Ezekiel 1*, 506; "Since the prophet was thirty years old at the time of his call, his wife may have accompanied him to Babylon five years earlier (1:2)."

cause of death and, with Joyce, I hold the view that מגפה mainly "conveys of divine agency."[20] As there is no explicit knowledge of the cause of death of the woman, it remains unclear if what YHWH does may be considered as an act of violence, a sort of 'femicide,' or merely a 'prophetic anticipation' of her natural death, happening precisely at that moment. The phrase "Son of man behold, I am taking from you the delight of your eyes" (v. 16) suggests a direct involvement of YHWH in the death of Ezekiel's wife, but the extent of such involvement may not be assessed.[21]

The use of the term מַחְמַד to describe Ezekiel's wife as, literally, the 'passion' or 'delight' of his eyes, precious, pleasant, and greatly beloved, serves to highlight the great affection of the people for the temple and the city.[22] The lexeme comes from the verbal root חמד used, for example, to indicate the prohibition of coveting the woman of another in Exodus 20:17, within the conceptual framework of the Ten Commandments. Considering a shared usage in the Hebrew Bible, this lexical choice accentuates the strong relationship of Ezekiel with his wife as the object of his greatest affection and desire. Schumpp[23] and Zimmerli,[24] among others, consider the phrase a simple expression of a happy marriage. This is evidenced by Block's definition of the marriage of Ezekiel as simply a "felicitous marital relationship."[25] I argue that these opinions weaken the metaphorical language and, therefore, the efficacy of the symbolic action. On the contrary, the strength

---

20 Joyce, *Ezekiel*, 167, "the phrase conveys divine agency and should not be made the basis for any speculation about the medical cause of death."

21 Several questions may be raised about YHWH's justice and the 'moral behaviour' in this regard. Would there not be a 'better' way to portray the destruction of the city than the death of Ezekiel's wife? Is the woman 'guilty' of anything that makes her worthy of death? Or, is the objectification of a woman an act of 'divine election' or merely a choice of a 'device' of a lesser value useful to divine purposes? Which form of divine agency may be involved?

22 In her book, Stiebert writes that "Ezekiel's unnamed wife is mentioned just once in the Old Testament, in Ezekiel 24:15–18 [...] Ezekiel and his wife were in exile together. We are told, too, that she was her husband's delight, that she died, and that Ezekiel is divinely instructed not to mourn for her [...] Ezekiel's (lack of!) response to his wife's demise puzzles the people of his community. Consequently, they conclude that it must have a wider significance, beyond Ezekiel's personal life." Stiebert attempts to reconstruct the feelings and experiences of Ezekiel's wife with the purpose of shedding light on the character of the husband, Ezekiel, and of the situation of women in exile. Stiebert provides interpretative insights into the socio-historical and religious situation of the exile, but dismisses the symbolic actions of Ezekiel as improbable, calling them merely symbolic instructions. See Johanna Stiebert, *The Exile and the Prophet's Wife: Historic Events and Marginal Perspectives* (Collegeville, MN: Liturgical Press, 2005), XIV.

23 Meinrad Schumpp, *Das Buch Ezechiel übersetzt und erklärt* (Freiburg: Herder, 1942), ref. Ezek 24:16.

24 Zimmerli, *Ezekiel 1*, 505.

25 Block, *Ezekiel 1–24*, 788.

of Ezekiel's symbolic behaviour rests on the sentimental implications of this marriage. Only in this case, it can rightly point to the bond of the people with the temple, and of YHWH with Israel.

4 Ezekiel's Uncommon Bereavement

The narrative reveals some questionable elements that turn out to be morally controversial: YHWH seems to be the agent of the death of Ezekiel's wife; he prohibits any form of externalization and pain processing, thus imposing an unusual behaviour on the prophet. All those common reactions to the painful demise of a dear one are forbidden here, as emphasised with וְלֹא, "and not" in verse 16. The prophet receives precise details about what he must (not) do. YHWH commands him to react to the death of his wife in a way contrary to the common course of action in the case of mourning a death.[26] He should not mourn (וְלֹא תִסְפֹּד), cry (וְלֹא תִבְכֶּה) or shed any tears (וְלוֹא תָבוֹא דִּמְעָתֶךָ). These three prohibitions tend to suffocate every instinct to express suffering or give space to any physiological and emotional reaction.[27] It would be desirable in Ezekiel's situation to express his emotions as a way of venting pain. The social context would have expected such behaviour; this makes more relevant the semantic characteristics of 'wonder' linked to the term מוֹפֵת for this symbolic behaviour. The uncommon behaviour of the prophet provokes and disturbs common sense. While irritating and amazing at the same time, it urges its audience to think over its meaning. This falls perfectly within the semantic boundaries of the lexeme מוֹפֵת as implied in other contexts of the Hebrew Bible, mainly when YHWH performs wonders.[28]

Ezekiel should also groan in deathly stiffness (הֵאָנֵק דֹּם מֵתִים), make no lamentation (אֵבֶל לֹא־תַעֲשֶׂה), bind a turban about himself (פְּאֵרְךָ חֲבוֹשׁ עָלֶיךָ), put shoes on (וּנְעָלֶיךָ תָּשִׂים בְּרַגְלֶיךָ), not cover the upper lip (וְלֹא תַעְטֶה עַל־שָׂפָם), and not eat the 'bread of lamentation' (וְלֶחֶם אֲנָשִׁים לֹא תֹאכֵל).[29] All these indications cancel any traditional form of managing pain and, in the words of Joyce, "Ezekiel is denied the customary rites of mourning."[30] Ezekiel may express his pain only silently

---

26 For further study on the ancient customs of death, see Zimmerli, *Ezekiel 1*, 506.
27 Zimmerli discusses the psychological component of the event, see Zimmerli, *Ezekiel 1*, 507.
28 Here are a few examples: Exodus 4:21; 7:3, 9; 11:9–10; Psalm 78:43; 105:5.
29 For further study on mourning rites and the use of the specific Hebrew terminology in the text, see Block, *Ezekiel 1–24*, 789.
30 Joyce, *Ezekiel*, 167.

and imperceptibly,[31] or in a close circle, mourning to one another, as verse 23 seems to suggest (וּנְהַמְתֶּם אִישׁ אֶל־אָחִיו).

The emotional character of the scene, so crucial for the effectiveness of the symbolic behaviour imposed on the prophet, sees Ezekiel embodying YHWH's relationship and feelings for Israel. At the same time, the prophet claims and manifests YHWH's presence in the experience of the exiles. Ezekiel's symbolic function points beyond himself to YHWH himself, as well as beyond the people; "their embodied existence testified to the reality of Yhwh as sovereign."[32]

Pain processing is prevented, and the sorrow following the event of death is here anticipated by YHWH's announcement to the prophet. Lipton sees mourning (in 24:15–27) as a form of petition preceding the event to divert or prevent YHWH's judgment.[33] This creative approach may have the advantage of cohering with the prophetic behaviour of Ezekiel in other passages of the book. In Ezek 3:24–26, the prophet is indeed secluded at home, deprived of his speech and commanded to restrict himself. In this train of thoughts, Wilson sees the dumbness[34] motif as a denial of the intercessory role of the prophet.[35] The behaviour of Ezekiel is bound to what the symbolic action wants to transmit, and his 'performance' is a clear replacement of verbal communication, a different and perhaps more effective means to express YHWH's oracles to the rebellious house of Israel unable to see and hear. Ezekiel's multi-faceted role in the drama is revealed through the symbolic actions he is commanded to perform. He is a prescriptive model to be copied, an example to imitate, and a visual message. Most of all, he is a paradigm for the house of Israel because what he is correlates closely with the meaning of what he does.[36] The self-understanding of Ezekiel is not a private

---

31 For psychoanalytical studies about Ezekiel's failure to mourn his wife's death, see David J. Halperin, *Seeking Ezekiel: Text and Psychology* (University Park, PA: Pennsylvania State University Press, 1993), 180–181; George Stein, "The voices that Ezekiel hears," *BJPsych* 196 (2010): 101.

32 Launderville, *Spirit and Reason*, 2.

33 Diana Lipton, "Early Mourning? Petitionary versus Posthumous Ritual in Ezekiel XXIV," *VT* 56 (2006): 185–202.

34 See also Moshe Greenberg, "On Ezekiel's Dumbness," *JBL* 77.2 (1958): 101–105.

35 Robert R. Wilson, "An Interpretation of Ezekiel's Dumbness," *VT* 22 (1972): 91–104.

36 For further studies on the question of Ezekiel as a model and paradigm, see Sheldon H. Blank, "Prophet as Paradigm," in *Essays in Old Testament Ethics, J. Philip Hyatt in memoriam*, ed. James L. Crenshaw and John T. Willis (New York, NY: Ktav, 1974), 111–130; Ellen F. Davis, *Swallowing the Scroll: Textuality and the Dynamics of Discourse in Ezekiel's Prophecy*, JSOTSup 78 / Bible and Literature Series 21 (Sheffield: Sheffield Academic Press, 1989), 83–84; Margaret S. Odell, "Genre and Persona in Ezekiel 24:15–24," in *The Book of Ezekiel: Theological and Anthropological Perspectives*, ed. Margaret S. Odell and John T. Strong, SBLSymS 9 (Atlanta, GA: SBL Press, 2000), 208 (though she rightly points out that 'Ezekiel is more than a moral exemplar'); Jacqueline Lapsley, *Can These Bones Live? The Problem of the Moral Self in the Book of Ezekiel*, BZAW 301 (Berlin:

one. In both cases in which מופת is used in reference to the prophet in chapters 12 and 24, Ezekiel is made a public מופת for the house of Israel, and he should recognize himself as such; he assumes a מופת identity.

5 Ezekiel's מופת Identity

The narrative of ch. 24:24–27 is a detailed testimony of how Ezekiel complied fully with YHWH's command. After the death of his wife, whenever that happened,[37] Ezekiel puts into action YHWH's instructions regarding how (not) to express the loss. The unusual behaviour serves the purpose of provoking the people, amazing them and pushing them to reflect on its meaning. Therefore, the request of the people is "Will you not tell us what these things that you do mean for us?" (24:19; הֲלֹא תַגִּיד לָנוּ מָה־אֵלֶּה לָנוּ כִּי אַתָּה עֹשֶׂה). The people ask Ezekiel to explain, declare what they should learn from what seems to be a symbolic attitude. Therefore Allen argues that the people "recognize the prophetic nature of the absence of mourning rites but not yet its significance."[38] Their question reflects the primary purpose of every symbolic action in Ezekiel, leading to reflection,[39] and indicates the recipient of such actions, the people ("for us", לנו). The question could be intended only as a rhetorical one, but this is unclear. It may be understood as a *prudens interrogatio dimidium scientiae*, a request done while already perceiving part of the meaning of what the symbolic action may mean. The question may suggest that the people anticipated a connection between the experience of the prophet and the fate of the city. This is also evident in the detailed 'prophecy' that Ezekiel

---

de Gruyter, 2000), 116–117; Nicholas J. Tromp, "The Paradox of Ezekiel's Prophetic Mission: Towards a Semiotic Approach of Ezekiel 3,22–27," in Lust (ed.), *Ezekiel and his Book*, 201–213.

37 Various scholars propose different solutions to the unclear timing of all the events related to the death of Ezekiel's wife (starting from v. 18). It may be worth noticing that if YHWH had communicated to Ezekiel his intention to take the life of his wife that same day, only a few hours could have passed between the announcement and the death. Ezekiel would have been thrown into a state of pain without even the time to process the loss. Even though there is uncertain whether the prophet's wife dies the same day he speaks to the people or the following day after the divine announcement, and uncertain is also the moment when Ezekiel acts on the instructions of YHWH, nevertheless, the interpretation of the symbolic action is here not affected at its core by the different options. See also Block, *Ezekiel 1–24*, 790.

38 Leslie C. Allen, *Ezekiel 20–48*, WBC 29 (Dallas, TX: Word, 1990), 61.

39 For example: "Son of man, has not the rebellious house of Israel asked you, 'What are you doing?'" (Ezek 12:9); "Now say to this rebellious house: 'Do you not know what these things mean?'" (Ezek 17:12); "When your people ask you, 'Will you not explain to us what you mean by these?'" (Ezek 37:18).

presents to the people. Ezekiel's behaviour is an oracle against the city of Jerusalem and the temple. The divine embodied character of Ezekiel's symbolic actions is implied while the people perceive that Ezekiel translates YHWH's oracle into a visual message with a bearing on his personal life.

The metaphorical language of this story becomes clear when Ezekiel's wife is understood as pointing to the city of Jerusalem; her death represents the profanation of the sanctuary and the destruction of the city; the love of Ezekiel towards her represents the love of the people for the temple; the woman's sudden death reflects the massacre of the people. Also, the lack of expression of emotion on the part of the prophet indicates the attitude Israel should have while facing the tragedy.

The phrase "you will do as I have done," reported in 24:22, highlights the demonstrative and exemplary character of Ezekiel's actions. The behaviour of the prophet serves as a 'standard' of reference for all those who pass through a similar experience when the city and the temple are destroyed. The prophet, being the מופת of YHWH, is placed in a position where his life becomes an observable and communicative sign. Ezekiel takes on a new persona, a מופת identity. His symbolic action is visible announcement, communicative example, and anticipation of the future.

At the same time, Ezekiel's embodied existence points to YHWH's presence because the prophet is the way in which YHWH's relationship with Israel is visualized. Even after the departure of the כבוד, and the apparent turning away of YHWH, represented by the permission of profaning the temple, Ezekiel's ministry as מופת made YHWH's presence tangible. In this sense, the profoundly paradoxical message of YHWH's promise of his presence as a מְקְדָּשׁ מְעַט (11:16) inevitably points to some form of divine presence among the exiles in a way different than in a building. Ezekiel himself may then be seen as a way in which YHWH became the מְקְדָּשׁ מְעַט for the house of Israel. Ezekiel is a form of special theophany, a substitute for YHWH's presence, and a demonstration of YHWH's intervention in human life. Ezekiel's מופת identity, through his symbolic actions and behaviour, points to a temporary relocation of YHWH's presence. Consequently, if Ezekiel is a sign and manifestation of YHWH's intervention in the life of Israel, then his ministry is a form of YHWH's מְקְדָּשׁ מְעַט presence.[40] Therefore, the prophet's experience in losing his wife becomes a crucial element to visualize the relationship of YHWH with Israel and his presence.[41] The sorrowful experience of Ezekiel,

---

40 For a comprehensive discussion on Ezekiel's relation to the question of the מְקְדָּשׁ מְעַט see Salemi, "Is Ezekiel a מְקְדָּשׁ מְעַט?" in idem, *A Linguistic-Theological Exegesis of Ezekiel as* Môphēt.
41 In line with the concept of Ezekiel visualizing YHWH's presence and glory, one might compare the way in which the physical face of Moses shone when he was speaking the law to the

unable to follow the usual rites associated with death, becomes the way Israel may encounter YHWH and process pain and judgment.

6 Female Objectification?

The death of Ezekiel's wife plays a pivotal role in the experience of the exilic community within the theology of the book of Ezekiel. In a way, she constitutes a metaphorical element of a traumatic narrative. Can she be considered divinely elected to die as a way of representing the fate of Israel? She is undoubtedly essential to the bizarre sign-act of Ezekiel. However, as previously discussed, there is no way of understanding which role YHWH plays in the death of the woman. Does he only anticipate a natural death, bizarrely coincident with the tragedy of the city of Jerusalem? Or, does he purposely cause her death? Whether we look at it in one way or another, directly or indirectly, she becomes the object of a story and of a sign act, or sign behaviour.

Not much may be said about her and nothing else is recorded on her life. The circumstances of her death remain obscure; therefore, YHWH may not be accused of 'femicide'. Approaching her story from the metaphoric perspective is what, so far, has de facto been the case. At the same time, the tragic experience of Ezekiel has been here portrayed as a sort of mimic of the experience of Israel with the city and the temple, and of YHWH with Israel as the delight of his eyes.

In this case, while Ezekiel's wife's death represents the experience of the destruction, the symbolic actions and behaviours of Ezekiel represent the new identity of the exiles. Odell argues that the focus of the narrative of 24:15–24 is on the transformation of the exiles, because "Ezekiel's actions provide a model for their own response to the destruction of Jerusalem."[42] Such a response is not, in the words of Odell, the result of an 'emotional paralysis' but rather "a paradoxical acceptance of their new status as the elect of God."[43] Ezekiel plays the role both of a symbolic representative of YHWH and of the people through his personal embodied experience. The role of his wife, as a symbolic image of the fate of Israel, is a pedagogical tool to prepare the people to face and accept the drama of Jerusalem, specifically of the temple, devoid of any concrete form of consolation.

The impotence in the face of this drama, well represented by Ezekiel's mutism, is furthermore marked by the abstention from all forms of sorrow and by

---

people in Exodus – perhaps an echo (or mirroring) of the 'terrifying' glory of YHWH himself manifesting on the top of the mountain.

42 Odell, "Genre and Persona in Ezekiel 24:25–24," 206.

43 Odell, "Genre and Persona in Ezekiel 24:25–24," 206.

the covered mouth. Odell argues that "Ezekiel is not only enacting the prophetic word, he is taking on a new significance as a model for the future."[44] In this sense, Ezekiel is a human sign, an embodiment or 'personification' of YHWH's presence, and a testimony of his power. Ezekiel, through his symbolic behaviour, is a 'living metaphor' as his wife is a 'death metaphor'. Both of them make visual what cannot be perceived yet. Odell asserts that "Ezekiel is more than a moral exemplar. He is the manifestation of divine reality in the lives of the exiles."[45] The relationship between Ezekiel and his wife symbolises the connection between the people and the temple, while also portraying the relationship between YHWH and his people.[46]

Ezekiel lives, feels, and acts anticipating, with his symbolic behaviour, the experience of the people in their loss of the temple and the city. At the same time, he assumes in his human existence the divine experience; thus, his experience becomes representative of that of YHWH. His pain serves to represent the bereavement of YHWH for the loss of the people.[47] I consider it essential to highlight that the sorrowful event may be seen as a paradoxical representation of YHWH's form of revelation of his own being. In this, I agree with Zimmerli's concept that somehow there is a parallel between the death of Ezekiel's wife and YHWH as the object of scorn in the eyes of the world.[48] The comparison may be extended to the point of understanding the silence of the prophet in parallel to the apparent absence of YHWH represented by the departing of the כבוד. There-

---

44 Odell, "Genre and Persona in Ezekiel 24:25–24," 207.

45 Odell, "Genre and Persona in Ezekiel 24:25–24," 208.

46 It is not unusual in the Hebrew Bible that YHWH refers to the people of Israel, or Jerusalem, as to his bride. See also Isaiah 54:1–15; 62:1–5. This seems implicit also in the metaphorical narrative of Ezekiel 16, where a symbolic history of Israel is described as a relationship between YHWH and an unfaithful woman. Hosea is also a prophet who vividly enacted YHWH's emotional marriage with His people.

47 Zimmerli, *Ezekiel 1*, 509, "This shows how remorselessly God's judgment must destroy and cannot even be held back before the holy ones, to whom rightly the most costly aspects of the love of the people of God belong (v 21). Because God acts in this way, he sets his own honor at stake in the judgment, and himself becomes an object of scorn and contempt in the eyes of the world. Into what depth of foolishness does God's judgement lead, where men regard it with their own cleverness! In his judgement does God not put himself to death in the eyes of the world? Yet even so the prophet holds unswervingly that in such an event God reveals himself to his world in the truth of his own being."

48 Zimmerli does not expand on this point. Perhaps, among different arguments, three senses may be implied here: (1) the scorn that YHWH might receive as the one responsible for causing the death of Ezekiel's wife; (2) the scorn that YHWH might receive as one like Ezekiel who does not even outwardly show grief for the loss of His people; (3) the scorn that YHWH might receive as the one bringing judgment upon Israel.

fore, Ezekiel does not only perform the function of a 'predictive' and visual demonstration of what will happen to the city. He also plays the role of a 'divine mime' embodying various emotions and replicating before the people the experience of YHWH's sorrow and grief.

In this train of thoughts, one certainly cannot avoid thinking about how a woman's death can serve to show divine feelings, or to be the 'place' for YHWH's self-disclosure, or how the traumatic experience of a woman's death can be a solution or 'cure' for the traumas of exile. The loss of Ezekiel's wife has paradoxically the function of preparing the people for the coming exile, and therefore – in some way – it serves to pre-process mourning and pain.

7 Conclusion

The story of Ezekiel's wife's death in chapter 24 provides a form of managing trauma, a sort of 'analgesic' solution.[49] Ezekiel mimics what YHWH lives. In this way, the prophet creates – where YHWH is apparently perceived as absent – an alternative form of presence. YHWH has not abandoned Israel. Conversely, he shares with them the experience of the destruction and the exile. He loves them as Ezekiel loves his wife. As YHWH is thus included in the experience of the exile, Ezekiel is the locus for YHWH's self-revelation.

While YHWH declares the imminent calamity to Ezekiel, he makes of his wife the most vivid representation of the incoming tragedy. Through King Nebuchadnezzar, YHWH would express his judgment against the people, the city, and the temple. YHWH's message, through Ezekiel's harsh personal experience, turns out to be a prophetic word.[50] The call to observe him and his actions in verse 16, הִנְנִי (הִנֵּה), underscores the theme of YHWH's self-revelation through the prophet and through his wife's death, while also ironically and paradoxically emphasizing the people's disbelief in the potential destruction of the Jerusalem temple by the Babylonian army. The temple's grandeur[51] provided a feeling of safety and was

---

49 See Ruth Poser, *Das Ezechielbuch als Trauma-Literatur*, VTSup 154 (Leiden and Boston, MA: Brill, 2012); Ruth Poser, "No Words: The Book of Ezekiel as Trauma Literature and a Response to Exile," in *Bible through the Lens of Trauma*, ed. Elizabeth Boase, and Christopher G. Frechette (Atlanta, GA: SBL, 2017), 27–48.
50 In the Targum (Ezek 24:15, 20), the reference is to a "word of prophecy from before the Lord," וַהֲוָה פִּתְגָּם נְבוּאָה מִן קֳדָם יְיָ עִמִּי לְמֵימָר.
51 For further study on the temple in Ezekiel, see Madhavi Nevader, *Exile and Institution: Monarchy in the Books of Deuteronomy and Ezekiel* (PhD diss., University of Oxford, 2008), 186–190.

cherished as a "glorious symbol of Israelite pride and identity."[52] It was a structure they admired as the joy of their eyes[53] and the desire of their hearts, leading them to view the city as secure, believing that no god would allow harm to his magnificent temple.

The symbolic behaviour of Ezekiel is a way to make the message tangible and sure.[54] His wife's death is the most drastic expression of YHWH's message and it ironically points to the end of the afflicting experience of Ezekiel's intermittent dumbness. The symbolic behaviour, initially a token of judgment, becomes paradoxically a token of mercy[55] and a revelation of YHWH. The death of the woman points to the opening of a new era, which is also marked by the removal of the dumbness of the prophet.[56] The extremely high price that Ezekiel has to

---

52 Block, *Ezekiel 1–24*, 792.

53 Lyons affirms that the use of this specific terminology here is merely the result of Ezekiel's technique of addition by the creation of word pairs. After several examples, he comments that Lev 26 is the source text for the borrowed locution, as follows: "As a final example of the creation of word pairs, we may note Ezekiel's transformation of the locution 'pride of your strength' (Lev. 26:19) into a series of paired phrases functioning as verbal objects in Ezekiel 24:21: 'sanctuary, pride of your strength ... desire of your eyes, longing of your soul,'" Michael A. Lyons, *From Law to Prophecy, Ezekiel's Use of the Holiness Code*, LHBOTS 508 (New York, NY and London: T&T Clark, 2009), 91. Nevader writes, "[...] a shared word should not necessarily be ground for presuming knowledge or use of a tradition," Madhavi Nevader, "Creating a *Deus non Creator:* Divine Sovereignty and Creation in Ezekiel," in *The God Ezekiel Creates*, ed. Paul M. Joyce, and Dalit Rom-Shiloni (London and New York, NY: Bloomsbury T&T Clark, 2016), 61 (see also 55–70). Therefore, I argue that the importance of the narrative function of this literal construction outshines the value of the analysis of literary techniques and possible sources. The focus is on Ezekiel in his role as a sign revealing the punitive judgment of YHWH and, at the same time, as the means for the people to understand that YHWH does not tolerate a behaviour contrary to his divine will indefinitely.

54 For a discussion on disagreements and controversies regarding the idea of the symbolic action as a 'prophecy after the fact,' see Ralph W. Klein, *Ezekiel: The Prophet and His Message*, Studies on the Personalities of the Old Testament (Columbia, SC: University of South Carolina Press, 1988), 47–48.

55 Te Stroete argues that the turning point from the catastrophic experience in which the exiles are prevented from mourning, is the idea of the transformation of the messenger of doom, who has managed to escape from the city, into a messenger of a new era of joy. Gerard te Stroete, "Ezekiel 24:15–27: The Meaning of a Symbolic Act," *Bijdragen: Tijdschrift voor Filosofie en Theologie* 38 (1977): 163–175; Joyce disagrees with a dismissal of the importance of the therapeutic nature of appropriate mourning because the non-mourning motif functions by conveying that the message of punishment is warranted and the refusal of proper mourning makes the trauma even harder to bear (Joyce, *Ezekiel: A Commentary*, 168).

56 For further discussion about the two versions of the removal of the dumbness in ch. 24 and 33, see Allen, *Ezekiel 20–48*, 61–62; see also Block, *Ezekiel 1–24*, 796, "the freeing of his mouth would open up the possibility of a new genre of message."

pay in bearing in his body the message he is called to proclaim is accompanied by the assurance that this will lead to a new relationship between YHWH and his people. This relationship will be based on new knowledge of him as evidenced by the ending of chapter 24 with the words "and they will know that I am YHWH." Thus, the death of Ezekiel's wife serves as a metaphor for Israel's destiny, encompassing both negative and positive aspects, but also mimicks their experience along with that of YHWH. It represents a deeply intricate embodied experience, where YHWH manifests himself in the prophet's life and humanity reflects the divine presence.[57]

---

57 See Stephen L. Herring, *Divine Substitution: Humanity as the Manifestation of Deity in the Hebrew Bible and the Ancient Near East*, FRLANT 247 (Göttingen: Vandenhoeck & Ruprecht, 2013).

Marvin A. Sweeney
Misogyny or Sign-act? Ezekiel's Embodiment of YHWH in Ezekiel 24

1 Introduction

Ezekiel's refusal to mourn for his dead wife in Ezekiel 24:15–27 troubles interpreters, who see gross insensitivity on the part of the prophet. Many see his refusal – as well as other actions and statements by the prophet – as an indication of his misogyny.[1] The prophet's failure to mourn for his wife demonstrates interpreters' failure to understand and account for Ezekiel's identity as a Zadokite priest. Scholarship on Ezekiel's remains heavily influenced by the 1924 monograph of Gustav Hölscher, who viewed Ezekiel solely as a prophet and stripped away much of the book as the product of later redaction designed to reconfigure him as a priest.[2] Hölscher's presuppositions about Ezekiel were based in his own Protestant theological identity, which followed earlier 19th century scholarship in holding up prophetic identity as the ideal means of relation to G-d rather than the priestly identity allegedly valued by Judaism and the Roman Catholic Church. But more recent scholarship affirms Ezekiel's identity as a Zadokite priest, who nevertheless is not ordained for service in the Jerusalem Temple due to his exile to Babylonia in 597 B.C.E. Facing a life in exile from the Jerusalem Temple, particularly after its destruction by Babylon in 587/586 B.C.E., Ezekiel would have been compelled to rethink his identity as a priest who would serve as a visionary prophet of YHWH in Babylonia.[3] Insofar as priests were forbidden to come into contact with the dead – unless they were blood relatives – Ezekiel could not mourn for his wife (Ezekiel 24:15–27), which would entail contact with her corpse at burial (Lev 21:1–4). Instead, he drew upon his identity as priest to devise an alternative to represent or embody YHWH, in this case as a sign-act that would depict his inability to mourn for his wife as symbolic of YHWH's refusal to mourn for Jerusalem.

---

1 E.g., David J. Halperin, *Seeking Ezekiel: Text and Psychology* (University Park, Pennsylvania; Penn State University Press, 1993), 177–183, esp. 181.
2 Gustav Hölscher, *Hesekiel. Der Dichter und das Buch. Eine literarkritische Untersuchung* (Giessen: Alfred Töpelmann, 1924), esp. 128–131.
3 E.g., Marvin A. Sweeney, "Ezekiel: Zadokite Priest and Visionary Prophet of the Exile," *Form and Intertextuality in Prophetic and Apocalyptic Literature*, FAT 45 (Tübingen: Mohr Siebeck, 2005), 125–143.

https://doi.org/10.1515/9783111521015-010

2 The Work of Gustav Hölscher

Hölscher's treatment of Ezekiel 24:15–27 is based on the fundamental dichotomy between poetry and prose that informs his overall treatment of the entire book of Ezekiel. In Hölscher's view, poetic expression emerged from the universalist human spirit that would give expression to monotheistic divine presence and the universal impulse toward ethical thought and action that characterized both the divine and the ideal human order. Apparently, World War I had not yet prompted Hölscher to rethink such ideals in relation to the breakdown of political order that led to World War I and the wholesale slaughter that ensued due to the use of modern weapons of war, such as the machine gun and mustard gas, to gun down infantry formations that were still based on Napoleonic principles of massed fire power and assault. World War II, which invoked racial privilege together with modern (including nuclear) weaponry to take mass slaughter to even higher and more outrageous levels, often against civilian populations, had not yet been realized to drive the point home.

Hölscher's division between poetry and prose viewed poetry as an expression of universal and enlightened ethical monotheism, whereas prose represented the work of reactionary, legalistic (Jewish) scribes, who understood neither the spirit of the divine nor the esthetic beauty of art, literature, or ethics.[4] Rather, the redactors were interested in "Judaizing" the poetic expression of Ezekiel to turn him into a priest, who would value particularistic, legalistic, and ritualistic Jewish notions of meaningless law, ritual, and Temple structure and service. Hölscher reads the poetry in Ezekiel 24:16–17, which focused on Ezekiel's loss of his wife, expressed in the poetry as "the delight of your eyes," Hebrew, *maḥmad ʿênêkā*, whom YHWH instructed him not to mourn, as a reference to his wife and family. This is well and good in itself, but Hölscher then argues that the poetry expresses no symbolic action, insofar as it lacks any reference to the statement as a "proverb," Hebrew, *māšāl*, or a "sign," Hebrew, *môpēt*. Instead, the unnamed (Jewish) redactor shifted the interpretation of the poetic instruction in his "midrash" on the poetry in Ezekiel 24:18–27 to a command not to mourn the destruction of the Jerusalem Temple. Such a move was – in Hölscher's understanding – not a true prophetic symbolic action; rather, it was a scribal interpretation, intended to transform the universalistic spirit of the prophet, Ezekiel, to the legalistic, ritualis-

---

4 For background on theological anti-Semitism, see, e.g., Alan T. Davies, *Anti-Semitism and the Christian Mind: The Crisis of Conscience after Auschwitz* (New York: Herder and Herder, 1969); Paul Lawrence Rose, *Revolutionary Antisemitism in Germany: From Kant to Wagner* (Princeton: Princeton University Press, 1990); Thomas Kaufmann, *Luther's Jews: A Journey into Anti-Semitism* (Oxford: Oxford University Press, 2017).

tic, and particularistic view of the Jewish priesthood. This view is rooted in the outlook of the New Testament, which in many of its writings views Jesus as a messianic prophet of G-d who opposes the legalistic, ritualistic, and particularistic Jewish Temple in Jerusalem as contrary to the will of G-d. The view was later mobilized in the Protestant critique of the Roman Catholic Church.

But Hölscher's universalist, Protestant world view prompted him to miss the significance of this passage. Ezekiel indeed appears in the Book of Ezekiel both as a visionary prophet of YHWH and as a Zadokite priest of the Jerusalem Temple, who was compelled to serve as the former after his exile to Babylonia in 597 B.C.E. but was prevented from serving as the latter.[5] According to the introduction for the book in Ezekiel 1:1–3, Ezekiel was born in 622 B.C.E. at the outset of King Josiah's reforms during the eighteenth year of his reign in which he sought to purify the Jerusalem Temple and reinstate it as the holy center of a revived Davidic empire that would comprise both the southern kingdom of Judah and the former northern kingdom of Israel in the anticipated aftermath of Assyrian collapse.[6] The enterprise failed, of course, when Pharaoh Necho of Egypt killed Josiah in battle at Megiddo while attempting to come to the aid of his Assyrian allies.[7] Josiah succeeded in delaying the Egyptians long enough to ensure Assyria's defeat at the hands of the Babylonians, and the result was a twenty-two year decline of Judah that saw the first exile of Judeans – including Ezekiel – to be deported to Babylon in 597 B.C.E., a second exile following the destruction of Jerusalem and the Temple in 587–586 B.C.E., and a third exile and flight from Judah following the assassination of Gedaliah ben Ahikim ben Shaphah, the Babylonian-appointed Judean governor of Judah, during the course of a failed attempt at revolt in 582 B.C.E. As for Ezekiel, who grew up in the Temple during the course of Josiah's reforms only to be exiled during the course of Judah's decline, the ideal of a restored holy Temple surrounded by the restored twelve tribes of Israel continued to inform his world view and his visionary, prophetic career.

---

5 Sweeney, "Ezekiel: Zadokite Priest and Visionary Prophet of the Exile"; Marvin A. Sweeney, *Reading Ezekiel: A Literary and Theological Commentary*, Reading the Old Testament (Macon, GA: Smyth and Helwys, 2013), 1–21, 124–125.
6 Marvin A. Sweeney, "The Royal Oracle in Ezekiel 37:15–28: Ezekiel's Reflection on Josiah's Reform," *Reading Prophetic Books: Form, Intertextuality, and Reception in Prophetic and Post-Biblical Literature*, FAT 89 (Tübingen: Mohr Siebeck, 2014), 219–232.
7 For discussion of the historical background of Ezekiel, see Marvin A. Sweeney, "Ezekiel, Historical Background," *The Oxford Handbook on Ezekiel*, ed. Corrine Carvalho (Oxford and New York: Oxford University Press, 2020), online, hard copy forthcoming.

3 Ezekiel's Symbolic Action

Most modern interpreters have come to understand that Hölscher erred in distinguishing the poetic material in Ezekiel 24:16–17 as the work of a presumed non-priestly prophet, Ezekiel, and the prose material in Ezekiel 24:15, 18–27 as the work of a priestly or Jewish redactor who sought to transform Ezekiel from a universal prophet to a legalistic and ritualistic priest. They have likewise largely come to understand that the passage entails a symbolic prophetic action,[8] insofar as it calls upon Ezekiel to refrain from mourning for his dead wife as a symbol for YHWH's refusal to mourn for the now destroyed Jerusalem and the Jerusalem Temple.

But it is not clear that interpreters have come to understand the full dimensions of the symbolic prophetic action, particularly the role that Ezekiel's priestly identity plays in the conceptualization of the act. Many balk at Ezekiel's refusal to mourn for his wife, insofar as a marriage relationship is generally perceived as the closest and most intimate relationship that a human being can choose to enter. How could a man refuse to mourn for his dead – and unnamed – wife, who had shared her life with him and died, perhaps brutally, when her husband likely refused to abandon the Temple during the Babylonian siege and assault?

Some turn to a different argument, viz., that Ezekiel was a misogynist; indeed, such an argument is not hard to make.[9] Ezekiel is a difficult personality to understand. He is a man who has visions of YHWH coming to him borne through the sky by four creatures, later identified as cherubim, who bear YHWH's throne chariot, modelled on a combination of the Ark of the Covenant and the imagery of the Mesopotamian gods, Assur, flying through the heavens at the head of his armies, and Marduk, with his four faces representing his world-encompassing presence. He ingests the Torah scroll of YHWH, declares it to be delicious, and later embarks on a visionary journey from his home in Babylon to Jerusalem, where he digs through the north wall, in an action understood by some to entail sexual repression, decries the image that provokes jealousy that he sees in the

---

8 For discussion of prophetic symbolic actions and communication, see esp. Georg Fohrer, *Die symbolischen Handlungen der Propheten*, ATANT 54 (Zurich: Zwingli, 1953); W. D. Stacey, *Prophetic Drama in the Old Testament* (London: Epworth, 1990); Kelvin G. Friebel, *Jeremiah's and Ezekiel's Sign Acts: Rhetorical Non-Verbal Communication*, JSOTSup 28 (Sheffield: Sheffield Academic Press, 1999); Soo J. Kim Sweeney, "Communications in the Book of Ezekiel: From the Iron Wall to the Voice in the Air," *The Oxford Handbook of Ezekiel*, ed., Corrine Carvalho (Oxford: Oxford University Press, 2021), published online, hard copy forthcoming.

9 See Halperin, *Seeking Ezekiel*, 181; cf. Julie Galambush, *Jerusalem in the Book of Ezekiel: The City as YHWH's Wife*, SBLDS 130 (Atlanta: Scholars Press, 1992), esp. 140–142.

Temple compound, and proceeds to envision the throne-chariot of YHWH hovering over the city and disgorging a man in white linen and his seven armed accomplices, who range through Jerusalem marking the foreheads of those who would survive, i.e., men of the age of majority, and slaughtering the rest, i.e., old men, women, and children. He is also capable of envisioning YHWH as a child abuser and rapist, who picks up a naked Jerusalem in the wilderness as a child, feeds, clothes, and raises her to maturity, and then "marries" her, only to see her run off with other lovers for which YHWH then condemns and punishes her. It is not difficult to see the makings of a disturbed personality and a misogynist in these oracles. In contemporary American culture, such a man would most likely end up in prison for child abuse and rape.

But Ezekiel is not a contemporary American man, who shares the world view of most modern American interpreters of the Bible or even the world views of European, Asian, African, and other contemporary interpreters, many of whom are women. He is portrayed in the Book of Ezekiel as a Zadokite priest of the Jerusalem Temple who was born to his station in life.[10] The fact that his exile from Jerusalem to Babylonia in the aftermath of the failed revolt against Babylon by King Jehoiakim ben Josiah of Judah does not change that fact. Ezekiel is never ordained as a priest for service at the Jerusalem altar; instead, his thirtieth year, 592 B.C.E., five years after his exile, the year in which his ordination would have taken place, becomes the year of his visionary experience of the presence of YHWH in Babylonia, which inaugurates his career as a visionary prophet of YHWH, much on the model of Samuel in 1 Samuel 3. Ordination does not confer priestly status in ancient Judah or Israel; it only qualifies one born to priestly status for service in the Jerusalem Temple. One, such as Ezekiel, who is not ordained due to exile or other circumstances, still undergoes the education from birth through age thirty that defines his world view as a priest who expects to be ordained for service in the Temple.

As Ezekiel's visionary career demonstrates, a priestly world view informs his prophetic vocation and oracles. One may see such influence in the inaugural vision, based especially on the imagery of the Ark of the Covenant which had been placed in the Holy of Holies of the Jerusalem Temple in Ezekiel 1–7; Ezekiel's vision of the destruction of Jerusalem and the Temple, which is overseen by the man in white linen, the garment worn by priests for service in the Temple, in Ezekiel 8–11; in Ezekiel's role as the watchman of his people who is commissioned to instruct them concerning their obligations to YHWH just as a priest would do (Ezekiel 3; 33; Leviticus 10:10–11); the vison of the restored Temple as the holy

---

10 Sweeney, "Ezekiel: Zadokite Priest and Visionary Prophet"; Sweeney, *Reading Ezekiel.*

center of a new creation in Ezekiel 40–48; and the overall chronological overview of Ezekiel's twenty-year career, from the age of thirty in the fifth year of Jehoia-chin's exile in Ezekiel 1–7, to the age of fifty, the twenty-fifth year of the exile in Ezekiel 40–48, the very years in which a priest who serves at the altar is expected to serve according to Numbers 4:3, 23, 30.[11] Ezekiel is portrayed throughout the book of Ezekiel and within the accounts of his own visionary experience as a priest.

4 Jerusalem as YHWH's Wife

An overview of prophetic world view, particularly in relation to Ezekiel's symbol-ic portrayal of his relationship with his wife as a symbolic expression of YHWH's relationship with Jerusalem or Israel, demonstrates that that such portrayals of typical of ancient Israelite and Judean prophets, many of whom are also priests.[12] The depiction of Jerusalem or Israel as the bride of YHWH is a common motif in prophetic literature. But the particular portrayal of the symbolic significance of the death of Ezekiel's wife is characteristic of priestly thought and practice. The symbolic act of Ezekiel's refusal to mourn for his dead wife constitutes a combina-tion of both prophetic and priestly world view.

The earliest portrayal of Israel as YHWH's wife appears in the account of Hosea's marriage to Gomer bat Diblaim in Hosea 1–3.[13] Hosea, who is recognized as a northern Israelite prophet – but not a priest – of the eighth century B.C.E., relates instructions from YHWH to marry a woman of harlotry, who will repre-sent the northern kingdom of Israel, and to have three children with her, Jezreel, a boy, who will symbolize the birthplace of the dynasty of the House of Jehu in a revolt against the House of Omri, Lo-Ruhamah, a girl, whose name symbolizes YHWH's lack of mercy for the House of Jehu; and Lo-Ami, another boy, whose name symbolizes the break in the relationship between northern Israel and

---

11 Sweeney, *Reading Ezekiel*, 1–21; Tyler D. Mayfield, *Literary Structure and Setting in Ezekiel*, FAT 2/43; Tübingen: Mohr Siebeck, 2010).

12 For discussion of the motifs of Israel or Jerusalem as the bride of YHWH in the prophetic literature, see Gerline Baumann, *Love and Violence: Marriage as Metaphor for the Relationship between YHWH and Israel in the Prophetic Books* (Collegeville, MN: Liturgical, 2003); R. Abma, *Bonds of Love: Methodic Studies of Prophetic Texts with Marriage Imagery (Isaiah 50:1–3 and 54:1–10, Hosea 1–3, Jeremiah 2–3)*, Studia Semetica Neerlandica (Assen: Van Gorcum, 1999). See also Galambush, *Jerusalem*, 35–59.

13 See Marvin A. Sweeney, *The Twelve Prophets*, Berit Olam (Collegeville, MN: Liturgical, 2000), 1:13–40.

YHWH. Altogether, Hosea's sign act is based on his apparently deteriorating marriage and represents YHWH's dissatisfaction with the House of Jehu, which was known for its alliance and trading relationship with the Assyrian Empire.

Zephaniah, a Judean prophet of the latter sixth century B.C.E., called for the restoration of Jerusalem's relationship with YHWH during the reign of King Josiah ben Amon of Judah (640–609 B.C.E.).[14] The prophet, again not a priest, metaphorically portrays Jerusalem as Bat-Zion, Daughter Zion, over whom YHWH rejoices with love at her return in Zephaniah 3:14–20. In a widely misunderstood verse in Zephaniah 3:17, the prophet states, "YHWH, your G-d, is in your midst; a warrior who delivers; he rejoices over you in joy; he plows (Hebrew, יַחֲרִישׁ) in his love; he shouts aloud over you in exultation." The Hebrew verb, יַחֲרִישׁ, normally translated as "he remains silent," appears to make little sense in this context, which portrays YHWH's loud exultation over the bride, Bat-Zion.[15] Consequently interpreters attempt emendations, such as "he will renew (Hebrew, יְחַדֵּשׁ) his love, but there is no textual evidence for such a reading. It is only when interpreters recognize that יַחֲרִישׁ, is derived from another example of the root, חרשׁ, "to plow," that the passage makes sense, in that the Semitic verb, חרשׁ, is often used as a metaphorical expression for sexual intercourse in Akkadian. When understood in this manner, the passage portrays YHWH metaphorically engaging in sexual intercourse with his newly restored bride.

Jeremiah ben Hilkiah, a prophet and priest of the line of Ithamar, Eli, and Abiathar from the town of Anathoth, likewise employs bridal metaphors to depict Jerusalem's relationship with YHWH. In Jeremiah 2:2–37, Jeremiah portrays Jerusalem as the bride of YHWH's youth who followed him in the wilderness (Jeremiah 2:2), but once in the wilderness, ran after other gods in an apparent reference to the apostasy at Baal Peor in Numbers 25.[16] The metaphorical portrayal of apostasy is presented in explicitly sexual terms when the prophet employs the metaphors of a camel or an ass in heat (Jeremiah 2:23–24), who will suffer punishment for seeking alliances with Egypt and Assyria in Jeremiah's time and thereby betraying YHWH (Jeremiah 2:36). Insofar as Jeremiah is a priest as well as a prophet, readers will see a manner in which a priest would use the wilderness traditions of the Pentateuch to teach the people about events in their own contemporary times when Jerusalem sought alliances with Assyria and

---

14 See Marvin A. Sweeney, *Zephaniah*, Hermeneia (Minneapolis: Fortress, 2003), 193–208; Sweeney, "Metaphor and Rhetorical Strategy in Zephaniah," *Reading Prophetic Books*, 323–333.

15 Sweeney, "Metaphor and Rhetorical Strategy," esp. 325–328.

16 Marvin A. Sweeney, "Structure and Redaction in Jeremiah 2–6," *Form and Intertextuality*, 94–108.

Egypt during the reigns of Josiah's predecessors, Manasseh ben Hezekiah (687–642 B.C.E.) and Amon ben Manasseh (642–640 B.C.E.).

Finally, there is the example of the anonymous prophet of the Isaian literature known only as Deutero-Isaiah, apparently a late-sixth century disciple or descendant of the eighth-century prophet, Isaiah ben Amoz. Deutero-Isaiah likewise employs the marriage metaphor to portray Bat Zion or Jerusalem (see, e.g., Isaiah 52:1–2) as an abandoned bride to whom YHWH returns (Isaiah 54, esp. v. 6).[17] The prophet announces YHWH's return to Jerusalem as well as the return of their children, a reference to the exiled tribes of Israel and Judah at the end of the Babylonian Exile. YHWH claims to have been gone only for "a short moment" (but never explains where he was or what he was doing!) as the exiled people of Jerusalem and Judah are called upon to return home following their exile in Babylonia. YHWH swears an oath like that of the covenant with Noah (Genesis 9:1–6) that YHWH will never be angry, withdraw his fidelity, or threaten their covenant again in taking Jerusalem back in love (Isaiah 54:9–10).

When interpreters turn to Ezekiel's use of the marriage metaphor in Ezekiel 16, they find a very different use of the metaphor in which YHWH came across Jerusalem in the wilderness as an abandoned baby girl of Amorite and Hittite descent whose umbilical cord remained uncut and who had not been washed in the immediate aftermath of her birth (Ezekiel 16:2).[18] The passage depicts YHWH's encounter of young Jerusalem, now sexually matured, when YHWH enters into a covenant, apparently a marriage covenant with her, and takes her for a wife. Although such an act might inspire charges of child abuse or rape in modern eyes, interpreters must remember that this is a depiction of a legitimate form of marriage in the ancient world, viz., the young woman is not related to YHWH and she is therefore eligible for marriage. Note the reference to the blood and nakedness of the baby/young woman throughout the passage which signal the concerns of the Holiness Code concerning the sanctity of blood (Leviticus 17) and incest, depicted in relation to uncovering nakedness (Leviticus 18; 20). Ezekiel portrays YHWH purifying young Jerusalem of blood and ensuring that there is a proper marriage relationship in keeping with the expectations of priestly conduct as articulated in the Holiness Code.

As in Hosea and Jeremiah, Jerusalem pursues other lovers following her marriage to YHWH which portrays Jerusalem's apostasy with other gods and especially with Egypt, which controlled Judah during the reign of Jehoiakim ben Josiah, 609–605 B.C.E. Following Babylon's defeat of Egypt in 605 B.C.E. and subsequent

---

17 Marvin A. Sweeney, *Isaiah 40–66*, FOTL (Grand Rapids, MI: Eerdmans, 2016), 168–206, 218–231.

18 Sweeney, *Reading Ezekiel*, 83–88.

subjugation of Judah, Jehoiakim revolted against the Babylonians, resulting in his death and the exiles of many prominent Jerusalemites and Judeans, including King Jehoiachin ben Jehoiakim and Ezekiel himself (2 Kings 24). Ezekiel 16 goes on to depict Jerusalem's apostasy as a consequence of her descent from the Amorites and the Hittites, who would among the pre-Israelite nations vomited out of the land due to their abominations in Leviticus 18:24–30 and 20:22–26. He likewise invokes the example of the Sodomites, which were written by E and J authors but figure prominently in the Priestly account of Sodom and Gomorrah in Genesis 18–19,[19] to depict the abominations of Jerusalem.

When interpreters turn to Ezekiel's sign action in Ezekiel 24:15–27 concerning the interrelationship between his refusal to mourn for the death of his wife and YHWH's refusal to mourn for the fate of Jerusalem, they find the underlying concerns of the marriage metaphor for the relationship between YHWH and Jerusalem defined in relation to the concerns for priestly sanctity as articulated in the Holiness Code.[20] The marriage motif portrayed in the preceding prophetic texts provides the context by which to understand Ezekiel's marriage relationship with his wife provides the model for conceiving YHWH's relation with Jerusalem or Bat Zion as an analogous and metaphorical marriage. In those cases in which the marriage between YHWH and Israel or Jerusalem is disrupted, i.e., Hosea 1–3; Jeremiah 2; and Ezekiel 16, Jerusalem – or Israel, in the case of Hosea – is charged with apostasy. With the death of Ezekiel's wife as model, however, there is no immediate marital model for the restoration of Jerusalem analogous to those presented in Zephaniah 3:14–20 or Isaiah 54; the placement of a new heart in the people and their purification by water in Ezekiel 36:22–32, together with the purification of the land from the dead in Ezekiel 37 and 38–39, serves as the basis for the portrayal of restoration in Ezekiel 40–48.

But Ezekiel's and YHWH's refusal to mourn cannot be explained simply as a matter of disregard for the wife or even misogyny in Ezekiel 24:15–27. Once again, the Holiness Code comes into consideration in explaining Ezekiel's and YHWH's refusal to mourn. Leviticus 21 presents a speech by Moses to the priests, here defined as the sons of Aaron, that they are not to defile themselves for the dead with the exception of those who are blood relatives, viz., his mother, his father, his son, his daughter, his brother, and his virgin sister who has not been married (Leviticus 21:2–3). For those who are related to him by marriage, which would

---

19 Antony F. Campbell and Mark A. O'Brien, *Sources of the Pentateuch: Texts, Introductions, Annotations* (Minneapolis: Fortress, 1993), 101–104; see also Marvin A. Sweeney, *The Pentateuch*, Core Biblical Studies (Nashville: Abingdon, 2017), 13–14.
20 Sweeney, *Reading Ezekiel*, 124–125; see also Risa Levitt Kohn, *A New Heart and a New Soul: Ezekiel, the Exile, and the Torah*, JSOTSup 358 (Sheffield: Sheffield Academic Press, 2002).

entail his wife and her family members, a priest may not defile himself (Leviticus 21:3). The passage goes on to forbid a priest to shave his head, cut the side growth of his beard, or gash himself as one does in mourning rituals, e.g., the behavior of the prophets of Baal who are mourning for their dead deity (2 Kings 18:25–29).[21] The passage further specifies marriage requirements of the priesthood and the conduct of the high priest. Fundamentally, the sons of Aaron, the priests (Hebrew, כֹּהֲנִים) of ancient Israel and Judah are forbidden to come into contact with the dead, unless it is a close blood relative. Death is the antithesis of sanctity in ancient Israelite and Judean thought, and the priest must therefore avoid contact with the dead, unless it is a blood relative. The wife of a priest is not included among his blood relatives, insofar as the relationship is established by marriage, not by birth.

In order properly to understand what is meant by mourning, interpreters must consider what mourning entails. Leviticus 21 specifies shaving the head and side-growth of the beard or gashing oneself, but such actions do not encompass the entirety of what must be done when one mourns for the dead. The body the dead must be prepared and cleansed for burial, it must be carried to the gravesite, and it must be buried. There is no indication of funeral homes in the ancient world to carry out such functions; instead, the immediate family is first and foremost the party responsible for such actions. In the case of the death of a woman, her surviving blood relatives, viz., her parents, her siblings, and her children, would be responsible for the mourning and burial of the dead. Her husband, however, is not a blood relative. In the case of a non-priest, the husband would presumably take part in the mourning and burial, but in the case of a priest, his sanctity as an ordained priest precludes such actions. As a priest of YHWH of the sons of Aaron, Ezekiel is forbidden to engage in mourning and burial rites on behalf of his wife because she is not a blood relative as specified in Leviticus 21.[22]

Ezekiel does not display disregard for his wife or misogyny in his refusal to mourn for her; rather, he observes the sanctity of his status as a priest and refrains from any behavior that would then compromise his priestly sanctity. His

---

21 Marvin A. Sweeney, *1 and 2 Kings: A Commentary*, OTL (Louisville: Westminster John Knox, 2007), 228.
22 For a study of the consequences of failure to observe priestly obligations concerning mourning for the dead, see my study, "Why Moses was Barred from the Land of Israel: A Reassessment of Numbers 20 in Literary Context," in *Seeking Wisdom's Depths and Torah's Heights: Essays in Honor of Samuel E. Balentine*, ed. B. R. Huff and P. Vesely (Macon, GA: Smyth and Helwys, 2020), 75–88, which argues that Moses and Aaron were barred from entry to the Land of Israel for their failure to purify themselves following the burial of Miriam when they appeared before YHWH at the rock.

behavior then serves as a symbolic action or model for YHWH's refusal to mourn on behalf of his own bride, Jerusalem or Bat Zion, which has just been conquered and destroyed by the Babylonians.

5 Conclusion

In conclusion, Ezekiel's decision to refrain from mourning for his dead wife is not an example of disregard for her, lack of love, or even misogyny. It is an example of how a Judean, Aaronite priest is expected to conduct himself in the event of the death of his wife. Ezekiel's actions then serve as the basis for a sign act that will illustrate YHWH's refusal to mourn for Jerusalem, metaphorically understood to be YHWH's bride in the prophetic tradition and perhaps beyond.

5 Conclusion

Penelope Barter
Unity and (Compositional) Disunity in Ezekiel 37:15–28

Ezekiel 37:15–28, tucked away between the vision of the dry bones (Ezek 37:1–14) and the oracles of Gog and Magog (Ezek 38–39), is easy to overlook. Once we do pay attention to this short sign-act, text-critical concerns rightly often take centre stage. Yet one of the most striking aspects of the text is one which is easy to miss by the time we reach Ezek 37: the formulas. In this chapter, I use the formulas in Ezek 37:15–28 as an entry point to discuss the composition and interpretation of the text, and demonstrate how these three elements (use of formulas, composition, and interpretation) impact one another. I ultimately argue for three main compositional units including an initial sign-act and interpretation (Ezek 37:15–19), and two supplements in vv. 20–23 and vv. 24–28. While the earliest form of the sign-act text made minimal use of formulas, the supplements introduce the relatively dense use of formulas in its current form and thereby invoke rhetoric from other parts of the book of Ezekiel.

In what follows, I treat this text as a literary sign-act; that is, exclusively as a textual phenomenon. Whether an Israelite prophet ever actually performed any part of this oracular roleplay is lost to us, and, in the case of Ezek 37:15–28, the instructions, the people's reaction, and the response the prophet must give are all couched as divine instruction and foretelling.[1]

1 Literary Structure

Ezekiel 37:15–28 is demarcated as a distinct textual unit by the presence of prophetic word formulas (PWF) in Ezek 37:15 and 38:1. While some have documented particular connections to the vision of the dry bones that begins the chapter, the

---

[1] This is, of course, contrary to Kelvin Friebel's conclusion in his influential *Jeremiah's and Ezekiel's Sign-Acts: Rhetorical Nonverbal Communication* (JSOTSup 283; Sheffield: Sheffield Academic Press, 1999), in which he argued that the sign-act texts "report nonverbal behaviors which were really and publicly performed by the prophets as part of their prophetic ministries" (34). Though I am also less confident that, as Friebel states, "it cannot be denied that the literary accounts of the sign-acts intend the reader to assume that the actions really took place" (his emphasis), Friebel is absolutely right to stress the value of the study of the rhetorical functions of these texts.

https://doi.org/10.1515/9783111521015-011

current literary structure nonetheless indicates a high-level division in v. 15.[2] The oracle presented in Ezek 37:15–28 has six occurrences of four different formulas in fourteen verses, and while not all should be considered structural elements, the placement and repetition invites our attention.[3]

Using these formulas as a guide, the structure of the unit can be seen as follows:

37:15	PWF
37:16–17	instructions for sign-act
37:18	people's response foretold
37:19	initial interpretation
37:19aα	first instruction to speak + messenger formula
37:19aβ–b	first interpretation of sign-act
37:20	conclusion of sign-act
37:21–28	expanded interpretation
37:21aα	second instruction to speak + messenger formula
37:21aβ–28	second interpretation of sign-act
37:21aβ–23	various restoration promises + covenant formula
37:24–27	extension and transformation of promises + covenant formula
37:28	extended recognition formula

The text has a fairly straightforward structure: after the PWF begins the unit, the divine speech begins with instructions for the sign-act, followed by the people's request for an explanation, followed by two interpretations of the sign-act. Between the two interpretations is Ezekiel 37:20, tentatively referred to here as the conclusion of the sign-act. The precise role of this verse both structurally and compositionally has garnered much attention. Broadly speaking, the crux of the structural issue is whether v. 20 is a resumption of the *instructions* to Ezekiel in

---

2 Christoph Barth, for example, argues for a thematic connection between Ezek 36:16–38; 37:1–14; and 37:15–28, and especially the recurrence of exodus and return in the two halves of Ezek 37 ("Ezechiel 37 als Einheit" in *Beiträge zur alttestamentlichen Theologie*, ed. Herbert Donner, Robert Hanhart, and Rudolf Smend [Göttingen: Vandenhoeck & Ruprecht, 1977], 39–52). The literary structure supports in particular the connection between the end of Ezek 36 and beginning of Ezek 37, since a consistent use of the PWF to delineate subunits in Ezekiel would mean the unit prior to Ezek 37:15–28 begins at Ezek 36:16, not at the start of Ezek 37 – see Tyler D. Mayfield, "Literary Structure and Formulas in Ezekiel 34–37" in William A. Tooman and Penelope Barter (eds.), *Ezekiel: Current Debates and Future Directions*, FAT 112 (Tübingen: Mohr Siebeck, 2017), 240–241.
3 PWF: Ezek 37:15; messenger formula (*Botenformel*): Ezek 37:19, 21; covenant formula (*Bundesformel*): Ezek 37:23, 27; recognition formula (*Erkenntnisformel*): Ezek 37:28.

vv. 16–17a and thus a part of the continuing sign-act, or recapitulation of the *outcome* of the sign-act (in v. 17b).[4] I read v. 20 in the current form of the text as more or less a repetition of the outcome of the sign-act, but with additional clarification. This, and the compositional considerations, will be discussed below.

The extent to which the second interpretation actually relates to the sign-act will be discussed later, but its opening structure mirrors that of the first interpretation. The second is comparatively expansive in both content and form though, with restoration promises made in successive steps, each ending with the covenant formula. An extended form of the recognition formula concludes the unit. The densely-packed formulas thus play a crucial role in forming the literary structure of the text, but also give helpful insight into the compositional structure. In what follows, each formula will be discussed in order of first appearance in Ezek 37:15–28, with attention paid to the function of the formula in this text, as well as the compositional insights to which it points.

2 The Formulas

2.1 Prophetic Word Formula (Ezek 37:15)

As noted above, the PWF in Ezek 37:15 (ויהי דבר־יהוה אלי לאמר) marks the beginning of the textual unit that continues until the next occurrence of this formula in 38:1. It is common for sign-act textual units to begin with the PWF, which is unsurprising given that they begin with divine instruction (e.g., Ezek 3:16–17; 12:1–6; 24:15–17). The PWF does not have any function particular to the sign-acts, however.

2.2 Messenger Formula (Ezek 37:19, 21)

The messenger formula (כה אמר [אדני] יהוה) appears throughout the book of Ezekiel, often preceded by an instruction to speak – such as the two uses in this sign-

---

4 For the former position, see, e.g., Friebel, *Jeremiah's and Ezekiel's Sign-Acts*, 367. Friebel proposes that v. 20 constitutes "a distinct command for the continued, extended performance of the nonverbal communication: the joined sticks were to be carried about ('and they shall [continue] to be in your hand') in the people's sight" (367). I find Friebel's reading very generous, but not entirely convincing. For the latter position, see, e.g., Ronald M. Hals, *Ezekiel*, FOTL 19 (Grand Rapids: Wm. B. Eerdmans Publishing Co., 1989), 272.

act text – but is sometimes used in a manner closer to the use of the prophetic utterance formula יהוה [אדני] נאם (e.g., Ezek 5:5; 20:39).[5] Although the messenger formula should not be used to structure the book as a whole, in some oracles it does appear to be used as a structural marker (e.g. Ezek 20).[6]

In Ezek 37:15–28, the messenger formula introduces both explanations of the sign-act. These two explanations, very different in scope and nature, each begin with an instruction for Ezekiel to speak to the people, followed by the messenger formula, then Yhwh's intended actions:

דבר אלהם כה־אמר אדני יהוה הנה אני לקח את־עץ יוסף אשר ביד־אפרים ושבטי ישראל חברו ונתתי אותם עליו את־עץ יהודה ועשיתם לעץ אחד והיו אחד בידי:	Ezek 37:19[7]	Say to them: "Thus says Lord Yhwh: Look, I will take the stick of Joseph, which is in the hand of Ephraim and the tribes of Israel, his companions,[8] and I will set them with it (with the stick of Judah), and I will make them one stick, and they will be one in my hand."
ודבר אליהם כה־אמר אדני יהוה הנה אני לקח את־בני ישראל מבין הגוים אשר הלכו־שם וקבצתי אתם מסביב והבאתי אותם אל־אדמתם:	Ezek 37:21	and say to them, "Thus says Lord Yhwh: Look, I will take the sons of Israel from the nations into which they have gone, and I will gather them from all around, and I will bring them into their land."

The repetition of the opening words and formula place the two explanations of the sign-act in parallel, yet it is important not to diminish the key differences between the two: while Ezek 37:19 is a direct response to a question that Yhwh presupposes the people will pose to Ezekiel, Ezek 37:21 is a resumption of a divine

---

5 This is not to say that the prophetic utterance formula and messenger formula are interchangeable, but rather that they sometimes have, as indicated by Daniel Block, "rhetorical equivalence". Block has also noted that the two may work together in a sophisticated way in some cases: there are twenty instances in Ezekiel of the prophetic utterance formula concluding an oracle which starts with the messenger formula (Daniel I. Block, *The Book of Ezekiel: Chapters 1–24*, NICOT [Grand Rapids: Eerdmans, 1997], 33). Note that Block refers to the messenger formula and prophetic utterance formula as the 'citation formula' and 'signatory formula' respectively.

6 For further discussion, see Mayfield, *Literary Structure*, 82. Mayfield argues that, while the messenger formula was sometimes employed as a structural marker within individual oracles, it "cannot be used for the macrostructure of the book since some genres within the book (e.g., the visions of chapters 8–11) do not use the formula regularly" and can occur either at the beginning or in the middle of divine speech.

7 As Greenberg notes, "The sense of vs. 19bα comes through ... but the text can hardly be in order." See his explanation of the problems and related text-critical issues in *Ezekiel 21–37: A New Translation with Introduction and Commentary*, AB 22A (New York: Doubleday, 1997), 755.

8 Reading חבריו with the qere.

speech after – in the final form of the text – Yhwh's tangent in v. 20.[9] Since there is no explicit (new) recipient, it is of course possible to read the two explanations in sequence, with v. 21–28 as a continuation and expansion of the first, but that does not account for the use of the messenger formula to reintroduce the divine speech.[10] While this double explanation is not unique among the sign-act texts (see for example the repeated use of the messenger formula to introduce successively broader statements in Ezek 5), it is worthy of closer attention.

Georg Fohrer already investigated this repetition of the messenger formula in the 1950's, though for him to entire phrase "and say to them, 'Thus say Lord Yhwh'" in v. 21 was to be understood as a gloss that became necessary after the insertion of of v. 19aβ–20 (in his notation), thus disrupting the original flow from the messenger formula in v. 19 to הנה in v. 21.[11] The repetition is also "a clear indication" of compositional disunity for Karl-Friedrich Pohlmann.[12] The shift of themes after Ezek 37:22 to those "which no longer correspond to the prophet's action" confirms for Pohlmann that there is a further compositional break after v. 22, and he ultimately reads Ezek 37:20–22 as a later addition to 37:15–19.[13]

---

9 Friebel states that the construction וכאשר "must be understood as indicating *certainty* and not just possibility or probability that the people would ask the question" (*Jeremiah's and Ezekiel's Sign-Acts*, 366 n650, my emphasis). In the context of this passage, we can confidently say that Yhwh anticipates that the people will pose a question about Ezekiel's bizarre actions, though it would also be reasonable to interpret this as a literary device (or at least a structural device within the divine speech) to move from the description of the physical act into its interpretations. The verbal response of the people plays a similar role in Ezek 12:9, where Yhwh begins "in the morning" by saying that the people have *already* questioned Ezekiel's actions and launches immediately into their explanation. In Ezek 24:19, the question of the people is reported as part of Ezekiel's rare first-person narrative, prompting him to recount the divine speech that explains the meaning of the sign-act. This is seemingly not a requirement of the genre, or its application in Ezekiel, however: in Ezek 5 Yhwh gives the instructions and the explanation without interruption.

10 See, e.g., Greenberg, who says Ezekiel "is to answer in two stages" (*Ezekiel 21–37*, 758).

11 Georg Fohrer, *Ezechiel*, HAT 13 (Tübingen: J. C. B. Mohr [Paul Siebeck], 1955), 211. Fohrer's reconstructed text of Ezek 37:19–21 thus reads "Sprich zu ihnen: So spricht Jahwe: 'Siehe, ich nehme die Israeliten zwischen den Böltern heraus, wohin sie gegangen sind, und sammle sie von ringsum und bringe sie in ihr Land'" ("Say to them: 'Thus says Yahweh, 'Behold, I am taking the Israelites out from among the nations where they have gone, and gathering them from all around and bringing them into their own land'").

12 Karl-Friedrich Pohlmann, *Der Prophet Hesekiel 20–48*, ATD (Göttingen: Vandenhoeck & Ruprecht, 2001), 501: "Aber auch für V.15–22 ist die zweimalige Redeanweisung (in V.19 und V.21) ein klares Indiz dafür, daß der jetzige Text nicht aus einem Guß ist."

13 Pohlmann, *Hesekiel 20–48*, 501. "Es erstreckt sich jetzt bis zum Ende des Kapitels (V.28), erweist sich jedoch nach V.22b als auf die vorausgehenden Darlegungen nicht abgestimmt, da hier verschiedene Themen angesprochen werden, die nicht mehr der Handlung des Propheten korrespondieren. Das spricht dafür, hinter V.22 eine Zäsur anzunehmen."

While I too see the double usage of the messenger formula and expanded scope of the interpretation in Ezek 37:21–23 (and further) as reasonable indications of an addition to the earliest form of the sign-act text, this does not in itself explain the origins of v. 20, which to my mind could feasibly 'belong' as the conclusion to vv. 15–19 or as a bridge introducing the supplement starting in v. 21. As Pohlmann himself notes, the "almost identical concluding remarks" of verses 17 and 19 form a neat framing of the people's response and the interpretation of the sign-act, which suggests that v. 20 is not needed to conclude the short original sign-act text.[14] Moreover, Anja Klein argues convincingly that v. 20 is what links the second interpretation to the sign-act: without it, v. 21–23 has no clear connection to Ezekiel's initial action.[15] There is in my view also a strong rhetorical argument for this position based on v. 17–19. After the insistence on the unity of the stick in the instructions and initial explanation, reverting to a plural form to conclude the text undoes the strength of the intended message, completing the sign-act text with:

והיו העצים אשר־תכתב עליהם בידך לעיניהם:	Ezek 37:20	And the sticks on which you wrote will be in your hand before their eyes.

I am thus inclined to agree that there is a compositional break between verses 19 and 20 (though I find myself less certain of Pohlmann's further division between verses 22 and 23). However, if this proposal is correct, this suggests that the earliest form of the sign-act text had only a PWF and single messenger formula, rather than the relatively dense use of formulas in its current form. The supplement(s), then, mimics the use of the messenger formula in the earlier text, while introducing three occurrences of two 'new' formulas. It is to these two that we now turn.

2.3 Covenant Formula (Ezek 37:23, 27)

The covenant formula, a future-oriented declaration that "they [the sons of Israel] will be my people and I will be their god" (והיו־לי לעם ואני אהיה להם לאלהים) appears in Ezek 37:23 and then in reverse order in v. 27. The formula envelopes the promises that David will be king over the people, that a covenant of peace will be established, and that Yhwh will set his sanctuary in the people's midst (Ezek 37:24–27).[16]

---

14 Pohlmann, *Hesekiel 20–48*, 501 ("fast gleichlautenden Schlußbemerkungen").

15 Anja Klein, *Schriftauslegung im Ezechielbuch. Redaktionsgeschichtliche Untersuchungen zu Ez 34–39*, BZAW 391 (Berlin: De Gruyter, 2008), 214.

16 See Franz Sedlmeier, "The Figure of David and His Importance in Ezekiel 34–37" in William A. Tooman and Penelope Barter (eds.), *Ezekiel: Current Debates and Future Directions*, FAT 112

In the rest of Ezekiel, the formula appears predominantly – perhaps exclusively – in later texts: Ezek 11:20; 14:11; and 36:28, with possible variant forms in 34:24, 30.

Zimmerli notes in addition that the covenant formula elsewhere in Ezekiel is found at the conclusion of units and suggests that the formula serves a similar purpose here in v. 27, where it "rounds off the divine proclamations before the expanded recognition formula follows in v 28".[17] It is precisely this typical usage in Ezekiel that also leads Zimmerli to be suspicious of the first occurrence of the formula, concluding that "it is likely that in the covenant formula in v. 23 b we find a hint that a section once ended here".[18] Supporting evidence for a compositional break after v. 23 can be found in both the expansion of the scope of the 'interpretation' and the language specific to the end of the unit, such as the five uses of עולם, which otherwise does not appear in the chapter.[19]

In his discussion of this formula, Zimmerli makes three related arguments that are relevant for our discussion here. First, despite the covenant formula ending the section in v. 23b, in Zimmerli's view the final compositional unit only begins at v. 24b ("and they will walk in my ordinances and keep my statutes and observe them"), since he finds that v. 23bβ and v. 24a together are dependent on Ezek 34:24 and "meant to call to mind the expression 'Yahweh their God and David their king'".[20] Second, however, he argues that this "statement about David" as king (which I understand to mean just v. 24a) is "clearly dependent" on v. 22, making it an addition to vv. 20–23. Finally, this resulting final section of vv. 24b–28 forms a bipartite proof-saying: an announcement of salvation in vv. 24b–27 which then ends with the covenant formula in v. 28.

Indeed, the description of David as 'king' (מלך) in v. 24a does pose some compositional questions, since later in v. 25 he will be referred to as 'prince' (נשׂיא).[21] As discussed above, Zimmerli's position solves this problem by assigning v. 24a as an addition to vv. 20–23 prior to the supplement in v. 24b–28, which also allows him to preserve the role of covenant formula. John Wevers, however, proposes

---

(Tübingen: Mohr Siebeck, 2017), 92–106, for a discussion of David's role in this chapter and its connections to other references to David in Ezekiel.

17 Walther Zimmerli, *Ezekiel 2*, trans. James D. Martin, Hermeneia (Philadelphia: Fortress, 1983) 271.

18 Zimmerli, *Ezekiel 2*, 271–272 (quotation on 271).

19 The term interpretation is used loosely here, since as a unit Ezek 37:24–28 has no clear connection to the initial sign-act, but is only woven in by the successively broader expansions to the text.

20 Zimmerli, *Ezekiel 2*, 271.

21 LXX neatly sidesteps the issue by referring to David as ὁ δοῦλός μου ἄρχων in both verses. See John W. Olley, *Ezekiel: A Commentary based on Iezekiēl in Codex Vaticanus*, Septuagint Commentary Series (Leiden: Brill, 2009), 494–495 for discussion.

that the references to the 'king' in v. 22 and v. 24 were added by a later author from the Ezekiel school, who is to be distinguished from the author of the supplementary vv. 21–28.[22] I remain open, however, to taking vv. 24–28 as a compositional unit and seeing the various descriptions of David as king, prince, and servant as an attempt to tie together various threads in the book of Ezekiel.[23]

Wherever the precise split falls, it is widely acknowledged among those who view vv. 24–28 as a separate compositional unit that the content has little, if anything, to do with the initial sign-act, even though it is presented in the final literary form as part of the second interpretation. Thematically, however, this final section has a connection to the general theme of unity via the covenant formula. Odell notes in her discussion of Ezek 11:18–20 that the covenant formula there is paired with the promise of giving people "one heart" (לב אחד), leading here to argue that "[f]or Ezekiel, there is no more concise or eloquent way to express the foundation of unity than this ancient formulation of a community centered in obedience to Yahweh."[24] Odell does not return specifically to this issue in her discussion of Ezek 37:15–28, though here we also encounter the covenant formula in the context of an emphasis on unity, as well as a gathering of the scattered people (Ezek 37:21; cf. 11:17) and obedience to Yhwh's statutes and ordinances (Ezek 37:24, cf. 11:20). This literary connection highlights another possible prompt for the further expansion of the sign-act. As well as making the promise of one king in v. 22 more specific, this final supplement indicates a broader impact of Yhwh's actions, since the establishment of the sanctuary in Israel's midst will ultimately serve as the tool for Yhwh's self-revelation to the nations (Ezek 37:28; see 2.4 below).[25]

---

22 John W. Wevers, *Ezekiel*, New Century Bible Commentary (Grand Rapids: Wm. B. Eerdmans Publishing Co., 1969), 194. Note that Wevers refers to these supplementing authors as 'traditionists of the Ezekiel school'. Blenkinsopp suggests that the author of Ezek 37:24–28 may be Ezekiel himself ("a possibility often overlooked"), though ultimately concludes that "since the end result is self-consistent and consistent with the book as a whole, it may be taken as it stands" (Joseph Blenkinsopp, *Ezekiel*, Interpretation [Louisville: John Knox, 1990] 176.).

23 Sedlmeier does not explicitly suggest this, but in my opinion offers suggestive evidence for this position (Sedlmeier, "The Figure of David", 101–104). He notes, for example, that the emphasis in v. 24a is still on unity, with David's role determined by his relationship with Yhwh (see also Ezek 34:23–24). In v. 25, where David is called נשיא, the emphasis is on David's subordination to Yhwh and, perhaps, suggests a particular *kind* of leadership: "Presumably this title, which occurs as a standard statement especially in Ezek 40–48, signals a critical distance from the behaviour of the real kings of Israel" ("The Figure of David", 104). To this point I would add that in Ezek 20:33 it is Yhwh himself who will reign – or "be king" – over the people (אמלוך עליכם).

24 Margaret S. Odell, *Ezekiel*, Smyth and Helwys Bible Commentary (Macon, GA: Smyth and Helwys, 2005), 124.

25 With regards to the identity of the king in v. 22, Joyce notes, I think rightly, that "it is at least possible [...] that v. 22 refers to *God* as the one king ruling over the reunited nation" (Paul M.

2.4 Recognition Formula (Ezek 37:28)

The core elements of the recognition formula (*Erkenntnisformel*) are the verbal element "and you/they/it will know" (יד"ע) and the object clause "that I am Yhwh" (כי אני יהוה). The book of Ezekiel has 71 of the 90 occurrences of this formula in the Hebrew Bible, and in Ezek 37:28 we encounter an expanded form with the distinctive feature that it is the *nations* who are the beneficiaries of this knowledge.[26] Although the role of the recognition formula is the focus here, the description of Yhwh as sanctifier is also conspicuous.

Zimmerli has famously examined the recognition formula at length, with two of his observations particularly relevant for this discussion.[27] First, he notes two kinds of recognition formula: the short form "and you/they shall know that I am Yhwh" and various expanded forms. Ezek 37:28 is a particularly interesting example of the recognition formula, as it is not only expanded in form, but also in scope, with Yhwh's sanctification of the Israel serving as his self-identification to the *nations*. This is of course not a unique occurrence, but unlike Ezek 20:41 or 36:20–23, where Israel's profanation of Yhwh's name among the nations will be reversed when Yhwh proves himself holy in the sign of the nations, the introduction of the nations here in Ezek 37:28 is unanticipated. Odell rightly points out that "[w]ithin the international context, the sanctification of Israel involves a radical separation from the nations", so a mention of the nations immediately following Yhwh's proclamation that his sanctuary will be in Israel's midst forever (Ezek 37.26–27) is not *jarring*, but it is striking.[28]

Second, Zimmerli notes that the recognition formula is found at the end of a divine speech in approximately 80 % of its occurrences in Ezekiel, "suggesting that this recognition of Yahweh is the final goal and actual culmination of what is spoken in the preceding divine discourse" and that this "tempts us to conclude that the end position is the formula's normal position".[29] It is thus unsurprising to find the formula used at the conclusion of this unit, but what is interesting is the interaction of this formula with the composition and interpretation of the text.

Joyce, "King and Messiah in Ezekiel" in John Day [ed.], *King and Messiah in Israel and the Ancient Near East: Proceedings of the Oxford Old Testament Seminar*, JSOTSup 270 [Sheffield: Sheffield Academic Press, 1998], 323–337 [328]). This suggestion can indeed be found elsewhere in Ezekiel (see n23 above). Joyce ultimately concludes however that "on balance, the natural reading of 37.22 is probably as a reference to a human king" (335).

26 Of the remaining 19 occurrences in HB, 10 are found in the Torah, all in Exodus.

27 Walther Zimmerli, "Knowledge of God According to the Book of Ezekiel" in *I Am Yahweh*, trans. Douglas W. Scott (Atlanta: Westminster John Knox Press, 1982), 29–98.

28 Odell, *Ezekiel*, 457.

29 Zimmerli, "Knowledge", 33.

If we are correct that Ezek 37:20 ff. is supplementary – be it one stage or multiple – then the conclusion of the unit with the recognition formula is also not original.[30] In ending the oracle this way, the supplementer uses a common Ezekielian style of conclusion, but in doing so also re-interprets the sign-act: the ultimate goal is no longer the 'simple' reunification of Judah and Israel, but rather the nations' recognition of Yhwh through his sanctification of Israel. Indeed, Hals already noted that this concluding formula,

> like all of the elaboration in vv. 24–27, makes no connection to the symbolic action or the hoped-for reunification [...] It seems clear, then, that original report of a symbolic action has been updated repeatedly in such a way that it has come to be a kind of summary collection of the most major items in Ezekiel's message of hope.[31]

Yhwh's self-description as 'sanctifier' arguably supports this conclusion in its reference to Ezek 20:12 (and, in turn, Exod 31:13).[32] By invoking the stylized history of Israel in Ezek 20, the author connects these promises of restoration to the overarching narrative of Yhwh's ongoing relationship with Israel and to the main themes of the book as a whole.[33]

2.5 Summary of Compositional Structure

In the text above, I have argued for three main compositional units:

37:15–19	Initial sign-act and interpretation
37:20–23	First supplement (second interpretation)
37:24–28	Second supplement (expansion of second interpretation)

---

30 This is, however, also the case with the use of the recognition formula in, for example, Ezek 16 and 20. A thorough investigation of the use of formulas in supplementary texts in Ezekiel is, in my opinion, long overdue.

31 Hals, *Ezekiel*, 274.

32 Yhwh as sanctifier is common in the Holiness Code (see Lev 20:8; 21:8, 15, 23; 22:9, 16, 32), though it is likely the author of Ezek 20 who first combines this with the recognition formula. See Penelope Barter, "Reuse and Innovation in Ezekiel 20 and Exodus 31:12–17", *CBQ* 82/3 (2020), 365–380 for further discussion. Note that Greenberg sees a broader connection between the "climactic summary of future blessing" in Ezek 37:23–28 and the covenant promises in Lev 26:2–13, though notes that the "different horizons of each document" result in notable divergences, such as the expectation of war, the provision of a king, and the location of Yhwh's presence (Greenberg, *Ezekiel 21–37*, 760).

33 As Odell notes, the reference in Ezek 37:25 to "the land that I gave to my servant Jacob" (הארץ אשר נתתי לעבדי ליעקב) also "envisions the fulfillment of Yahweh's oath in chapter 20" (*Ezekiel*, 456).

As discussed, v. 20 *could* be read as the conclusion to the initial interpretation and there are arguments for viewing v. 24a as an independent supplement prior to the addition of vv. 24b–28. On balance, however, this division seems the more convincing at this stage.

This tripartite division fits relatively cleanly with the literary structure of the text, but nonetheless impacts our interpretation and invites a new reading.

3 Rereading Ezekiel 37:15–28

If Ezek 37:15–28 was indeed composed in the stages outlined above, we may ask what the original sign-act text and the intermittent stages communicated.[34]

The initial sign-act text seems quite straightforward. The PWF (Ezek 37:15) begins the new unit, indicating a structural division from the preceding vision. The divine speech introduced by the PWF contains the instructions for the sign-act, the people's response to it, and the interpretation of the sign-act (Ezek 37:16–19). Ezekiel is instructed to take two sticks, write on each one, and join them in his hand. Although Ezekiel is not explicitly instructed to do this publicly, we may assume from v. 18 that that is the intention, since the people will ask Ezekiel for the meaning of his action (see also below). The messenger formula introduces the first-person divine response to the people's question: Yhwh will take the two 'sticks' and they will be one in Yhwh's hand. Zimmerli rightly notes that this interpretation is quite strange, as it is largely a recapitulation of the description of the sign-act itself, though now with "the word of Yahweh emphasized as strongly as possible: It is I who do all this".[35]

But why is the interpretation largely a recapitulation? On the one hand, this could suggest that the sign-act was already sufficiently clear, so further explanation would be superfluous. On the other, perhaps this initial interpretation does not go far enough: what does it mean for them to be joined in Yhwh's hand? The fact that the ramifications of the sign-act are not particularly explicit may have been one of the factors in the expansion of the interpretation.

As discussed in 2.2 above, Ezek 37:20 may or may not belong to this initial layer. If it *does*, it may have served to round off the narrative. Greenberg notes

---

34 I make no grand claims here about the extent to which the intermittent stages of the text were known or circulated. I do assume that the intermittent stages were considered 'complete' by their authors rather than unfinished, though broader questions about the expectations of ancient authors and readers around coherence are unfortunately far outside the scope of this chapter.
35 Zimmerli, *Ezekiel 2*, 274–275.

of this verse that the "visual, concrete union of the sticks promises realization of the verbal message" and, as such, would be a fitting end to the sign-act text.[36] It also clarifies that the sign-act will be performed in the sight of the people (לעיניהם): readers can infer this from v. 18, but only in v. 20 is this made explicit. This may seem like a technicality, but in Ezek 12 and 24 – the other sign-act texts in which the people respond to Ezekiel's actions – we have a confirmation that Ezekiel completed the sign-act prior to the people's response to it. In Ezek 12:7 it is also notes specifically that he did so in their sight (לעיניהם).

Ultimately, however, I concluded that v. 20 more likely belongs to the first expansion of the base text (Ezek 37:20–23). In that case, we can agree with Hals that it is "a rather awkward resumption".[37] I remain unsure as to how to understand this verse as an introduction to the second interpretation. It could, in a straightforward narrative sense, be a link back to the sign-act in vv. 16–17 to connect that as directly as possible with the not-so-clearly-related interpretation in vv. 21–23. In a more metaphorical sense, the idea that the sticks are still in Ezekiel's hand (and thus Yhwh's) could be intended to indicate that the restoration described can *only* take place under Yhwh's protection: as Odell describes, "[o]nce the people are in his "hand," they will no longer fall prey to these other takers".[38] Yet to my mind there can be no confusion in vv. 21–23 that the restoration will only come about through Yhwh's will and actions.

The second interpretation of the sign-act begins proper in Ezek 37:21, with the use of the messenger formula mimicking the opening of the divine speech in v. 19. In what follows, Yhwh promises to take the sons of Israel out of the nations, gather them, and bring them into their own land. The supplement has no clear connection to the original sign-act except for the emphasis on two nations becoming one in v. 22:

ועשיתי אתם לגוי אחד בארץ בהרי ישראל ומלך אחד יהיה לכלם למלך ולא יהיה־עוד לשני גוים ולא יחצו עוד לשתי ממלכות עוד:

And I will make them one nation in the land, on the mountains of Israel, and one king will be king over all of them, and they will not be two nations again, and they will not be divided into two kingdoms again.

Greenberg argues that the restoration is "described nonfiguratively" here, "with just enough repetition of key terms to show that it is a decoding of the symbolism".[39] In the context of this supplement though, it is mainly the juxtaposition with vv. 15–19 that allow us to read vv. 21–23 as an interpretation of the sign-act.

---

36 Greenberg, *Ezekiel 21–37*, 755.
37 Hals, *Ezekiel*, 273.
38 Odell, *Ezekiel*, 456.
39 Greenberg, *Ezekiel 21–37*, 755.

Indeed, the main role of this supplement is to expand upon and tease out the reunification of the two nations. While the initial text already had a strong theocentric flavour, the supplement promises a new political order, under which the people will no longer defile themselves (v. 23). The final words of v. 23 succinctly conclude the text with the covenant formula, which is commonly used in Ezekiel and already has connotations of unity in the book (see 2.3 above).

In the final supplement, the promise of a future king in v. 22 is made more specific with the introduction of David, though the theme of unity under the ruler remains key. Although David is variously referred to as Yhwh's servant, prince, king, and shepherd (see 2.3 above), the message is clear: in this new order, the people will live in the land given to Jacob under an everlasting covenant of peace (וכרתי להם ברית שלום ברית עולם יהיה אותם). Indeed, the repeated use of עולם in this supplement adds a new tone to the sign-act text, transforming the meaning of the sign-act from a one-off event (the people will be regathered and the two nations made into one) into a promise of one leader, one land, and one covenant for עולם, with Yhwh's sanctuary in the people's midst from then on. The ending of the first supplement with the covenant formula (v. 23) is mirrored here in the conclusion of the interpretation (v. 27), albeit with the order reversed.

The final transformation of the initial sign-act and interpretation takes place with the final formula. In Ezekiel, it is only here and Ezek 20:12 that Israel itself – rather than Yhwh's name – will be sanctified. The interpretation of the sign-act ends with the recognition formula, but specifically the claim that the *nations* will acknowledge that Yhwh sanctifies Israel. In the context of this final layer, it is clear that Israel has been set apart by Yhwh to be the home of Yhwh's sanctuary. While the interpretation of the sign-act has been expanded beyond recognition, the themes of the book of Ezekiel are well-represented in the final form of the text.

William A. Tooman
"Is he not a Riddle Monger?"
הלא ממשל משלים הוא – Ezekiel's Sign-acts as a Coordinated Sequence

1 Introduction

The book of Ezekiel is best known, perhaps, for its evocative visions and redolent sign-acts. The book's visions (1:1–3:15, 8:1–11:25, 36:1–14, 40:1–48:35) are intricately connected with one another. Their revelations address a number of interconnected problems and questions and culminate in the book's final vision of restoration.[1] It is, perhaps, less appreciated that the book's many sign-acts have a parallel design and purpose. Sign-acts appear in 3:22–5:17, 6:11–12, 12:1–20, 21:11–12 [Eng. 6–7], 24:15–27, and 37:15–28.[2] They too have been coordinated with one another and represent a logical sequence that culminates with a sign-act of restoration. The coordination of the sign-acts is signalled by verbal and topical links and by a step-by-step development of shared motifs, topics, and arguments within them.[3] In this paper, I explore how Ezekiel 12:1–20 has been crafted to sit strategically between chapters 2–5(6) and 24 before stepping back to offer some global comments on Ezekiel's sign-acts as a coordinated sequence.

---

1 See, e.g., H. van Dyke Parunak, "The Literary Architecture of Ezekiel's *Mar'ôt 'Ĕlōhîm*," *JBL* 99/1 (1980): 61–74; Frank-Lothar Hossfeld, "Die Tempelvision Ez 8–11 im Licht unterschiedlicher methodischer Zugänge," in *Ezekiel and his Book. Textual and Literary Criticism and their Interrelation*, ed. Johan Lust, BETL 74 (Leuven: Peeters, 1986), 151–165; and William Tooman, "Covenant and Presence in the Composition and Theology of Ezekiel," in *Divine Presence and Absence in Exilic and Post-Exilic Judaism*, ed. Nathan MacDonald and Izaac J. de Hulster, FAT II/61 (Tübingen: Mohr Siebeck, 2013), esp., 151–82.
2 Some interpreters include 21:13–22 among the sign-acts. I address this later in the paper in n. 27.
3 A few scholars have argued for coordination between a few of sign-acts. Paul Joyce, for example, has argued that the sign-acts in chap 4–5 are "distinct and yet interrelated, with some cross-referencing" (*Ezekiel: A Commentary*, LHBOTS 482 [London: Bloomsbury, 2009], 84). Likewise, Yip has recognized that "Ezek 3:16–27 and 4:4–8 are bound together by a sort of cross reference system of thematic resemblance" (Hei Yin Yip, *Ezekiel's Message of Hope and Restoration: Redaction-Critical Study of Ezekiel 1–7*, BZAW 532 [Berlin and Boston: de Gruyter, 2021], 125–26, quote on 126).

https://doi.org/10.1515/9783111521015-012

2 Ezekiel 12:1–20 between 2:1–5:17 and 24:15–27

Ezekiel 12:1–20 describes two sign-acts. First, the prophet is commanded to prepare an exile's baggage and break through a wall (12:3–16). The prophet is then instructed to eat and drink with anxiety and trembling (12:17–20). The command to perform each sign-act (vv. 3–7, 17–18) is followed by an interpretation of that act (vv. 8–16, 19–20). The interpretation of the first sign-act is also divided into two parts. One concerns the prince in Jerusalem (vv. 8–13) and the other his retainers (vv. 14–16).[4] Each text-segment (vv. 3–7, 8–13, 14–16, 17–18, and 19–20) is linked to another of Ezekiel's sign-acts.

Heading (12:1–2). Ezekiel 12:1–2 is a heading under which all of 12:3–20 sits. "The word of the LORD came to me: O mortal, you dwell among a rebellious house. They have eyes to see but see not, ears to hear but hear not; for they are a rebellious house."[5] As the heading indicates, the fundamental problem that the chapter will address is rebellion. The house of Israel is 'blind' and 'deaf'. Whether this is the cause or the consequence of the rebellion is not immediately clear. The nature of the rebellion is also unclear. Is it religious, political, ethnic, cultural, interpersonal, or some other type? Is it rebellion against God, the prophet, Judah's political masters, one another, or none of these? These opening verses contain a number of locutions that are identical or similar to locutions from the call-narratives and the book's first sign-act in chaps 2–3. When recognized, these links help clarify the heading's opaqueness:

Ezek 2–3	Ezek 12:1–2
– you dwell among (אתה יושב) scorpions ... for they are a rebellious house (כי בית מרי המה). 2:6 – for they are a rebellious house (כי בית מרי המה). 2:6; 3:9, 26, 27 (2:7, 8)[6] – whether they listen or not (אם־ישמעו ואם־יחדלו). 2:5, 7; 3:11 (cf. 3:27) – the house of Israel will refuse (לא) to listen (לשמע) to you, because they refuse to listen (לשמע) to me. 3:7 – he who listens will listen, and he who does not will not (השמע ישמע והחדל יחדל). 3:27	[1] The word of the LORD came to me: [2] O mortal, you dwell among (אתה יושב) a rebellious house (בית־המרי). They have eyes to see but see not, ears to hear but hear not (ולא שמעו); for they are a rebellious house (כי בית מרי הם).

---

[4] In Codex Leningrad, the chapter is divided by *petûḥot* into the following paragraphs: vv. 1–7, 8–16, and 17–20.

[5] All translations are adapted from the NJPS.

[6] The locution מרי (ה)בית is unique to Ezekiel. It is distinctive of the call-narrative (2:1–3:21), the first sign-act (3:22–27), and the present sign-act (12:1–20). Outside of these pericopae, it only appears at 17:12; 24:3; and 44:6.

In the call-narratives, Ezekiel was summoned to announce "lamentation, moaning, and woe" (2:10) that will befall Israel for her rebellion against God (2:3 [and implied in 2:8]). Chapter 2 emphasized that the house of Israel was unlikely to listen to Ezekiel because they are rebels and have long been rebels (esp. 2:3). Chapter 3 claims that although they should be able to hear and understand what Ezekiel says, they will not. Their 'blindness' and 'deafness' has made them less comprehending even than a people who do not speak the same language as the prophet (3:5–7). Ezekiel 12:1–2 revisits the subject of Israel's rebellion against God and, in doing so, it presupposes the arguments presented in chaps 2–3.

The first sign-act (12:3–7). The chapter's first sign-act is reported in vv. 3–7. The divine command to enact it is reported in vv. 3–6 and prophet's obedience in v. 7. God commands the prophet to prepare the baggage of an exile and "go into exile by day before their eyes." This is only the first element of the sign-act. As a second element, God requires the prophet break through a wall and "carry the baggage out through it." That these are two distinct acts is clear. The first acts happened "by day." The second must happen "in the dark." There remains a third element that occurs simultaneously with the second. The prophet must perform the night act with his face covered. Three actions occurring at two different times are presented in Ezek 12 as a single sign-act and given a single interpretation.

At the transition between the divine command to enact these signs (vv. 3–6) and the report of Ezekiel's obedience (v. 7), two lines appear that will resurface in 24:15–27:

Ezek 2–3	Ezek 12:3–7	Ezek 24:15–27
– for they are a rebellious house (כי בית מרי המה), 2:5, 6; 3:9, 26, 27; 12:1, 2, 3	[3] Therefore, mortal, get yourself gear for exile, and go into exile by day before their eyes. Go into exile from your home to another place before their eyes; perhaps they will take note, for they are a rebellious house (כי בית מרי המה). [4] Carry out your gear as gear for exile by day before their eyes; and go out again in the evening before their eyes, as one who goes out into exile. [5] Before their eyes, break through the wall and carry [the gear] out through it; [6] before their eyes, carry it on your shoulder. Take it out in the dark, and cover your face that you may not see the land; for I make you a portent to the house of Israel (כי־מופת נתתיך לבית ישראל). [7] I did just as I was commanded (ואעש כן כאשר צויתי): I took out my gear by day as gear for exile, and in the evening I broke through the wall with my own hands. In the darkness I carried [the gear] out on my shoulder, carrying it before their eyes.	– Ezekiel shall become a portent for you (יהיה יחזקאל לכם למופת) 24:24 – So you shall be a portent for them (והיית להם למופת), and they shall know that I am the LORD. 24:27 – I did as I had been commanded (... ואעש כאשר צויתי). 24:18

Despite the fact that numerous sign-acts have already been described in the book
(3:22–5:17, 6:11–12), this is the first time that Ezekiel is described as a מופת, a
dynamic symbol of the fate of Zedekiah and those surrounding him.[7] The only
other time he will be referred to in this way is in reference to the sign-acts of
chap 24. Likewise, Ezekiel is explicit about his obedience in both cases ("I did as
I was commanded," 12:7; 24:18).

Interpretation of the first sign-act (12:8–16). The interpretation of the first sign-
act unfolds in two parts. In the first part (vv. 8–13) the sign-act is explained as a
prediction of Zedekiah's fate. This half of the interpretation uses a number of
locutions that reappear in 24:15–27.

Ezek 12:8–13	Ezek 24:15–27
[8] In the morning (בבקר), the word of the LORD came to me: [9] O mortal, did they not ask you, the House of Israel (הלא אמרו אליך בית ישראל) that rebellious house (בית המרי), "What are you doing?" (מה אתה עשׂה) [10] Say to them: "Thus said the Lord GOD: This pronouncement concerns the prince in Jerusalem and all the House of Israel who are in it."[8] [11] Say: "I am a portent for you (אני מופתכם): As I have done, so shall it be done to them (כאשר עשׂיתי כן יעשׂה להם); they shall go into exile, into captivity. [12] And the prince among them shall carry [his gear] on his shoulder as he goes out in the dark. He shall break through the wall in order to carry [his gear] out through it; he shall cover his face, because he himself shall not see the land with his eyes." [13] I will spread my net over him, and he shall be caught in my snare. I will bring him to Babylon, the land of the Chaldeans, but he shall not see it; and there he shall die.	– "the people asked me (ויאמרו אלי העם), 'will you not tell us what these things mean for us, that you are acting so?' (מה ... אתה עשׂה)," 24:19 – "Ezekiel shall become a portent for you" (יהיה יחזקאל לכם למופת), 24:24 – "so you shall be a portent for them" (והיית להם למופת), 24:27 – "you will do as I have done" (ועשׂיתם כאשר עשׂיתי), 24:22 – "just as he has done, you will do" (כל אשר עשׂה תעשׂו), 24:24.

---

7 There is a distinction between the use of מופת and אות in Ezekiel. מופת is reserved for the
prophet himself and is never used for the prophet's actions. אות is not used for the prophet, but
is applied to the sign-act of the iron-plate in 4:3 and to the people in 14:8. Randall Bailey, "Prophetic Use of Omen Motifs: A Preliminary Study," in *The Biblical Canon in Comparative Perspective: Scripture in Context 4*, ed. K. Lawson Younger, William Hallo, and Bernardo Batto (Lewiston,
NY: Mellen, 1991), 205; cf. Sheldon Blank, "The Prophet as Paradigm," in *Essays in Old Testament
Ethics: Festschrift for J. Philip Hyatt*, ed. J. Crenshaw and J. Willis (New York: Ktav, 1974), 123–24.
8 Considered from a text-critical vantage, v. 10b is the most problematic in the chapter. The MT
reads (literally): "the prince is this oracle in Jerusalem, and the entire house of Israel who are
in their midst." There are three problems: LXX[A], T[J], and Symmachus all presuppose -ל or על
before הנשׂיא. Both LXX[A] and LXX[B] translate המשׂא as if it were משׁלים/המשׁל, i.e., "the prince and
leader(s)." Finally, there is no plural antecedent for the pronoun המה. I have tentatively concluded
that the original text was המשׂא הזה על הנשׂיא and became על הנשׂיא המשׂא הזה by metathesis. MT
corrected it to הנשׂיא המשׂא הזה. The *Vorlage* of LXX[B] corrected to [הזה] הנשׂיא והמשׁל (or LXX[B] corrected
in translation), and LXX[A] corrected to [הזה] על הנשׂיא והמשׁל. (The third problem may simply be a
case of המה concording with the referent of בית ישראל rather than its morphology.)

The sign-act is an unvoiced, theatrical prophecy about the fate of Zedekiah. He will escape the siege of Jerusalem by night and (possibly) in disguise. However, he will be captured by the Babylonians and taken into captivity, where he will die, never to see the land of Israel again. Indeed, his eyes will be put out in Babylon (2 Kings 25:1–7; Jer 53:4–11).[9] The similarities between 12:8–13 and 24:15–27 are not limited to shared locutions. The evening and morning pattern, in 12:7–8, is also in 24:18 (and 33:21–22). More importantly, 24:2 announces the beginning of the fulfilment of Ezekiel's many sign-acts, especially 12:1–20, the final fulfilment of which is declared in 33:21–22.

The focus shifts in verses 14–16 to Zedekiah's retainers. It is important to note that vv. 14–16 do not correspond to the first sign-act. Ezekiel's three actions all have to do with Zedekiah, not with "all those around him." Their fate is connected to the sign-acts in chaps. 4–5:

Ezek 5	Ezek 12:14–16
– When the days of siege are completed, destroy a third part in fire in the city, take a third and strike it with the sword all around (בחרב סביבותיה) and scatter a third to the wind (תזרה לרוח) and unsheathed a sword after them (וחרב אריק אחריהם). 5:2 – I will scatter all your survivors to every wind (וזריתי את־כל־שאריתך לכל־רוח). 5:10 – One third of you shall die of pestilence (בדרק) or perish in your midst by famine (ברעב), one-third shall fall by the sword (בחרב) around you (סביבותיך), and I will scatter one-third to every wind (לכל־רוח) and will unsheathe the sword after them (וחרב אריק אחריהם). 5:12 – abominations (תועבות). 5:9; 11	[14] And all those around him (סביבתיו), his helpers and all his troops, I will scatter to every wind (אזרה לכל־רוח); and I will unsheathe the sword after them (וחרב אריק אחריהם). [15] Then, when I have scattered them among the nations and dispersed (וזריתי) them through the countries, they shall know that I am the Lord. [16] But I will spare a few of them from the sword (מחרב), from famine (מרעב), and from pestilence (מדבר), that they may recount all their abominable deeds (תועבותיהם) among the nations to which they come; and they shall know that I am the Lord.

Some few of Zedekiah's "helpers and troops" (עזרו וכל־אגפיו) – most of whom will have died from famine, pestilence, and sword (v. 16) – will be scattered among the nations and pursued by violence (v. 14). These pronouncements are derived from the sign-act of the hair in 5:1–17, and bear no relationship to the sign-act commanded in 12:3–7.

---

9 A detailed discussion of the relationship of the elements of the sign-act with the fate of Zedekiah can be found in Kelvin Friebel, *Jeremiah's and Ezekiel's Sign-acts: Rhetorical Nonverbal Communication*, JSOTSup 283 (Sheffield: Sheffield Academic Press, 1999), 268–71.

The second sign-act and its interpretation (12:17–20). The second sign-act and its interpretation are treated together here, because they are presented as a single paragraph in the masoretic text and because they only comprise four verses altogether.

Ezek 4	Ezek 12:17–20
– And he said to me, "O mortal, I am going to break the staff of bread in Jerusalem, and they shall eat bread (ואכלו־לחם) by weight, in anxiety (ובדאגה), and water (ומים) by measure, in horror (ובשממון). ¹⁷ Lacking bread and water (לחם ומתם), they will be desolate (ונשמו) ..." 4:16–17	¹⁷ The word of the LORD came to me: ¹⁸ O mortal, eat your bread in trembling (לחמך ברעש תאכל) and drink your water in fear and anxiety (ברגזה ובדאגה תשתה). ¹⁹ And say to the people of the land: Thus said the Lord GOD concerning the inhabitants of Jerusalem in the land of Israel: They shall eat their bread in anxiety (לחמם בדאגה יאכלו) and drink their water in horror (ומימתהם בשממון ישתו), because their land will be desolate (תשם) of its multitudes on account of the lawlessness of all its inhabitants. ²⁰ The inhabited towns shall be laid waste and the land shall become a desolation (שממה); then you shall know that I am the LORD.

The second sign-act (12:17–20) is clearly a reprise of the sign-act from 4:16–17. In chap 4, the sign-act presaged starvation accompanying the siege of Jerusalem. In chap 12, the same action is a portent of deprivation following the siege, due to the extensive destruction of inhabited areas and agriculture. The sign-act indicates that there will be continuity of conditions for the people in Jerusalem during the siege and the people throughout the land after it.

The main literary connections between 12:1–20 and chaps 2–5 and 24, can be sketched as follows:

Call-narratives, "they are a rebellious house" ←	12:1–2 – Accusation Israel is a rebellious house	
	12:3–7 – Sign-act 1 baggage of an exile & breaking through a wall (day & night) →	24:15–27, מופת, evening & morning
5:1–17, famine, pestilence, & sword; survivors scattered ←	12:8–16 – Interpretation pronouncement against the prince in Jerusalem: he will be captured and taken to Babylon pronouncement against the people surrounding the prince: many will die of famine, pestilence, & sword; survivors will be scattered →	24:15–27, מופת
4:16–17, eating & drinking in anxiety & horror ←	12:17–18 – Sign-act 2 eating & drinking with trembling, anxiety & horror	
←	12:19–20 – Interpretation pronouncement against survivors in the land	

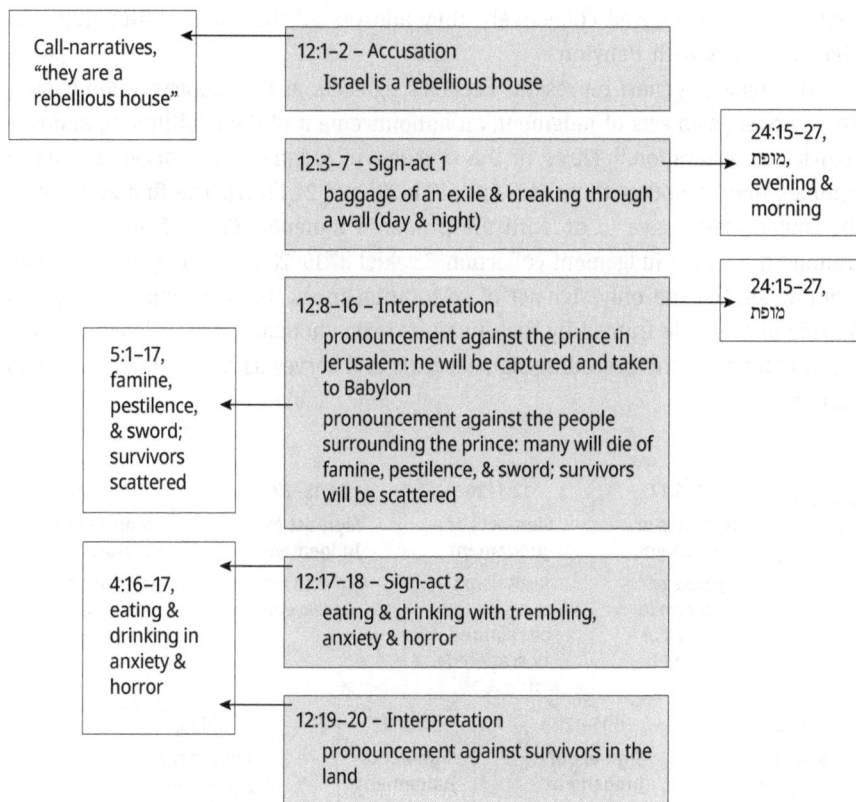

3 Ezekiel's Sign-acts as a Coordinated Sequence

Ezekiel's sign-acts, when viewed as a collection, represent a coordinated sequence. It is, admittedly, a bit unnecessary to say that they are a "sequence." Any group of items presented one after the other is in a sequence. It is another thing altogether to say that they are a "coordinated sequence." What I will suggest is that the sign-acts are coordinated in two ways. They are connected to one another by common topics and repeated locutions. They are also coordinated in that the sequence itself is meaningful. It is significant that 3:22–27 is the first, that 37:15–28 is the last, and that each of those in between falls where they do. This is because the sign-acts, in addition to being presented chronologically, have been organized as a logical sequence. All of the sign-act texts after the first one presume information from preceding ones. They are logically and topically contingent, and, when viewed collectively, they address all the communities that survived the wars with Babylon.

The following chart represents Ezekiel's sign-acts, as they appear in the book.[10] There are six sign-acts of judgment, an announcement of their fulfilment, and one sign-act of restoration.[11] Three of the sign-acts of judgment are larger and more complex than the other three (4:1–5:17; 12:1–20; and 24:15–27). The first and last of the smaller texts have to do with the prophet's muteness (3:22–27 and 33:21–22), framing the whole judgement collection. Ezekiel 37:15–28 is not a sign-act of judgment at all, but the only sign-act of restoration in the book. It appears to stand outside of the cycle framed by the muteness texts, though, as we will see, it is still coordinated with the preceding sign-act texts and serves as a hopeful rejoinder to them all.

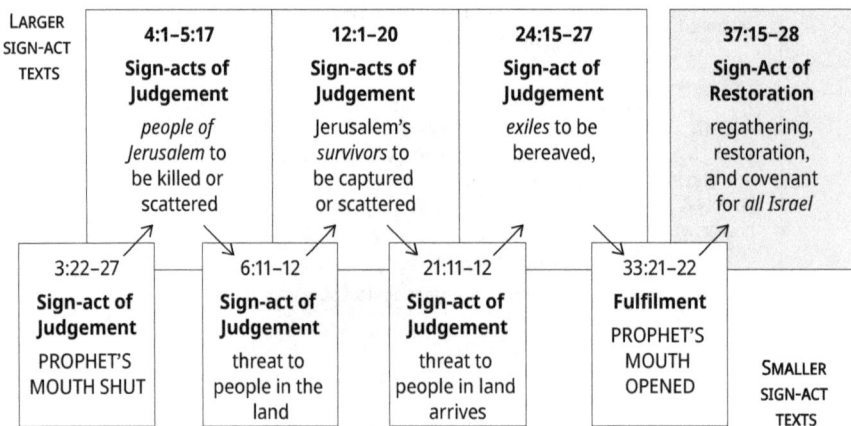

LARGER SIGN-ACT TEXTS	**4:1–5:17**	**12:1–20**	**24:15–27**	**37:15–28**
	Sign-acts of Judgement	**Sign-acts of Judgement**	**Sign-act of Judgement**	**Sign-Act of Restoration**
	people of Jerusalem to be killed or scattered	Jerusalem's *survivors* to be captured or scattered	*exiles* to be bereaved,	regathering, restoration, and covenant for *all Israel*

3:22–27	**6:11–12**	**21:11–12**	**33:21–22**	
Sign-act of Judgement	**Sign-act of Judgement**	**Sign-act of Judgement**	**Fulfilment**	
PROPHET'S MOUTH SHUT	threat to people in the land	threat to people in land arrives	PROPHET'S MOUTH OPENED	SMALLER SIGN-ACT TEXTS

In the following paragraphs, I will concentrate on ways that Ezekiel's sign-act texts have been coordinated and sequenced, culminating in 37:15–28.[12] I will ad-

---

10 Cf. Franz Sedlmeier, *Das Buch Ezechiel: Kapitel 1–24*, NSKAT 21/1 (Stuttgart: Katholisches bibelwerk, 2002), 51–53, 66–67.

11 The announcement of the sign-acts' fulfilment in 33:11–12 could be considered part of a sign-act. The opening of the prophet's mouth is the second half of the sign-act initiated in 3:22–27, where the prophet's mouth was closed. opening the prophet's mouth is a sign that the prophet is again able to act as their reprover.

12 In this part of the essay, I will not be mapping the locutions repeated in different sign-acts. That there are many has been illustrated with 12:1–20. Likewise, though the coordination between sign-act texts was achieved redactionally, I will not be charting those redactional operations. I will be describing their results.

dress the sign-act texts serially, and I will describe the argumentative and themat-ic connections to preceding sign-acts in each.

4 The Sign-acts of Judgement

Ezekiel 3:22–27. It is the first sign-act that makes all the others necessary. God shuts the mouth of the prophet, so that he may not act as "reprover" of his rebellious people (בית מרי). As a result, the prophet is forced to act out many of his oracles, and these actions are signs (מופתים) for those who can read them. The prophet does continue to receive visions and oracles, as a prophet normally would, but in most cases we are not told if he ever passed them along to the other exiles.[13] The prophet's role as watchman (צפה) or reprover (מוכיח) is constrained in three ways. He is confined to his house (3:24); he is bound with ropes so that he "cannot go out among" the people (3:25), and God makes him mute (אל״ם; 3:27). Strictly speaking, only the third of these is necessary. As we will see, though, the second one has a coordinating function that is not yet apparent.[14] The prophet's mouth will only be opened in 33:21–22 when news arrives that Jerusalem has fallen and that all his sign-acts have been fulfilled.

Ezekiel 4:1–5:17. Ezekiel's first public sign-acts are described in 4:1–5:17. Zimmerli has argued (convincingly, in my view) that a number of different sign-acts have been combined and conflated to produce MT-Ezek 4:1–5:17. The MT is structured in three parts: 4:1–8, 9–17, and 5:1–17. In each part the prophet performs multiple sign-acts simultaneously. In 4:1–8, the prophet is given three sign-act pairs: six actions in a single performance lasting four-hundred and thirty days.

---

13 In some cases, we are told that the elders called on the prophet (e.g., 8:1; 20:1), presumably to receive prophecies. On other occasions he is told to "prophecy," נב״א (e.g., 6:1), or "preach," נט״ף (e.g., 21:7 [Eng. 21:2]), or "take up a lament," נש״א קינה (e.g., 19:1), etc. These cases seem to fall under the exception granted in 3:37, "when I speak to you, I will open your mouth."
14 Greenberg argues that all the sign-acts were performed inside of the prophet's house, using domestic objects one might find there (brick, pan, razor, etc.) (*Ezekiel 1–20*, AB 22 [New York: Doubleday, 1983], 117). For some reason, he does not also argue that the prophet remained bound while performing sign-acts. Greenberg's conclusion, it seems to me, defies the logic of a sign-act, which must be performed before the whole community. In fact, the sign-act in 12:1–20 requires the prophet to be outside of his house. I suspect that the line to "shut yourself up in your house" has been included as a measure-for-measure action again the exiles. Because they are a rebel-lious *house*, their prophet is shut away in his *house* where he cannot serve their needs.

4:1–3	4:4–6	4:7–8
1. prophet inscribes a brick with "Jerusalem" & places it under siege 2. prophet sets an iron pan between himself and the brick	3. prophet lays on left side 390 days to "bear the sins of Israel" 4. prophet lays on right side 40 days to "bear the sins of Judah"[15]	5. prophet bears his arm against the brick "Jerusalem" 6. prophet bound while lying on his side

These sign-acts do not receive explicit interpretations. For some, the meaning is obvious (e.g., "set up a siege against it" in 4:2). Others are obscure. The significance of the specific numbers of days that the prophet is bound and why he is bound, for example, are neither obvious nor explained.[16]

Ezekiel 4:9–17 is also a double sign-act. The prophet is instructed to prepare a six-grain bread and to cook it on a fire fuelled by human solid-waste.[17] Considering what these actions portend – lack of sufficient grain and firewood – it seems likely that 4:9–11 were performed together with 4:1–8. (Perhaps the unclean six-grain bread was Ezekiel's food for the days of the siege.) Verses 16–17 interpret the mixed-grain bread as a symbol of starvation in Jerusalem. Verses 12–15, though, break from the rest of 4:1–17. All the sign-acts relate to the coming siege of Jerusalem and focus (almost exclusively) on the Jerusalem community. Cooking food over excrement signals something different. It indicates uncleanness: "the people of Israel shall eat their bread, unclean, among the nations to which I will banish them." These four verses shift focus to conditions after the siege and anticipate 5:1–17, which speak to the fate of the siege's survivors.[18]

---

15 Based on an extensive allusion to Lev 10 (and 16) Yip argues that "Ezekiel is called upon to bear Israel's iniquity/punishment and to atone for them in a way reminiscent of the high priest. Ezek 4:4–6 recalls the action of Ezekiel's priestly role of suffering for the Israelites" (*Ezekiel's Message*, 119–24, quote at 124).

16 The scholarly proposals about the 390/40 days are numerous and need not detain us. See: J. Lust, K. Hauspie, and A. Ternier, "Ezekiel 4–5 in Hebrew and in Greek: Numbers and Ciphers," *ETL* 77/1 (2001): 132–52; Friebel, *Sign-acts*, 211–13, 216–222, 247. One aspect of the binding will be addressed momentarily.

17 The mixing of many types of grain indicates shortage. During the coming siege of Jerusalem, there will not be enough grain of any one type to make a loaf.

18 Allen misunderstands 4:13. He assumes that it applies the whole sign-act to conditions after the siege, but 4:13 only applies to cooking food over excrement. See Leslie C. Allen, *Ezekiel 1–19*, WBC 28 (Grand Rapids: Zondervan, 2018), 70.

4:9–11	4:12–17
Two signs	*Interpretation*
preparing a mixed-grain bread	Israel will eat unclean food among the nations
cooking over excrement	starvation in Jerusalem

The sign in 5:1–17 is similarly complex. In this multifaceted sign-act, the prophet is commanded to shave his head and beard, divide the hair into three equal parts and perform a different action against each third. One third is placed on the brick (4:1) and burned. One third is placed around the city and struck with a sword. One third is scattered to the winds and a sword drawn after it. A pinch of hair is removed and bound in the prophet's skirt. All these actions are to be performed "when the days of siege are completed" (5:2), that is, when the four-hundred and thirty days described in 4:4–6 are completed. They are directed at the people who endured the siege of Jerusalem and at its survivors. The three judgements are interpreted in light of Leviticus 26:25–33. One third will die of famine in the city. One third will die of pestilence outside the city, and one third will be scattered.[19] A remnant will survive the fall of the city, but they too will be destroyed, because they bear the seeds of their own destruction (v. 4).[20]

Versus 5–17 do more than just interpret the signs. They also provide God's reasons for afflicting his people in these ways.

5:1–4	5:5–17
Signs	*Reasons (5:5–9, 11a)*
1. shave hair and divide into thirds: $^1/_3$ burned, $^1/_3$ struck, $^1/_3$ scattered	1. Jerusalemites broke the Torah (abominations)
	2. Jerusalemites defiled the sanctuary
	Interpretation (5:11b–17)
2. a few hairs bound in prophet's skirt	1. $^1/_3$ will die of pestilence, $^1/_3$ will die by violence $^1/_3$ will be scattered among the nations.
	2. "you" will be a ruin and a mockery to the nations; you will endure ongoing famine, death (by wild animals), and pestilence[21]

---

19 דם in 5:17 is not a separate punishment, "bloodshed," as it is rendered in many translations. See William Tooman, "On the Meaning of דֶּבֶר וָדָם in Ezekiel (5:17, 14:19, 28:23, 38:22)," *VT* 60 (2010): 666–68.
20 Friebel argues that the antecedent of "these" (ומהם; v. 4) is the third that are scattered (v. 2), so those bound in Ezekiel's skirt can be considered the remnant that are saved from destruction and exile. *Ezekiel's Sign-acts*, 241–42; cf. Karin Schöpflin, *Theologie als Biographie im Ezechielbuch. Ein Beitrag zur Konzeption alttestamentlicher Theologie*, FAT 36 (Tübingen: Mohr Siebeck, 2002), 210–11. I understand it differently. The hairs bound in the prophet's skirt represent the exiles of 597 BCE, who are consistently presented in Ezekiel as corrupt and doomed (e.g., 12:16).
21 Verses 16–17 rewords the punishments derived from Lev 26:25–33, 39 to include verbiage from Deut 32:23–24.

One verse does not obviously fit into this pericope. In 5:10, the prophet is told "parents will eat their children in your midst, and children shall eat their parents." This obviously relates to the starvation that will accompany the siege of Jerusalem, but it does not seem relate to any of the signs. It does, though, further align the interpretation with Lev 26: "you shall eat the flesh of your sons and the flesh of your daughters" (Lev 26:29; cf. Deut 28:53; 2 Kings 28:53–54; Jer 19:9; Lam 2:20; 4:10). Also, as we will see, its addition introduces a theme that will reappear in a subsequent sign-act: parent/child bereavement.

Ezekiel 4:1–5:17 is the longest and most complicated of the sign-act texts. For this reason, many of the subsequent sign-act texts will recall topics, actions, and arguments first presented here. Looking back to 3:22–27, Ezek 4:1–5:17 continues from and is connected to it. The most obvious dependence is that the prophet must now act out his oracles, which only became necessary when muteness was inflicted on him in 3:26–27. Likewise, the two texts share a particular symbolic action. In both the prophet is bound with ropes (3:25; 4:8). This action is deployed to different effect in each. In 3:25 the binding is a sign to the exiles that the prophet is prohibited from reproving them.[22] In 4:8 it is a sign that there will be no respite from the coming punishment until Israel and Judah have atoned in full for their sins.[23] It was observed above that this action is not necessary in chap 3. One of the reasons that it was included there was to enhance the cohesion of 3:22–27 with 4:1–5:17.[24]

Ezekiel 6:11–12. The actions required from the prophet are trifling in this case. The prophet is instructed to stamp his feet, clap his hands, and exclaim "Ah!" (אָח). These interjections are, apparently, a testimony of indignity against "the abominations of the house of Israel." Elsewhere in Ezekiel הֶאָח is used as an exclamation of gladness (25:3, 6; 26:2; 36:2). This sign-act appears to be a declaration of joy that Israel is being punished at last (per Deut 28:63).[25] The sign-act indicates that Israel will "fall by the sword, by famine, and by pestilence" (6:11b). These three punishments, which first appeared in 5:1–4, are applied to those who are "far off," "near," and who "survive" (v. 12). "Near" and "far" are not oriented with respect to any person or place in 6:12. That has to has to be supplied from chap 5, i.e., those who are far *from Jerusalem*, or near *to Jerusalem*, or who survive *the*

---

22 That this sign-act is directed to the exiles with Ezekiel in Tel-Aviv implicit in the line "you have been bound, and *you will not go out among them*" (3:25).

23 See Friebel, *Ezekiel's Sign-acts*, 220 n. 323.

24 So Karl-Friedrich Pohlmann, *Der Prophet Hesekiel/Ezechiel 1–19*, ATD 22.1 (Göttingen: Vandenhoeck & Ruprecht, 1996), 89; Yip, *Ezekiel's Message*, 110.

25 The use of הֶאָח in 21:20 [Eng. 21:15] partakes of the same ambiguity as 6:11.

siege of Jerusalem.[26] In these ways, Ezek 6:11–12 assumes the content and context of 5:1–4.

Ezekiel 12:1–20 is described above.

Ezekiel 21:11–12 [Eng. 21:6–7]. Like 6:11–12, this is another minimal sign-act.[27] All that is required of the prophet is that he "moan." When the people ask "why do you moan?" the prophet is to reply that it is due to news (שמועה) that is coming (באה), news of the siege of Jerusalem (21:6–10 [Eng. 21:1–5]). The messenger does not arrive in this chapter but in chap 33, when he brings tidings of the city's fall, but his arrival will be predicted again in chap 24.

This little sign-act text announces the arrival of the fulfilment of Ezekiel's preceding sign-acts from 4:1 to 12:20, assuming all of their content.[28] It also shares a particular similarity to 6:11–12 and 24:15–27. All three of these sign-acts involve a verbal exclamation (6:11–12; 24:15–27). In 21:11, the prophet is ordered to "moan" (האנח) to show his grief. In 6:11–12 he is required to shout "Ah!" (אח), which, conversely, signals joy.[29] In 24:15–17 the prophet is commanded to "moan, groan" (האנק דם), but he is prohibited from lamenting or weeping (also 24:22).[30] All three of these verbal exclamations – whether communicating joy or grief or bereavement – are directed at the same event, the outpouring of divine punishment on Jerusalem.

Ezekiel 24:15–27. Ezekiel's final sign-act of judgment opens with a divine announcement that God is going to take "the delight of your eyes" from the prophet. That very evening, Ezekiel's wife dies.[31] The death is not the sign, though. The sign is the prophet's response. He is commanded to "Moan, groan; observe no mourning for the dead. Put on your turban and put your sandals on your feet; do not cover over your upper lip, and do not eat the bread of comforters" (v. 17).

---

26 Many commentators assume this without discussing it, e.g., Greenberg, *Ezekiel 1–20*, 136. Cf. Sedlmeier, *Ezechiel: Kapitel 1–24*, 127–28.

27 Surrounding this sign-act text is the whetted sword oracle (21:6–10 + 13–37 [Eng. 21:1–6 + 8–32]). The sword oracle gives the impression that it was composed from three sign-acts: drawing the sword and whetting it, and setting up a sign-post. The only part that is still presented as a sign-act is 21:11–12. The others are presented as oracles.

28 Greenberg, *Ezekiel 21–37*, 420.

29 See n. 25.

30 Many translations read דם as "in silence" or "in motionlessness" from Iדמ״ם. I read it as IIדמ״ם, "wail, groan" (so Isa 23:2; Lam 2:10). See Baruch Levine, "Silence, Sound, and the Phenomenology of Mourning in Biblical Israel," *JANES* 22 (1993): 99–100.

31 Her death was caused by מגפה (v. 15), which could be translated "blow" or "plague" (e.g., Exod 9:14). If the latter option is adopted, it is a synonym of דָּבָר וָדָם and presents another connection to 5:3.

When the people ask why he is behaving this way, he is to reply "I [God] am going to desecrate my sanctuary, your pride and glory, the delight of your eyes and the desire of your heart; and the sons and daughters you have left behind shall fall by the sword" (v. 21).[32] God's desired response is that the people should "not lament or weep, but you shall be heartsick because of your iniquities and shall moan to one another" (v. 24). Because this moment brings all the prophet's sign-acts against Jerusalem to fulfilment, there is no longer a reason for him to be mute. When news of Jerusalem's fall comes, he will be freed to speak normally again (v. 27). The parts of this sign-act all carry symbolic weight. The desecration and destruction of the temple is so grievous, that normal mourning rites are insufficient to the moment. The exiles will lose family members back in Judah, just as Ezekiel lost a family member. News of Jerusalem's woe should provoke the exiles to regret the part they played in it. They should moan, like the prophet moans, mourning their guilt.

This sign-act text repeats many of the themes and topics from the sign-acts in chaps 4–5, 12, and 21. Verses 15–27 continue the message of fulfilment begun in 21:11–12. There it was announced that news (שמועה) of Jerusalem's fate was coming (באה). Here it is again predicted that news (שמעת) is coming (באה), by means of a survivor, a fugitive from Judah (24:24, 26). Entailed in the report is information about widespread death, in particular the demise of the children of the exiles (24:21, 24). This motif was first encountered in 5:10. As part of his actions symbolizing this tragedy, the prophet was prohibited from eating (21:22), just as the Jerusalemites were destined to starve in the city (esp., 4:16–17; 5:10). In 4:17, the purpose of the starvation was to make the people "heartsick over their iniquity" (ונמקו בעונם). The present sign-act has the same objective, to make the people "heartsick because of your iniquities" (ונמקתם בעונתיכם). Finally, the trope "evening and a morning" occurs in 24:18 and in 12:1–8. In all this, the prophet himself (not the actions) has become a sign (מופת) for the people, just as he was in 12:6, 11 (// 24:24, 27).

Ezekiel 33:21–22. After six and half years performing sign-acts concerning the fate of Jerusalem, news arrives that the city has fallen. A fugitive from Judah brings word to Ezekiel "in the morning." Before the fugitive can makes his announcement, during the prior "evening," Ezekiel's mouth was opened and his muteness lifted. There is no sign-act in 33:21–22. Rather, it is the report that all the previous sign-acts are now fulfilled.[33] It reverses the divinely initiated mute-

---

32 Both the temple and the sons and daughters of the exiles who remain in Jerusalem are referred to as the "delight of your eyes" (vv. 21, 25).
33 See the qualifying comments in n. 11.

ness placed on the prophet in 3:22–27, and it relates directly to the prediction of news coming in 21:11–12 and 24:27.

The sign-acts of judgment are interconnected. Each deploys locutions found in other sign-act texts. Each has some thematic or topical connection(s) to other sign-act texts. Each depends on at least one preceding sign-act text, even if only in some small way. There is yet another way that the sign-acts of judgment represent a comprehensive collection. Taken altogether, they address the fate of each of the Judean communities: the people who remained in Judah and Jerusalem after 597 BCE; the exiles of 597 BCE in Babylon; the scattered survivors of 587/6 BCE; the survivors of 587/6 BCE who remained in the land; and the exiles of 586/7 BCE.

– Ezekiel 3:22–27 restrained Ezekiel's ability to act as a reprover for the exiles of 597 BCE in Babylon.
– Ezekiel 4:1–5:17 was directed to several communities. Chap 4 focused on the people who remained in Judah and Jerusalem after 597 BCE., though vv. 12–15 discussed ritual conditions for those who would be scattered after the siege. Chapter 5 turned attention to the scattered survivors of 587/6 BCE and to the exiles of 586/7 BCE, who would be sent to join their compatriots in Babylon. Though one verse, 5:10, looked back on the siege and predicted cannibalism among the city's inhabitants.[34]
– Ezekiel 6:11–12 repeated the threats of chap. 5. Though no target was named, the chapter in which vv. 11–12 are embedded addressed the population of Judah between 597 BCE and 586/7 BCE, and the two adjectives "far" and "near" (רחוק, קרוב) presuppose the same communities as 5:1–9, 11–17.
– Ezekiel 12:1–20 concentrated on Zedekiah and those around him, those who would attempt to escape Jerusalem in 587/6 BCE. In the interpretation portion of the first sign-act (vv. 8–16), the fate of these few was applied to all those who would go into exile in Babylon in 586/7 BCE (v. 10–12). The second sign-act predicted starvation for the survivors of 587/6 BCE who remained in the land.
– Ezekiel 21:11–12, the first prediction of the news that would arrive in 33:21–22, warned that every "spirit shall grow faint and knees turn to water" among the exiles of the first deportation.
– Ezekiel 24:15–27 is a sign-act to the exiles of 597 BCE, a sign that the temple was about to be destroyed and the exiles' "sons and daughters" slaughtered.

In the final sign-act of the book, 37:15–28, the prophet will finally offer a message of hope, hope for all these communities, hope for regathering, for rebuilding, and for reconciliation with God.

---

34 See n. 20 above.

5 The Sign-act of Hope. Ezekiel 37:15–28

It would be reasonable to think that the book of Ezekiel should not contain any more sign-acts after Ezekiel's mouth is opened in 33:21–22. But, just a few chapters later in 37:15–28 Ezekiel is ordered to perform one last sign-act. It is a sign-act of hope not of judgment, and it reverses many of the judgments announced against the communities of Israel in the preceding sign-acts.

The prophet is commanded to take two sticks and to inscribe "belonging to Judah and the sons of Israel associated with him" on one and "belonging to Joseph and all the house of Israel associated with him" on the other. The prophet is then to join the two sticks into one.[35] Because the prophet's mouth is now open, he can immediately declare the sign's interpretation. The most obvious thing that the joining of the sticks could signify is the reunification of the tribes of Israel, and indeed the sign-act does represent this hope. All Israel's remaining communities (the survivors of Jerusalem still in the land, the exiles of both deportations in Babylon, and the diaspora communities scattered throughout the nations), each of whom were addressed in the sign-acts of judgement, will be reunified as a single people. But it symbolizes much more too. It represents the regathering of all exiles, in all countries, to the land of Israel. It represents the restoration of a single monarch over all twelve tribes. It represents the permanence of the reunification. It represents adherence to the Torah, such that the people will "never again defile themselves by their fetishes and their abhorrent things, and by their transgressions" (v. 23). It represents God's cleansing of Israel and his (re)adopting them as his people. Additional details are supplied in vv. 24–28. The king will be David; this future condition will be eternal, and so forth. The main point, for the purposes of this essay, is this: the sign-act of thee two-sticks (37:16–17) only symbolizes reunification. Every other topic raised in its interpretation appears in the preceding sign-acts of judgment. Scattering was predicted in 4:12–15, 5:1–4, 6:11–12, and 12:14–16. The monarchy was the particular focus of 12:3–16. Defilement of the people and temple was directly addressed in 4:12–15 and 5:11. The charge of disregard for the Torah was levelled in 5:6–9, 12:19, and 24:24. In short, 37:15–28, like all the sign-acts of judgment before it, engages with the whole sequence of sign-acts that came before it, reversing them, annulling their consequences, and closing the whole coordinated sequence.[36]

---

35 Whether the prophet is meant to bind them together mechanically, or whether he is to perform a miracle is impossible to tell.

36 Viewed in this light, I doubt that it is accidental that the first sign-act performed by Ezekiel (as opposed to performed *on* Ezekiel) was to "inscribe" (חקק) a brick (4:1), and his last sign-act was to "inscribe" (כרות) two sticks (37:16).

6 Conclusion

I have argued in this essay that every sign-act text in Ezekiel after the first (3:22–27) is linked with at least one other preceding sign-act text. Each contains topics, themes, and locutions that appeared previously. Each depends in some way on the content of at least one preceding sign-act text. Occasionally, a sign-act text anticipates information in a subsequent sign-act text (e.g., anticipation of the messenger in 21:11–12 and 24:26), but the dependence mainly runs in a single direction. I have no doubt that this coordinated sequence is the product of redaction, that the sign-acts have been purposefully reshaped to coordinate them. As a result, they no longer reflect historical events without interference. The degree to which the words and deeds of a six-century prophet are reflected in them is not recoverable (if it ever was). What were once actions, symbolic theatre for a particular community living in a period of particular crisis, have been reframed as interconnected stories, as integral parts of a larger work of literature. They are not sign-acts at all. They are mutually dependent, mutually informing sign-act stories.[37]

---

[37] I have not suggested that Ezekiel's sign-act texts are not also coordinated with other parts of Ezekiel, with its oracles, visions, and allegories. Of course they are. I have not suggested that they are not coordinated with other texts outside of Ezekiel. Of course they are. I have only suggested that the degree to which the sign-act texts are linked with one another wanted further description.

Addendum

Repeated actions & motifs in the sign-acts of judgment.[38]

	3:22–27	4:1–5:17	6:11–12	12:1–20	21:11–12	24:15–27	33:21–22
prophet's mouth shut/opened	✓						✓
prophet bound with ropes	✓	✓					
prophet eats & drinks in fear		✓		✓			
God will unsheathe his sword		✓		✓			
death of children		✓				✓	
triad: sword-famine-pestilence		✓	✓	✓			
temple desecration		✓				✓	
verbal exclamation			✓		✓	✓	
show/hide joy/grief			✓		✓	✓	
evening & morning				✓		✓	✓
message/messenger from Jerusalem					✓	✓	✓

---

38 This chart makes two things visible: the largest sign-act text, Ezekiel 4–5, sets about half of the subjects and motifs that appear in subsequent sign-act texts; and sign-act texts tend to share subjects and motifs with texts that are proximate to them.

Index of Ancient Sources

Apocrypha

Aramaic Sefire Treaty

BM 40183+

Boghazköy tablet

Gilgamesh, Enkidu, and the Netherworld

Hebrew Bible

https://doi.org/10.1515/9783111521015-013

Josephus

K 2175+

Necyomantia

Nergal and Ereshkigal

Vassal Treaty of Esarhaddon

Index of Modern Authors

https://doi.org/10.1515/9783111521015-014

Subject Index

audience 10, 16–18, 23, 24, 26, 42, 45, 49–51, 53, 57, 58, 61, 64–66, 71, 72, 76, 77, 79, 82, 91, 92, 98–100, 112, 120, 137–141, 143, 144, 148, 149, 151, 154–156, 158, 166

Babylon and Babylonians 9, 14, 22, 38, 39, 50, 53, 58, 64, 66–68, 75, 76, 80, 85, 86, 89, 94, 96, 97, 105–108, 121, 122, 127, 129, 131–134, 147, 153, 156, 164, 172, 176, 178–180, 183, 186, 205, 206, 208, 209, 216, 217
body 8, 21, 30, 33–45, 49, 50, 52, 65–68, 70, 71, 75–77, 81, 88, 106, 125, 127, 138, 139, 142, 144, 151, 163, 174, 185

communication 8, 10, 14, 15, 29, 32, 34, 40–46, 64, 65, 75, 149, 167, 169, 179, 190
confinement 51, 53, 59, 62, 63, 65, 66, 68, 69, 71–74, 76, 83, 90, 97, 100, 101, 104, 161, 210
corpse 130, 157, 176
corpses 35, 126, 127, 133, 153, 157
covenant 25, 58, 63, 70, 72, 73, 77, 116, 126, 134, 153, 183, 189, 190, 193–195, 197, 200, 209

David 18, 24, 25, 28, 29, 35, 39, 42, 51, 56, 59, 62, 65, 66, 68, 117, 129, 134, 144, 145, 147, 152, 163, 167, 176, 178, 193–195, 200, 217
death 9, 10, 18, 29, 30, 35, 37, 61, 73, 76, 80, 95, 97, 124–127, 129–132, 134, 136, 143, 145, 149, 160–173, 181, 184–186, 212, 214, 215, 219

eating 15, 21, 22, 40, 68, 69, 76, 91, 109, 110, 126, 138, 139, 148, 166, 203, 207, 208, 211–215, 219
eschatology 145–148, 150, 152, 153
exile and exiles 9, 10, 16–18, 20, 22, 25, 26, 38, 49, 50, 52–55, 57–61, 64, 66–68, 76, 82, 88–90, 92–95, 97, 98, 100, 109, 120, 121, 123–125, 127, 131–134, 137, 141, 143, 144, 146–157, 162, 163, 165, 167, 169–173, 176, 178, 180, 181, 183, 184, 203–205, 208–210, 212, 213, 215–217

https://doi.org/10.1515/9783111521015-015

formula(e) 10, 50, 81, 83, 84, 86, 92, 93, 111, 155, 156, 188–200

genre 28, 39, 42, 49, 50, 64, 78, 82, 98, 99, 129, 155, 173, 192

identity
– national 144, 163
– priestly 10, 40, 50, 68, 74–76, 176, 179
Israel and Israelites 12, 14, 16, 17, 20–25, 29, 39, 42, 45, 58, 61, 62, 68, 69, 71, 72, 74, 75, 79, 81, 85, 87–95, 97–99, 101, 111, 117, 123–126, 131, 133, 134, 137, 144–147, 151–153, 156, 160–163, 166–174, 178, 180, 181, 183–185, 188, 191–193, 195–197, 199, 200, 203–209, 211–214, 217

Jerusalem 8–10, 14, 18, 21, 22, 25, 29, 33, 35, 38, 39, 41, 43, 53, 55, 58, 63, 64, 66–70, 72–74, 76–80, 82, 85, 86, 88, 91, 92, 94–98, 100, 101, 105–107, 110, 111, 117, 121, 122, 132, 144, 147–150, 154, 156–158, 160, 162, 164, 169–172, 176–184, 186, 203, 205–217, 219
Josiah 178, 180, 182, 183
Judah and Judahites 8, 9, 14, 20–25, 29, 31, 39, 45, 59, 64, 67, 69, 70, 72, 73, 75–77, 89, 95, 97, 122, 132, 144, 149, 153, 178, 180, 182, 183, 185, 191, 197, 203, 211, 213, 215–217

magic 50, 52, 78–80, 98, 100, 101, 132, 134
marriage 14, 163, 165, 171, 179, 181, 183, 184
metaphor 10, 14, 20, 32, 38, 53, 54, 68, 76, 79, 88, 90–92, 94–96, 100, 105–107, 112–114, 116, 117, 119, 120, 130, 149, 160, 163, 165, 169–171, 174, 182–184, 186, 199
mourning 10, 18, 40, 73, 95, 134, 136, 149, 151, 156, 165–168, 172, 173, 176, 177, 179, 181, 184–186, 214

performance 8, 10, 14–16, 18–20, 23, 24, 26, 28, 41–45, 48, 49, 51, 60, 65, 66, 78, 80, 82, 83, 85, 86, 88, 90–101, 104, 105, 108–110, 120–122, 136–144, 148–151, 154, 155, 157,